FLOWER ARRANGING

a step-by-step guide

Susan Conder   Sue Phillips   Pamela Westlake

FLOWER ARRANGING

a step-by-step guide

Susan Conder   Sue Phillips   Pamela Westlake

MALLARD
PRESS

MALLARD
PRESS

An imprint of BDD Promotional Book Company, Inc.
666 Fifth Avenue
New York, N.Y. 10103

"Mallard Press and its accompanying design and logo are
trademarks of BDD Promotional Book Company, Inc."

Copyright © The Hamlyn Publishing Group Limited 1990

First published in 1988 by Orbis Publishing Limited

First published in the United States of America in 1990
by The Mallard Press

ISBN 0792-45322-0

Produced by Mandarin Offset
Printed in Hong Kong

CONTENTS

INTRODUCTION

Flowers are for everyone. They help to make a celebration of daily life and they can provide a satisfying way to develop creativity and stamp your own personality on your surroundings. Many more varieties of flowers are now readily available and anyone of any age, from children to grandparents, can enjoy the relaxing and rewarding craft of flower arranging.

Creative expression with flowers can be achieved regardless of artistic ability. You don't need to be a painter to produce beautiful floral designs and the possibilities for experimentation are boundless. Flower arranging is a flexible skill and you can try out your own ideas and follow your own inclinations once you have mastered the basic techniques of holding flowers in place, extending their life, choosing and using different containers. Surprisingly little equipment is necessary and the best way of learning more about flower arranging is by creating different kinds of displays.

Whether you prefer an easy natural style where the flowers hardly look as though they have been formally arranged, a traditionally structured approach or an innovative modern look, the arrangements in this book will provide both inspiration and instruction to achieve impressive displays. The step-by-step illustrations help you to learn basic techniques and design principles of flower arranging while your lovely creations enhance every room in your home.

The wide range of floral arrangements offered in this book will give you fresh ideas to explore. Experiment with exotic blooms, Oriental designs or dramatic fruit and flower fabrications, or perhaps see what you can do with wild flowers gathered from field and forest. Try an exciting landscape arrangement resembling the vibrant border of a cottage garden or a large scale display with branches and berries to fill the corner of a dull and bare room.

You will find novel ideas for the actual placing of flower arrangements. Perhaps you have not thought of hanging a floral display on a wall or high up in a cupboard or on a shelf, or even out of doors.

Containers need not be limited to the conventional cut-glass or ceramic vase. Many likely ones come from the kitchen. Baskets, bowls, crocks and jugs are always useful, but try also boxes, chests or hampers for an original arrangement, or even borrow from nature and use a hollow log.

Making flowers a part of your life is infinitely pleasureable. It is a pastime from which you will reap the benefits every day.

CLASSIC
ARRANGEMENTS

Start with the classic ways of presenting and arranging flowers to create beautiful floral displays for your home. Clear, easy to follow, step-by-step photographs using various kinds of flowers make professional looking results easy. Innovative ideas for containers help you make the most of your displays. These classic arrangements can provide inspiration, instruction and a spark for your imagination.

Every room in the home can be perfect for flowers. Make them part of your decorating scheme to emphasize the style you want to create. This traditional arrangement echoes the classic mood of the lamp table.

lowers are the most versatile accessory in the home. They alter the atmosphere in a room, and can be used to change colour balance. Choose flowers carefully to complement the colour, proportion and style of a room and they will provide the perfect finishing touch. As an added bonus, in the right setting a simple bunch of tulips will look just as attractive as a showy arrangement.

Flowers in the warm tones of red, orange and golden yellow help to bring an extra glow to any room and therefore they are a welcome addition to rooms with a north-facing aspect. By the same token, light-coloured flowers, such as pastel pink, lemon-yellow, cream and white, can brighten a dark corner and are a perfect choice for the home.

Kitchen Arrangements

Kitchens are often neglected as ideal settings for flowers, yet they are the very hub of the household. The golden rule for kitchen flowers is to keep arrangements simple. Anything too elaborate looks as if it has been put in the wrong setting, and can appear inappropriate in a functional kitchen.

Most kitchens are treasure troves full of containers. A tall, narrow storage jar, with its lid propped wide open, will serve as an elegant and functional vase for a handful of spring flowers and, if there is room, a bundle of twigs. A striped china pudding basin can be decorative as well as serviceable if you display a mound of daffodils, sweet williams or lungwort raised just above the rim. In a wide-necked container of this kind, the stems will need to be held in foam or crumpled wire.

Alternatively, two or three pottery beakers or mugs, each holding a different flower variety, make an ideal kitchen display, providing that the containers are matched to a principal colour in the room.

If space on working surfaces is at a premium try to find a raised position in which to display flowers and use any space on top of a wall cupboard, dresser or a tall broom cupboard. Dried flowers are best-suited to an elevated position as they need little attention and can be left for several weeks at a time.

Do not neglect dried flowers com-

pletely, however. After a while, take them down and blow the dust from them. If a kitchen suffers from a high level of condensation, the dried flowers will eventually re-absorb some moisture. Should this happen, dismantle your display and hang the flowers in an airing cupboard or on a clothes line on a warm, sunny day to dry.

At ceiling level light can be minimal, so bright or pale flowers are most suitable in this position if the flowers are to be seen. Suitable flowers for elevated locations include: lemon-yellow, gold, pink and cream statice and strawflowers; pale-pink and pastel-blue hydrangea heads; orange Chinese lanterns; and silver-white sea lavender

ABOVE A simple shelf unit over an oak chest in a shallow recess provides the perfect setting for potted primulas placed among the china and a large preserving pan planted with daffodils.

and honesty. For a country-kitchen look hang several bunches of dried flowers from the ceiling.

Sitting room flowers

If you have a sitting room which is furnished and decorated in pale colours, a matching flower arrangement will be perfectly in keeping. However, sometimes an exact colour match is not

LEFT Attention is drawn to the buffet table by this bright diagonal design arranged in foam on top of a glass vase.

BELOW A kitchen cupboard is perfect for flower displays. A bunch of violets in a tankard stands beside lemon narcissi. A warm glow comes from the Chinese lanterns at ceiling level.

wholly appropriate, especially where cool colours are concerned. In such a case, the introduction of a few deep-orange or strawberry-pink flowers brought as bright highlights into a cream and yellow colour scheme would lift the whole room delightfully.

Another way to add a glow to a room is to create small areas of warm colour. To achieve this effect, place a pot of marmalade-orange begonias on an occasional table, a tall vase of cyclamen-pink gerberas on the mantelpiece, or a bowl of anemones on a coffee table.

Rooms which are furnished in deep, rich colours may suit toning flowers in the winter. In spring cooler tints are more effective. Introduce colour contrast – perhaps in the form of a tall jug of pale pink and cream ranunculus placed where it will be viewed against a red wall, or a glass jug of spring-green foliage, yellow and white flowers in an orange environment. This will bring a spring-like freshness to the room.

Coffee-table arrangements

In a room where a coffee table forms the focal point and chairs are positioned around it, display low flower arrangements. These look best viewed from above and the table top forms a frame around the flowers. To make a domed display, fit a shallow bowl with crumpled chicken wire and mix short-stemmed roses, garden pinks and lady's mantle; hellebores, marsh marigolds and periwinkle; or primulas, lilies of the valley and freesias.

In a sitting room with well-spaced seating, place individual flower arrangements on small tables positioned beside the chairs, thus creating splashes of colour around the room. Choose small, narrow containers as chair-side tables tend to be of limited size.

Window magic

Windows are an ideal setting for flowers, providing a natural background with changing lighting effects.

A basket of spring flowers on a wide windowsill provides a visual link with the view beyond. Casual designs with spiky twigs and deliberately untamed outlines look impressive against a garden background. Include a few branches of catkins, some hedge clippings, and

11

LEFT Purple clematis, pink mallow and lime-green lady's mantle grouped together in slim vases make a dramatic all-round design for a table. For a pretty finishing touch a single viola flower has been placed on each dish.

A buffet table is a different matter. The role of flowers here is to draw attention to the display of food and provide visual unity to an otherwise-disparate spread.

When displays are placed in any location that has a distracting background, whether it is a tempting selection of colourful dishes or a heavily-patterned wallpaper or fabric, both the choice of flowers and the way in which they are arranged is important. A random placing of soft, green foliage, red and white striped alstroemeria, yellow carnations and mimosa may look enchanting, but it could also look careless and confusing against an equally busy background. It is far more effective to design an arrangement for such a setting in which the colours are grouped in solid colours to form a regular pattern.

Bedside blooms

There is a case for having two types of flower arrangement in a bedroom. One should be a light, bright and cheerful arrangement that catches every shaft of early-morning light and makes it a pleasure to leap up and draw back the curtains. A jug of apple blossom, doronicums and golden tulips placed on a table in front of the window or at the foot of the bed would certainly give a lift to the spirits upon waking.

Alternatively, create a relaxing display. This could be as simple as two or three bunches of violets situated beneath a lamp on the bedside table, a specimen vase filled with freesias or a stem of fuchsia on the dressing table.

If the surfaces in a bedroom are cluttered, resort to a little visual trickery and place flowers where they will be reflected in the dressing-table mirror. Small bedrooms are greatly enhanced, and enlarged visually, by the clever placing of wall or free-standing mirrors. Turn this design feature to added advantage by placing an earthenware jug of lilies and carnations in a position where they will have double the impact.

fallen twigs or tree prunings in such a display. Among all this unruly material, spring flowers such as daffodils, irises and mimosa make an attractive contrast.

Narrow windowsills can be enhanced by a line of old pearly-glass medicine bottles, each holding a single flower. To ensure that the bottles do not topple over, you could secure each container temporarily to the sill with a sticky adhesive fixing pad or a small blob of florist's adhesive clay.

Another way round the problem of a narrow windowsill, which ultimately gives you more flexibility, is to fix a very narrow wooden trough or box to the sill. Line it with plastic, insert a piece of soaked stem-holding foam, and arrange flowers and foliage so that it twines up the window frame. At night it would be advisable not to draw your curtains, or you could end up knocking your carefully-arranged display.

Flowers and food

No special meal would be complete without a floral accompaniment, but flowers play a quite distinct role on the dining and buffet table. On a dining table it is the role of a flower arrangement to enhance the scene, but not dominate it visually.

SHAPING UP

Curves, crescents and triangles, the traditional shapes of flower design can help you to transform a simple bunch of flowers into a spectacular display.

ew flower arranging enthusiasts are surprised to find it is easier to create a flower design based around a traditional floral shape such as a triangle, than starting one with no planned outline.

Floral arrangements can be created to conform strictly to basic outline shapes – the triangle, the vertical, the horizontal, the L-shape and all kinds of curves.

Yet, within these formal outlines there are limitless variations open to you whether designing with foliage alone, or with a mixed collection of seasonal or artificial flowers. You can create any of the designs on any scale, from a composition large enough for a public hall to a miniature cluster to decorate your dressing table.

The essential difference

Whether a flower arrangement conforms to a traditional design shape or not, proportion plays a large part in the overall effect of the design. Half-a-dozen mopheaded chrysanthemums would look totally unbalanced in a jam jar, as would a bunch of violets resting on the rim of a tall spaghetti jar. By following some simple guidelines and gauging what looks best, you will be able to create professional-looking flower designs. These more formal arrangements are particularly suitable for special parties or social functions.

There are two basic differences between traditional flower compositions and the more informal kind. Traditional designs are composed to a code based on specific proportions, centred around the relationship between the length of the principal stem or stems and the container.

These more stylised arrangements are composed to taper gracefully towards each of their points, the three tips of a triangle or the extremes of a curve, for example. To achieve this effect a selection of plant materials in different shapes is generally needed. When choosing fresh, dried or artificial flowers and foliage, try to include some slender, pointed stems or sprays to mark the outer points of your display; medium-sized flowers or seedheads to fill in the design; and larger, rounder flowers or individual leaves to provide a focal point at the centre.

In traditional flower arrangements, the height of a vertical container or the width of a horizontal one gives a strong guideline to the finished design's overall size. Generally, the height of the main central stem in an upright design, or each of the sideways stems in a horizontal design, should be at least one-and-a-half times the height or width of the container. With this in mind, you need to select the upright vase or shallow trough carefully. If you decide upon a very tall vase or a particularly long, flat one, you may find yourself with an uncomfortably large design.

Judging the proportions

This doesn't mean you have to measure every stem and with experience, you will be able to judge at a glance that the proportions of your designs are correct.

If you choose a 25cm (10in) tall vase for an upright design, you need a central stem at least 37cm (15in) long – it could be a twig, a spray of evergreen privet or a chrysanthemum bud. Don't forget to allow for the extra length to be pushed into the foam, or concealed in the vase.

With a 25cm (10in) tall container and 37cm (15in) long stem, your design will be just over 60cm (25in) tall.

The same principle applies to designs of all sizes, however small and delicate. Gather several winter jasmine stems and early spring flowers to compose a triangular arrangement in an egg cup and follow the same plant-to-container ratio. If the egg cup is 4cm (1¾in) high,

FAR LEFT A pedestal design suits a special occasion and this spectacular triangular arrangement enhances its corner to perfection.

LEFT Slender beech twigs and pointed iris and daffodil buds provide the vertical lines of this design, while cyclamen leaves and a handful of glass chips conceal the pinholder.

BELOW A graceful figurine supports a Hogarth curve design based upon a stretched S-shape with both upward and downward movement.

the main upright stem will extend about 6cm (2in) above the rim, giving a total height of 10cm (4in).

Taking a sideways look

The proportion principle is simply turned sideways when you are measuring horizontal designs. If you want to compose a low, wide triangular shape in a shallow baking dish, first measure the dish, say it is 15cm (6in) wide. The visual length of each sideways stem, which will form the lower points of the triangle, should be at least 22cm (9in). Don't forget to allow for the extra stem length to be hidden by the container.

Never trim stems randomly, only to find you have no stems long enough. It is better to cut a little off at a time, measure the stem against the container for size, and then cut more if necessary.

Triangular designs

Once you understand how to calculate the proportions, it becomes easier and more fun to create traditional designs. Anyone who has had to arrange a pedestal of flowers for a church or other public place has good reason to be grateful to the neat, symmetrical triangle. Triangular designs can be composed in any size and proportions: tall and steeply-pointed like a church spire, or squashed almost flat, with a very short, central, vertical stem.

The triangle shape is particularly suited to any tall container, from a floor-standing pedestal or a china cake stand, to a tall candlestick or a Grecian-style urn. The lift of the container above the floor or table top encourages you not to take the geometrical shape too literally – it can look uninspiring – but to bring the side points down in graceful sweeps.

Never use a ruler to create straight lines linking the top point and the two side angles. An outline with a gentle and shallow curve dipping in at each side looks far more natural and attractive. The finished flower design will not be a perfect triangle, but a soft and pretty interpretation of the shape.

Long and short

An L-shaped arrangement is a variation on the triangular theme. These designs are especially easy to arrange in shallow containers and troughs or on trays and

LEFT The wooden and basket-weave box, an interesting combination of textures, lifts the L-shaped arrangement above the table surface allowing for the softening outlines of trailing eucalyptus sprays.

Use stems of broom, eucalyptus, ivy, or gladioli in tight bud that curve naturally to each side to form the top and bottom loops of the S-shape.

Position the stems in the foam so that they appear to be a single harmonious line, with no join at the centre. Here again the tapering rule applies, and you will need willowy materials to continue the graceful lines right through to the centre. Position the central focus flowers to visually anchor the design to the container.

Using the measurement rule

The same measurement rule applies to the curved designs as to angular ones. Measure the design from tip to toe, if it forms an upright S, or from side to side if the S is lying down.

Inverted crescent and horseshoe shapes are all variations on the theme and would suit a side table, the centre of a dining table or, on a small scale, on the dressing table.

If the arrangement is to be viewed from all sides ensure it is equally attractive from all viewpoints. Turn the design around frequently when you are making it, so that you can assess and compose it from both sides.

As you get used to creating traditional and floral arrangements, you will develop an eye for choosing the best gnarled and knobbly twig for an upright line, the right graceful sweep for a curve, and the right container to suggest a particular style.

---

boards. Select a straight stem for the main upright and place two slightly shorter ones one on either side of it. As ever, be careful to avoid a forced and unnatural effect.

The one-to-one-and-a-half rule applies only to the main upright stem. The principal horizontal, placed at right angles to the vertical to make the foot of the shape, can be of equal length or considerably shorter.

Define the shape with apple, beech or hawthorn twigs. Taper the top and side with mediumweight materials such as narcissus, and place a single large bloom such as a lily, or a cluster of three flowers close to the base angle as your focal point.

An L-shape display is economical with flowers, a bonus in the autumn, without looking sparse. Place an arrange-ment towards one end of a sideboard or windowsill, with the foot pointing along the length, and it will appear to decorate the whole space.

Gentle curves

Designs that feature graceful, romantic curves look welcoming in the hallway, elegant in the drawing room and femi-nine in the bedroom.

The most romantic design is the Hogarth curve. It takes its name from the 18th-century English painter, who called flowing curves 'the line of beau-ty'. It is also called the 'stretched' or 'lazy S', a name which fits its shape.

Containers for such an arrangement should suit the easy, flowing lines. Porcelain, pottery or plastic figurines, tall candlesticks and table-top pedestal stands all enhance the graceful outlines.

CURVING FOLIAGE

If you want to design a curved arrangement and can't find any stems with the right graceful curves – cheat. Use slender stems of broom, in leaf or in flower, and carefully tie them into a hoop. Leave them for a few hours, untie the string and they will remain curved in shape.

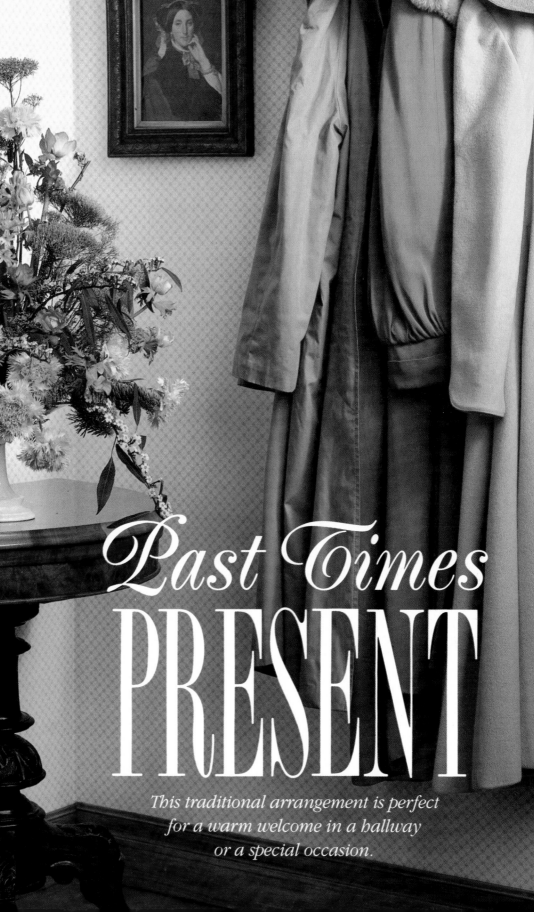

Past Times
PRESENT

*This traditional arrangement is perfect
for a warm welcome in a hallway
or a special occasion.*

Although experimenting with flowers can be great fun, it's nice to return to more traditional styles of arranging occasionally. Formal displays can be very reassuring, and restful to the eye, simply because of their familiar style and shape.

If you prefer a more traditional style of flower arranging, this display is perfect for you. However, even if modern arrangements are your speciality, a change is always refreshing. Sometime in the future you could well be asked to create a formal display for a party or an occasion in a church, and experience will help to build your confidence for such an event.

Arrangements of the past

Traditional flower arranging goes back to Edwardian, or even Georgian, times, when huge, generous displays of garden, greenhouse and wild flowers, loosely arranged into oval, bouquet-like bunches, filled English country and suburban houses. In the late 1940s and 1950s, the geometry became more pronounced and stylized, with tighter, more controlled displays replacing exuberant ones. The arrangement shown here combines the obvious geometry of a symmetrical triangle with the relaxed generosity of earlier Edwardian times.

Choosing the flowers

No one flower is dominant in this theme, and though the combination here is especially attractive, other flowers could be substituted. Florist flowers are often available out of season, and commercially-grown and imported blooms can always be found. However, some flowers do symbolize certain times of the year: the distinctly wintery *Euphorbia fulgens* used here, for example, and spring-like hyacinths. By

PREVIOUS PAGE A traditional, triangular-shaped arrangement for an old-fashioned, gracious welcome. The warm pink tones, hyacinth fragrance and graceful arrangement of foliage and flowers combine to create a feeling of hospitality at its best. Here, the setting is an equally traditional entrance hall.

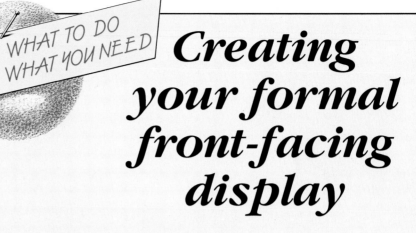

WHAT TO DO
WHAT YOU NEED

Creating *your formal front-facing display*

1 *6 hyacinth stems*	**6** *12 stems (from one branch)*
2 *20 anemones*	*of blue pine*
3 *13 'Fantasy'*	**7** *block of fresh florist's foam*
carnations	**8** *prong and adhesive clay*
4 *12 blue trachelium stems*	**9** *florist's knife*
5 *10 pink euphorbia stems*	**10** *china pedestal vase*

1 Attach a prong to the base of a clean, dry pedestal vase, with adhesive clay. Saturate a foam block, then cut it to fit, and fix it on the prong. Divide one branch of blue pine into 12 sprigs, 15-20cm (6-8in) long, then remove the lower needles. To form the basic frame-work of the display, evenly space nine sprigs horizontally around the sides of the block and three upright sprigs in the centre.

2 Snip the ends off six hyacinth stems, cutting straight across, not at an angle, and varying the stem lengths from 10cm (4in) to full size. Insert the stems close together in the centre of the block. Hold the stems at the bottom; if you push them in from the top, the stems will bend or snap. Try not to leave hyacinth stems out of water for long, as they quickly lose their moisture content and wilt.

3 Snip the ends off 13 carnations, varying the heights. Cut between the bumps, or nodes, so the stems can take up water. Use the tallest four stems to set the display's height, placing them behind the hyacinths. Use seven to form a horizontal cluster to one side of the display and group two on the other side. Insert the stems above the blue pine sprigs, angled outwards or slightly downwards.

4 Strip the lower half of ten euphorbia stems of leaves and flowers, to avoid overcrowding the centre of the display, and allow maximum water to reach the remaining foliage and flo wers. Distribute the arching branches in a ten-pointed, star-shaped pattern, with the rear branches upright; the side branches, horizontal; and the longest branches arching downwards in the front.

5 Strip off any lower leaves from 12 trachelium stems. Snip the ends, varying the lengths, then fill out an imaginary triangular frame. Use short-stemmed blooms to build up the density in the middle, and use the tallest ones to reinforce the vertical carnations. Angle a few downwards in the front side of the foam block so breaking the solid outline of the vase, and create a softer line.

6 Snip the stems of 20 anemones, varying the lengths, but leaving most stems in bud long and cutting those with more open flowers shorter. Put fully open blooms in the centre, to build up visual weight and interest, and use the long-stemmed buds to fill out the triangle's outer points. Check the display from the front for bare patches and imbalances, and make any final adjustments needed.

changing the flowers within the same basic structure you could create summer or autumn displays. For a summer arrangement lilacs would aptly replace the hyacinths, and arching sprays of white bridal wreath the euphorbia.

The colour theme here is pink, with touches of blue. It avoids being 'sugary sweet' by ranging the shades and tints of each colour from fresh to subtle and smoky. You could substitute a cream and white theme; or a yellow, apricot and orange one, with perhaps rich brown glycerined beech foliage instead of the blue foliage used here.

Large-flowered Dutch hyacinths are chosen for their delicious fragrance as well as their bright pink colour. Buy hyacinths when the florets are showing colour, and have started to open, but before they're fully open, to get the maximum display life of about a week. If the stems are twisted when you buy them, carefully and tightly wrap the bunch in newspaper, then soak it in a deep bucket or jug of cool water for several hours, or overnight.

Flowers for arching sprays

Euphorbia fulgens, a tender relative of poinsettia, garden spurges and some indoor plants is included for its arching sprays of tiny pink flowers and eucalyptus-like, blue-grey leaves. It is available in late autumn and winter; buy stems with most of the flowers open, and handle gently. You will probably have to order it from your florist; if unavailable, use arching sprays of eucalyptus instead.

FRONT-FACING DISPLAYS

- All displays should be made up proportional to the height and width of the container. In an upright display, the height of the main stem should be one-and-a-half times the height of the container. This principle can be turned sideways when measuring horizontal designs.
- In front-facing displays foliage can be placed at the back to hide the foam.

Standard 'Fantasy' carnations, with their heavily-fringed petals, are more graceful than ordinary, large-flowered types, which have a dense, massive appearance. However, solid pink carnations are suitable and they are more widely available. Whichever you choose, buy them half open, for the longest display life.

Single-flowered 'de Caen' anemones are featured, but you could use double-flowered forms instead, or even single pink chrysanthemums. Pink-red anemones are ideal, but you may have to buy two bunches of mixed colours, and extract the pink flowers. In that case, choose bunches with the most pink, or pink and cream blooms. Don't waste the scarlet and purple ones – use them in another arrangement, or display them alone, in a tall glass tumbler. Anemone stems, like hyacinths, can twist; so straighten them carefully, as you did with the hyacinth stems.

The most unusual floral ingredient is the trachelium, or throatwort. A member of the *Campanula* family, trachelium resembles sedum, with its flat heads of tiny, lavender blue flowers. Sedum could be substituted, especially in an autumnal arrangement, when russet-red tones are needed. Both are suitable for drying. Trachelium can be grown in the garden, and although perennial, is often treated as a half-hardy annual.

Choosing the foliage

Blue pine, or *Abies procera* provides the foliage for this display. Its branches are densely covered with stiff blue needles, and sprigs of it are excellent for adding bulk to a display, without adding the sombre tones usually associated with conifer foliage.

Blue pine is available from florists, but is hardy, so you could cut a small branch from a tree growing in the garden. If you want to plant one to supply you with foliage all year round, choose the variety 'Glauca', which is a beautiful silvery-blue. For this display, you could also use blue-grey juniper or pine, or dark-green spruce foliage.

Choosing the container

You need a stemmed container for this display, to allow the euphorbia branches to arch. Here, a simple white-glazed pedestal vase is used, but you could use a plain china or glass cake stand instead. If you do, fix the florist's foam block onto a shallow plastic base, then attach the base to the cake stand with florist's adhesive tape. Then you can water the display, without risking spills.

Choosing the setting

This is a front-facing display so it looks most attractive with its back against a wall. An ideal location would be on a hall table, as shown, a broad mantelpiece or sideboard. The triangular shape needs plenty of space around it to avoid looking cramped, so corner tables, unless wide-angled, are less suitable.

A traditional display like this looks best against a plain background, and a mirror is an excellent backdrop if the display is quite simple.

The setting needs to be reasonably cool in temperature to prevent the conifer needles dropping, and to extend the life of the hyacinths and anemones.

QUICK TIP

SEALING EUPHORBIA STEMS

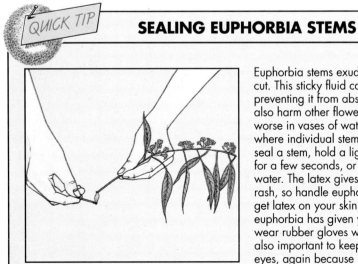

Euphorbia stems exude a milky latex when cut. This sticky fluid can block the stem, preventing it from absorbing water, and can also harm other flowers in the display. It is worse in vases of water than in foam blocks, where individual stems are more isolated. To seal a stem, hold a lighted match to the end for a few seconds, or dip it briefly in boiling water. The latex gives some people a skin rash, so handle euphorbia with care. If you get latex on your skin, wash it off at once; if euphorbia has given you a rash before, wear rubber gloves when handling it. It is also important to keep latex out of your eyes, again because it is an irritant.

SPOTLIGHT

LARGE DISPLAYS

There are times and places when large-scale flower arrangements come into their own: you may have a room corner that looks rather empty; a long blank stretch of wall that has yet to be furnished; or you may want to make a display that will be eye-catching in a hall for a party.

Large arrangements are fun to create and need not be unduly expensive. One practical and attractive way to create height and width without incurring too much expense is to use twigs and branches. Versatile foliage from which to choose includes: pussy willow with its little furry clusters; catkins with long fronds of yellow pollen; may tree in pale-green leaf; and forsythia with its bright yellow flowers. Even dead branches and twigs that you find beside a hedgerow have good decorative potential. The more gnarled and knobbly the branches, or covered with moss or silver-grey lichen, the better.

Using twigs need not stop you from making elegant designs. You can blend the most wayward of branches to good effect with elegant and dainty flowers such as spray carnations, roses, gypsophila and ranunculus.

Junk shops and jumble sales are good sources for extra-large containers and any slight imperfections can be disguised easily. For a homely appearance choose brown and beige earthenware jugs and preserve jars, large pottery casseroles and storage containers. Tall wooden flour bins and baskets will give a rustic look to large displays.

A large container will need supplementary mechanics if the arrangement is to stay firm. Fix a piece of crumpled wire mesh netting into the opening of a large or wide-necked container to hold the stems upright. Alternatively, if the arrangement calls for some stems to slant downwards over the container rim, wedge in several blocks of soaked foam extending above the aperture. Large displays can be weighted with pebbles at the bottom of the container to prevent them from tipping over.

LEFT A study in woody textures. This classically simple pot is a perfect choice for a bunch of tall, silvery-green eucalyptus sprays.

BELOW A family sized glazed pottery casserole cooks up a vibrant blend of country-garden flowers arranged in clustered groups of cool and brilliant shades.

Spring Spectacular

A simple way of bringing the freshness of spring into your home to create a classic arrangement using fresh flowers and foliage.

In spring gardens and florist shops, the bright, sunny yellows of daffodils and forsythia dominate the scene, together with the heady fragrance of mimosa, narcissus, hyacinth and lilac. As the temperature rises, flower prices start to drop, so you can afford to create extravagant displays.

This arrangement combines traditional and informal styles: a loose collection of flowers and foliage making a roughly symmetrical, triangular shape. If you're on a tight budget you can scale the project down, using a smaller jug or vase.

This is called a 'frontal' display, as it is designed to be seen only from the front, which is another advantage if you want to save money, since you get the maximum impact from each flower.

Choosing the flowers and foliage

Yellow, white and blue form the basis for this display, with splashes of red and green adding depth and contrast. Spring colours go with most schemes, but if you have a specific room in mind, you could alter the colour of the tulips, iris and narcissi accordingly.

Tulips, through the skills of commercial growers, are available nearly all year round. Here, 12 yellow tulips, striped with red, are used. Although you could use plain yellow tulips instead, the red creates attractive abstract patterns, especially when the flowers are open. For the best value, buy tulips in bud, with at least half of each bud showing colour.

'Soleil d'Or' (French for 'golden sun') is the name of the popular multi-flowered narcissus used here. It is delightfully fragrant, inexpensive and widely available in winter and spring. The double-flowered, yellow and orange 'Cheerfulness' or the white

'Paper White' could be used instead. Buy a bunch when the tiny buds are just starting to open.

When to buy

Forsythia is another symbol of spring. Buy three fairly large branches in bud, with the buds just showing colour.

Mimosa is fragrant and charming, but its little flowers can be short-lived. For best results, buy it when about half the flower balls are open, and try to keep it cool and out of direct sunlight.

Buy almond blossom, on the other hand, in tight bud, with minimum colour showing, and the small flowers will open over a span of two weeks. Ten almond stems are needed here, but you may have to order them, and the eight stems of forced white lilac, in advance from your florist. The lilac flowers should just be starting to open; avoid any with brown or papery edges.

From the garden, there are several early-flowering cherries, to use in place of the forced almond. Clusters of *Mahonia japonica* flowers could replace the mimosa; and the first of the magnolias, *M. campbellii*, could be used in place of the lilac.

Seven blue iris are used in the display. The blue colour (verging on purple) complements the yellow flowers, while the yellow markings on the iris petals, or 'falls', repeat the main colour theme. Buy iris in bud, but with the buds showing colour.

The flat, round heads of dill add a lacy touch, and the charm of a wild

flower. Buy five stems, with the small, greenish white florets open. Finally, four stems of fern-like evergreen ruscus are included. Ruscus is good value for money, lasting for two weeks. From the garden, semi-woody stems of ivy would be ideal foliage for the display.

Conditioning the material

'Conditioning' means preparing cut flowers and foliage, so they remain attractive for as long as possible. Conditioning is very important with woody stems, such as almond, forsythia and mimosa, to prevent the stems drooping and their flowers wilting.

Recut all the material as soon as you get it home, and stand the stems in a bucket of deep water overnight. Cut off the white ends of the narcissi, iris and tulip stems, which are not able to absorb sufficient water. Tightly wrap the tulip flowers and stems in grease-proof paper before placing them in water, as the petals will turn transparent. This also helps to straighten any strongly-curving stems.

Lilac and daffodil stems have sap that can shorten the life of other cut flowers, so condition each in its own container of water overnight, before adding to a mixed display. Cut these flowers to the lengths needed for the display at this point, so they don't have to be recut when you use them.

Choosing the container

A simple, creamy white, wide-necked jug, 30cm (12in) high, is used. The spout

---

HOW-TO

USING TULIPS AND NARCISSI

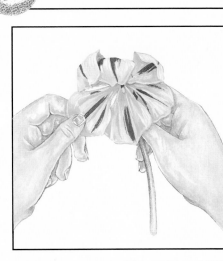

- To give tulips an exotic, lily-like appearance, try opening out their petals, so they turn back on themselves; such petals are technically called 'reflexed'. Very gently curl each petal backwards between your finger and thumb, repeating the process until it retains a graceful line.
- If you want to use tulip stems without their leaves, a quick way to neatly remove them is to cut round the stem (without breaking it) using a sharp knife. Pull the foliage off.
- Daffodils and narcissi, such as 'Soleil d'Or' used here, come complete with natural papery covers over the flower buds. To remove them, carefully pull down the protective cover and, using a sharp knife, cut it off neatly where it joins the stalk.

and handle add interest, but a wide-necked vase of a similar size would do equally well. You could repeat one of the flower colours in the vase: pale or deep yellow, red or blue.

Avoid heavily multi-coloured or dramatically patterned containers, which would distract from the flowers. A glass container is not really suitable, as the muddle of stems and wire mesh netting is anything but attractive! Avoid, too, narrow-necked containers, which are liable to give displays a pinched look.

Choosing the setting

This front-facing display looks best against a plain or lightly patterned background; the delicate floral detail would be lost seen against a strong pattern. It's a generously large arrangement, so place it in the centre of an occasional table, or on a sideboard in the dining room. If space allows, a cool bright entrance hall would make a lovely setting for this display, and the fragrance would be especially noticable in such a small room.

It is important to remember that iris and mimosa are sensitive to ethylene gas, which is released by ripe fruit and vegetables, so try to keep them away from the display.

Looking after the display

Tulips, lilac and narcissi need to absorb large amounts of water. As the stems displace much of the water in the jug, check the water daily, and top up as needed. The warmer the room, the more water the flowers will need. Remove any wilting flowers as soon as possible. As well as spoiling the look of the display, they release ethylene gas, which harms the iris and mimosa.

To refresh the flowers, lightly spray-mist them daily; you can buy inexpensive plastic misters from florists and garden centres. Give the ruscus an especially heavy spray, but try to avoid the tulips and daffodils, which turn papery and transparent if their petals come into contact with water. Shield them with a piece of greaseproof paper as you spray, and leave it in position for a few seconds, while the mist falls. Be careful too, of water stains on furniture! With your care, this glorious celebration of spring will grace your home for a week or more.

Creating a spring flower display

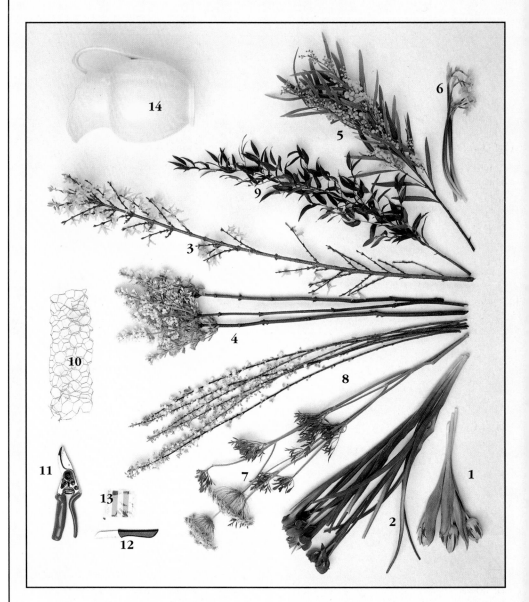

1 *12 yellow tulips with a red stripe*
2 *7 irises*
3 *3 forsythia stems*
4 *8 stems of white lilac*
5 *3 mimosa stems*
6 *1 bunch of 'Soleil d'Or' narcissus*
7 *5 stems of dill*

8 *10 stems of almond blossom*
9 *4 stems of ruscus*
10 *30cm (12in) square of chicken wire*
11 *secateurs*
12 *florist's knife*
13 *cut flower food*
14 *wide necked jug*

1 Fill the jug ¾ full of water. Add a sachet of cut-flower food to the water, according to manufacturer's instructions, and stir to dissolve. Form a piece of 2.5cm (1in) mesh chicken wire, roughly 30cm (12in) square, into a cylinder, wide enough to fit snugly in the jug. Insert the cylinder, check that it is secure, then fold over the top of the wire mesh, to make a 'lid' for holding the stems.

2 Cut three forsythia stems diagonally, snipping the stems upwards so they can take up water. Cut one stem about 75cm (30in) long, and two stems 60cm (2ft) long. Strip off the lowest branches. Insert the tallest stem in the centre, to set the height, and one on each side, to create a fan shape. Cut four lilac stems 60cm (2ft)long; and four stems 45cm (18in) long. Insert in front of the forsythia.

3 Using secateurs, cut off the lower leaves of four ruscus stems, and thin out the upper leaves. Cut two stems 50cm (20in) long; insert one on each side, to set the width of the display. Insert two stems, 30cm (12in) long, to arch over the front rim. Using a knife, cut the iris stems diagonally, stripping away some leaves and varying the stems from 20cm (8in) to full length. Group them in the centre.

4 Recut the tips of the almond stems, using secateurs, and strip any leaves or flowers that would be under water. Insert the stems to reinforce the fan shape, gently bending the outer stems to create slight curves. Trim any mimosa foliage which is hiding the flowers, then cut the stems, varying the lengths. Build up a dense mass of mimosa in the front centre, to highlight the forsythia.

5 Use the dill to add softness to the display, and as contrast to the linear forms of the stems. Remove the side shoots, which deprive the main flowerhead of water, and, using secateurs, cut five stems ranging from 30-60cm (1-2ft) long. Insert the shorter stems to fill out the base of the triangle, and use the taller ones to make a staggered pattern slightly off centre.

6 Snip the tulip stems, and open the petals of five buds (see 'How-to' box). Place them in a tight, short-stemmed mass in the centre of the display. Place longer-stemmed buds round the edges of the jug. Remove the papery wrappings from the ready-cut narcissi (see 'How-to' box), then insert them low in the front. Check that the display is balanced and top up with water.

COFFEE TABLE
CLASSIC

Combine bright spring flowers and colourful foliage in a domed display that is ideally suited for a coffee table.

colourful mixture of the very best that spring has to offer, this exuberant display is the perfect arrangement for a coffee morning, tea party or drinks party. That's because it is low and small enough to be stable and to leave space for glasses, cups and plates, while being large and colourful enough to make a lasting impression.

A domed display, such as this one, with a collar of foliage round its base, is called a Biedermeier. Named after a style popular in 19th-century Germany, Biedermeiers are based on the idea of a hand-held bunch of flowers. They are classic enough to fit into any decor, simple enough for anyone to make, and can be scaled up or down, according to your budget and the available space.

The colour scheme used here is typically spring-like: rosy pinks, creamy yellows and blues, softened by fresh greenery. It could, however, be easily translated into a single colour, or 'monochromatic' scheme, using shades of pink, for example, or all white.

Choosing the flowers

Two bunches of deep pink tulips are used, but you could use a bunch of pink and a bunch of white, or a bunch of pale pink and another of deep pink. Buy them when the buds are shut, but showing colour, and re-cut the stems when you get them home, followed by a long drink of water.

One bunch of blue hyacinths is called for in this arrangement. Buy them when the lowest florets are showing colour, but the top buds are tightly closed, and they will delight you for a week or more with their vivid colour and heavenly fragrance. Condition hyacinths by re-cutting the stems straight across – not diagonally, like most flowers – and giving them a long drink of water.

The kaffir lily, or schizostylis, is the 'odd-flower-out' in this display, since its natural flowering season is autumn.

Buy them from the florist when one or two of the lower flowers on each stem are showing colour and beginning to open. A deep-pink variety is shown here, but for a softer effect, choose a pale-pink kaffir lily.

Pink lilies are year-round favourites, but their main season is spring and summer. Buy lilies with all their buds showing colour, but not more than one flower open. When you get them home, cut off the lower, white portion of the stems, and give them a long drink. Be careful of the dust-like lily pollen; some people prefer to carefully snip off the stamens, so the pollen doesn't stain clothes or furnishings.

Festive touch

Creamy-yellow spray carnations, rimmed in red, add a festive touch. Pale or deep-pink, or plain creamy yellow, varieties could be used instead. Try to buy a bunch with half the flowers open, half in bud, and avoid bunches that have an unpleasant odour or yellow lower leaves and stems.

A mixture of dark-green and colourful foliage adds contrast and helps to hide the florist's foam base. If the types

CREATING A BIEDERMEIER SHAPE

1 Create the symmetrical outline of the display by positioning the stems of leather leaf fern around the outside edge of the florist's foam. Place a few sprigs in the centre as a site for the first flowers. Alternatively, use a few fronds of a Boston fern houseplant.

2 Place the hyacinth stems in a cluster in the centre to set the height of the dome, and the focal point of the design. Place some of the carnations at right angles to the hyacinths around the outside, then begin to fill out the dome shape by angling the others upwards.

3 The symmetrical dome effect is achieved by placing flowers of different lengths throughout the display and angling them at varying degrees to 'round-off' the arrangement. Turn the display to check the shape is consistent from every angle.

shown here are not available, aim for a variety of leaf shapes and include some dark-green foliage.

Even the smallest garden will have a few shrubs, so if the foliage used here is not available, use any attractive greenery that you can find .

Lacy foliage

Leather leaf is a florist's fern, as tough as its name. Lacy, flat ferns, such as leather leaf, are traditionally used for collars round the base of Biedermeiers and Victorian posies.

Laurustinus is a hardy evergreen shrub, worth growing for year-round foliage for flower arranging. Though not strikingly beautiful, the dark-green foliage adds bulk to arrangements, and provides a cool backdrop for more colourful material. In this display, its pretty, pink-white flowers are a bonus.

Florists sometimes stock laurustinus, but you may have to order it in advance. You could also use eleagnus or even bay foliage from the garden, or sprigs of florist's eucalyptus.

Slender, colourful grevillea leaves add an unusual touch. Grevilleas are Australian shrubs, too tender for growing outdoors in cool temperate climates, but sometimes available as cut foliage. To get the same effect, use a few leaves from a narrow-leaved variety of croton, instead. Finally, leafless twigs are included to break up the outline, or silhouette, of the display, and add vertical, linear contrast to the rounded flower forms.

Choosing the setting

The container plays a secondary role in this display, being almost entirely hidden by ferns. When making a Biedermeier you can use a plastic container, though a china one always feels nicer to work with and being heavier, is more stable than a plastic one of the same size and shape.

A coffee table is one of the natural focal points in a living room. Placed in front of the sofa, or in the corner of an 'L'-shaped arrangement of two sofas, a coffee table is where your eye rests naturally. And because coffee tables are low, you can look down on the display, and enjoy its rounded form from above. End tables, or even a dressing table, would be equally suitable locations.

WHAT TO DO
WHAT YOU NEED

Six steps to a coffee table display

1 *3 stems of laurustinus*
2 *leafless twigs*
3 *10 stems of pink tulips*
4 *5 stems of red and yellow spray carnations*
5 *4 stems of pink lilies*
6 *1 bunch of kaffir lilies*
7 *1 stem of grevillea*
8 *2 stems of leather leaf fern*
9 *5 blue hyacinth stems*
10 *fresh flower florist's foam*
11 *shallow, round ceramic bowl*
12 *florist's knife*

1 Fill the bowl a third full of water and secure the wet florist's foam. Insert the leather leaf fern around the outside of the foam to form a collar of foliage. Cut two hyacinth stems to 20cm (6in) and three to 16cm (4in), and place them in a cluster in the centre of the foam. Cut hyacinths straight across and place them in the foam immediately as they quickly lose their sap.

2 Define the outline of the display using the carnations. Trim the stems to 12-15cm (5-6in) and remove most of the foliage. Place some of the stems at right-angles to the hyacinths, at intervals between the fern. Insert the other stems at varying angles, building up a dome shape, and making sure the display is fairly symmetrical.

3 Intersperse the laurustinus with the carnations, reinforcing the rounded outline by angling the foliage towards the centre. Cut the lilies very short (just below the flowerheads) and discard the foliage. Place a few near the hyacinths in the centre, and at various intervals throughout the arrangement, following the dome-shaped frame.

4 Trim the kaffir lily stems to about 15cm (6in), leaving a few leaves near the top. Insert the flowers throughout the arrangement, varying the stem lengths to fit into the overall shape. The vivid colour of these tiny flowers is a delightful contrast to the cream hue of the carnations, and gives bright splashes of colour to the whole display. The kaffir lily is sensitive to ethylene gas,so keep away from fruit and vegetables.

5 Remove the leaves from most of the tulips (using a sharp knife). Trim the stems quite short – 12-15cm (5-6in) – and place them at intervals in the display. The tulips complement the colour of the lilies, while contrasting with the hyacinths, for an unusual, but attractive effect. Retain some of the cut-off tulip leaves, curve them around your finger and insert them around the outside of the display.

6 Break one stem of grevillea down into several small stems. Curl some of the leaves over and dot them throughout the display; leave others straight so that they stand higher than the flowers, softening the outline slightly. Insert the twigs to add a spring touch, again snipping them slightly longer to break up the rigid dome shape. Water the display regularly by parting a few flowers and using a small watering can.

A few branches of arching cherry blossom make a stark, angular silhouette against the window and shutter. Using a second flower type would spoil this effect.

All of a Kind

Make an impact with inventive, natural-looking displays using a single flower type.

An arrangement featuring just one flower variety emphasises the essential beauty of the blooms whose subtle qualities may be lost in a mixed flower design. You can also concentrate the fragrance of a delicately-scented plant, without fear that it will be overwhelmed by stronger-smelling flowers. In addition, limiting yourself to flowers and foliage from one variety of plant can be challenging: the interest in a display has to come from some other element than just the contrast in plant materials, and this forces you to be imaginative in your flower arranging.

Floral Focus

One of the main reasons for choosing flowers of a single type is to focus attention solely on the flower colour. A massed-dome design does just this, and its use of compactly-packed flower-heads highlights the colour of the blooms. Spring is one of the best times of year to experiment with displays of a single flower type as spring flowers have some of the most vibrant colours.

To make a domed display, use a fairly shallow, straight-sided dish – a soufflé, casserole or baking dish, or a short storage jar would be ideal. Fill the top of the container with a piece of crumpled wire mesh and fix it firmly in place with two lengths of florist's adhesive tape. Cut the stems of four or five flowers to the maximum height required, and place them in the centre of the dish. Cut other flowers to increasingly shorter lengths and arrange them around the first stems until those at the outside appear to be sitting on the container rim. These last flowers will hide the supporting wire.

Flower varieties suitable for this treatment include daffodils, irises and hyacinths. Freesias can also be used if cut short and placed in a small cylindrical glass; this design does not require any anchoring wire.

Individual beauty

The inverted cone is a variation of the massed-dome design in which all but the central stems are positioned at an angle. Viewed from above, the effect is also one of a mass of flowers, but each flowerhead is separate and therefore can be seen in detail. This is a gracious and adaptable style much favoured in stately homes. Inverted cone designs look very good on a side table beside a wall, on a dining table or, in the right proportion, on a coffee table.

Use any fairly shallow bowl as a container, although sloping sides which follow the direction of the stems are an advantage. Fix a large, round, heavy pin-holder with a few pieces of florist's adhesive clay to the bottom of a dry bowl. Partly fill the bowl with water, cut the chosen flower stems to a single length and press the stems onto the pin-holder. When the arrangement is finished the stems should spread out evenly so that from whichever side the design is viewed it will look like a fan.

Ensure that the stems are positioned close enough together so that the pin-holder is concealed completely.

Shaping up

Traditionally, an elegant, geometric-style design such as a triangle or a crescent comprises a selection of flowers of varying shapes – some long and pointed, others full and rounded, and a few in between. However, although it is easier to achieve stylized shapes with flower types of graduated sizes and shapes, it is not essential.

If you include some flowers that are in bud and others at more advanced stages of development, you can achieve a considerable variety of shape with a single flower type. For example, use irises that are both half-opened and fully-developed; or team underdeveloped freesia buds with their lovely, fully-opened, cone-shaped flowerheads. You can create stylish traditional designs simply by using two or more colours of your chosen flower type.

With the addition of a selection of foliage all shapes are possible. For example, you can create a triangle shape on a pedestal. To do this secure a piece of soaked florist's foam in a container and outline the triangle shape with slender stems of foliage. Position short, leafy sprays or more substantial individual leaves close to the foam. Fill in the shape by placing buds at the points and fully-opened flowers to form the central focal point of the arrangement.

Creating a crescent or curving shape is just as simple. Outline the shape with gently arching foliage stems or branches – slender pussy willow, broom or berberis would be appropriate – and fill in the shape with flowers that are at every stage of development.

Less rigid designs

It is impossible to impose the same degree of discipline on flowers which grow with wayward or naturally arching stems, such as forget-me-not, tobacco plants and gypsophila. These, therefore, need different treatment when they are to be displayed as a single flower group.

In such a simple arrangement the relationship between the blooms and their container is one of the central elements of the design, so care must be taken in choosing the container. Minute blue flowers such as forget-me-nots and the even more delicate speedwell can look like a generous mass of blue, as long as they are not overshadowed by a dominant container. A deep, straight-sided bowl in grey, mint-green or misty blue would be ideal. As the stems will drape naturally, very little of the container will show. In these circumstances a margarine tub spray-painted in a

ABOVE Country-style pottery with broad bands of bright blue and yellow makes a sunny group, and gives a lead to a pretty floral touch in the form of a simple bunch of buttercups trailing over the jug handle.

RIGHT Golden mimosa positively glows against this blue and white kitchen pottery. A block of soaked foam fitted in the neck of the container enables some stems to be angled downwards for a natural-looking display.

LEFT Trails of yellow-green periwinkle break up the golden profusion of a bunch of yellow and orange daffodils in a teapot. A trio of flowers in a matching sauce boat provides more amber interest.

patchwork or an intricately-woven Persian carpet.

If you wish, you can extend the design up and over the basket handle to make a feature of it. Twist a slender trail of ivy leaves, periwinkle, clematis, or any suitable foliage available round the handle. Add a splash of colour by tucking a single flower among the leaves. For a more lasting handle-decoration, wrap a tiny block of soaked fresh-flower foam in a self-adhesive clear plastic wrapping, and wire it to the handle. Push flower stems into the foam, their lines following the curve of the handle. Conceal the foam with some short-stemmed flowers or foliage.

A variation on the floral patchwork theme, which makes a lovely table centre for a party, can be made using a wire cooling rack in a shallow baking dish. Choose flat-faced flowers such as single spray chrysanthemums with their array of lovely colours; blue, pink and white cornflowers; or yellow, orange and bronze marigolds. Fill the dish with water. Cut the stems short to equal length and place a flower in each 'hole' in the wire mesh. You can make regular stripes of colour, reproduce an intricate quilt design, or draw a draughtboard design of contrasting colours.

Flowers and seedheads

One way to carry out the single flower variety theme is to combine flowers and seedheads from the same plant. You can often cut flowers and seedheads at the same time from the same plant. Combine a bunch of bright mauve honesty flowers with their purple and cream seed carriers and silvery-paper 'moons' in a jug to make a brilliant display.

Lupins and love-in-a-mist can also be used in flower and seedhead combinations. The lupin seed pods appear to be covered in silver velvet, and love-in-a-mist has pale pink, blue and white flowers with a touch of green and ball-like, purple and cream striped seedheads.

REGULATING DEVELOPMENT

If you buy flowers such as daffodils and irises in tight bud, but want to include a variety of shapes in your arrangement you can regulate their development to some extent.
Cut all the stems at an angle as soon as you get the flowers home. Put those stems that you wish to stay at the bud stage in cold water and keep them in a cool, dark place. Place the stems that you do not want to open fully in tepid water, and those you want to open completely in hot, but not boiling, water. Leave the latter flower stems in a warm place and they should have opened fully by the morning.

suitable toning colour would look just as attractive as an expensive piece of Wedgwood china.

Random Patterns

A pretty way to display a multi-coloured selection of flowerheads, for example primulas, zinnias or pansies, is to arrange them facing upwards in a shallow basket. Fit the basket with a waterproof lining (a margarine tub or an old glass baking dish, according to size) and fix a piece of crumpled wire flat across the top. Place the flowers side by side, their heads touching but not over-crowded, to fill the container, blending the colours to give the look of a random

TULIPS

AVAILABLE IN THE SPRING AND WINTER MONTHS IN MANY VIBRANT TONES, TULIPS ARE SOME OF THE CHEAPER FLOWERS TO BUY. TRY THESE SIMPLE ARRANGEMENTS AND FOLLOW THE TIPS FOR LONGER LASTING BLOOMS.

Although tulips are now available earlier in the winter, their natural flowering time is spring. During spring the flowers are of the best quality and least expensive. There are hundreds of varieties of tulips on sale in a wide range of bright colours – red, yellow, orange, pink, purple and white – as well as the more unusual bi-coloured blooms. We are using 'Appledoorn', a very popular variety which has single, red, goblet-shaped flowers.

Tulips are interesting and sometimes frustrating flowers to work with because however you decide to arrange them, they will always move in response to the light. Many florists think this makes them difficult to manage, but if you adopt a slightly less rigid style of arranging, you will achieve pleasing results. As you can see from our three displays even traditional flowers like tulips can look stunning arranged in more unconventional ways. With a little imagination and confidence you can show off your tulips to their best advantage.

As with other bulb flowers, avoid using tulips in florist's foam. Use alternative forms of stem support such as chicken wire, pinholders or pebbles, or just arrange them simply in a vase. Top up the vase water frequently as tulips are heavy drinkers. Tulip stems also twist and turn naturally towards the light. If you want to have straight-stemmed flowers, wrap several tulips in damp newspaper, secure the bunch well and place it in a deep container of water overnight.

QUICK TIP

BUYING AND CONDITIONING

Buy tulips when the buds are tightly closed but their colour is clearly showing. The upper half of the bud should be coloured while the rest of the bud is still green. Tulips showing no colour rarely open. Tulips will take about three or four days for their petals to open out fully and should then last a further week in displays.

It is important to condition tulips thoroughly before you begin arranging to get the maximum flower life. If you have bought tulips from the florist cut off the white lower end of the stem 2.5cm (1in) and place them in deep, tepid water as soon as you get them home. Before you begin arranging, allow them a few hours to take up water. A type of cut-flower food is sold specially for tulips. Add this to the vase water to keep it clean and free of bacteria.

1 Fill a white tulip-shaped vase two-thirds full with tepid water and add cut-flower food. Arrange two long sprays of eucalyptus, cut to a length of 45cm (18in) to the right and left of the vase. Position the eucalyptus so that it arches outwards over the two lips of the vase.

2 Insert four tulips about 38cm (15in) long, complete with their foliage, into the vase. Place them at equal distances apart in the vase. Allow their stems to overlap one another to form a criss-cross network of support in the vase. Place a fifth stem standing upright in the centre.

3 Continue adding about another eight tulips of the same height to the vase, positioning the flowers to the left or right, depending on the direction they naturally lean towards. Pack the vase with flowers and their foliage, turning the vase as you work to ensure it looks full from all angles.

Tulip fan

The long elegant stems of tulips combine beautifully with pale-green scented eucalyptus sprays to create this graceful, arching fan-shaped display. No holding tricks are needed as the shape of this white china vase provides all the necessary stem support.

1 Secure a pinholder to the centre of a shallow white dish with a blob of florist's adhesive clay. Fill the dish two-thirds full with tepid water and add cut-flower food. Insert a bleached branch firmly into the centre of the pinholder so that it stands up straight. Use the branch as the frame for your arrangement.

2 Cut the tulips to different lengths. Measure the tulips against the branch to determine their approximate height. Cut the three tallest stems with tighter buds so that they are about 5cm (2in) smaller than the highest branch. Position the tall tulips into the centre of the pinholder, close to the branch. Place two more slightly shorter tulips about 5cm (2in) further down the display to create a middle level and to show off all the flowerheads. Gently ease back the outer petals on these two tulips to open up the flowerheads fully.

3 Insert another two tulips, with more open flowers, low down in the display to mask the pinholder. Alternatively you could use pebbles or marbles to hide the mechanics if your flowers are in tight bud.

BELOW This vertical, front-facing arrangement uses only a few tulips to create a strong visual impact. The tulips follow the simple curving line of a bare bleached branch which adds an oriental look to the display. Top up the shallow dish regularly as tulips drink a lot of water.

Red hot and oriental

1 Cover the base of a large, rectangular, clear glass vase with a layer of sand to a depth of about 5cm (2in). Rinse some small pebbles or shingle thoroughly under clean running water to remove any dirt particles. Cover the sand with a layer of pebbles. Arrange the pebbles to form a curvy line to add interest to the bottom of the vase.

2 The more tulips you use the more stunning the result. We have used six bunches for this large vase. Cut all the red tulips to a length of about 25cm (10in) so that they do not stand too tall above the rim of the vase. Cut the stems at a slant and leave the foliage on the stems to bulk out the display. Begin arranging the tulips around the rim of the vase.

3 Fill the entire vase with tulips, working your way into the centre of the vase. Allow some leaves to overlap the edge of the container. The flowers will support one another so do not push the stems right into the sand. It will not be possible to arrange each flowerhead so that they all face forward, as tulip stems tend to curve towards the light.

Red sea of tulips

A rectangular, clear glass vase brimming with vibrant red tulips creates a stunning array of flowers in a bed of sand and pebbles. Place this simple modern arrangement at eye level. Note how your display changes as the flowers start to open.

WHITE LILIES

JUST PURE WHITE LILIES AND A LITTLE FOLIAGE FOR CONTRAST, IN THREE DELIGHTFULLY DIFFERENT STYLES – CLASSIC, INFORMAL AND MODERN. USE LILIES TO CREATE LONG-LASTING ARRANGEMENTS COMBINING ELEGANCE AND SIMPLICITY.

Longiflorum lilies (florists call them 'longis') have such a luminous quality that wherever an arrangement is placed, the flowers almost seem to 'glow'. The purity of their colouring, symbolising peace and tranquility, makes them an appropriate choice for your home at Christmas.

Long-lasting lilies will see you right through the twelve days of Christmas. Use them to brighten up a dark corner or to provide a strong highlight against a plain wall. Or place your arrangement in the hallway so that guests are greeted by a magnificent display and the heavenly scent of the flowers is carried all around the house.

Buying lilies
At the florist, you pay for the number of flowerheads – not the number of stems. Choose those with slightly open buds – tightly-budded flowers may have been 'forced' and will open into sub-standard flowers.

HOW-TO AVOIDING LILY POLLEN STAINS

A vase of elegant lilies looks beautiful, but falling pollen can leave unsightly stains on clothes and furnishing fabrics. To prevent showers of pollen, nip off each lily stamen between thumb and forefinger while preparing the flowers.

However, if the worst happens, sprinkle a little talcum powder over pollen-stained patches and brush off briskly with a clothes-brush. Repeat until the stain fades.

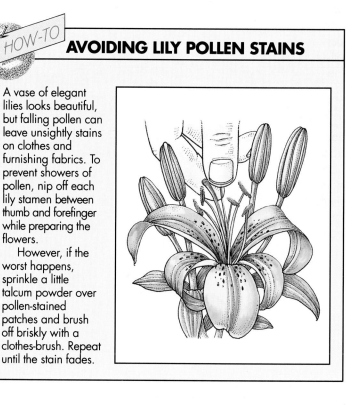

1 No extra foliage is needed here: just seven lilies. As a rough guide, the height of the arrangement should be about two thirds that of the vase. The central lily stem is tallest in this design. Hold the flower by its stem upside down against the vase to judge the correct height. Cut the stem, then remove the lower leaves.

2 Place the tallest lily in the centre of the vase, then, using it as your maximum height guide, add more lilies with stems cut to different lengths. To help you decide where to place individual stems, hold each one up to see which way it leans naturally. Insert the lilies so that they are all leaning outwards. The stems should support each other, keeping the blooms in place so that the flowers open in the right direction.

3 Add the rest of the lilies – let your eye be your guide as to how long or short each stem should be. As more stems are added they will give firm support to the others, and the individual flower-trumpets will stand proudly without drooping. Lastly, angle the flowerheads to face outwards so that the arrangement can be appreciated from all sides.

RIGHT White on white gives a stunning effect, while green foliage provides strong contrast. Make this an eye-catching feature by setting it against a plain wall. Or use it to light up a neglected corner or dark area in the house.

Informal elegance

1 For this strikingly modern arrangement you will need just two stems of lilies and bear grass (or delicate-looking foliage of your choice). Cut one stem so that it is about two thirds the height of the vase. Remove the lower leaves and place the stem in the centre of the vase. Because the vase is tall and narrow, you won't need to use stem-holding props.

2 Cut the stem of the second lily to a shorter length and place it in the vase next to the first stem. Trim the ends of the bear grass, removing the dried brown ends. Place a delicate spray to one side of the arrangement, fanning it out slightly so that it curves in a graceful arc over the side of the vase.

3 Place another spray of bear grass on the opposite side of the arrangement to balance the overall shape. This design is meant to be seen from the front, so make sure that the flowers and foliage have their 'best face forward'. As a finishing touch, loosely knot a few straps of bear grass to form a 'loop' in the centre of the arrangement. The delicate arching sprays set off the lilies to perfection.

BELOW A magnificent contrast – jet black coupled with pure white. The slightly abstract design is inspired by Japanese flower arranging styles.

'Sculpture' in black and white

1 You will need a glass bowl, tree grass and five lily stems. Trim the ends of the tree grass sparingly as the sprays should be left fairly long. Fill the bowl with grass, fanning it out gently over the rim.

2 Cut five lily stems to short lengths. To create the circular display, begin in the centre of the bowl. Place the longer stems just off centre, then insert the other lilies carefully among the foliage.

3 When you have added all the lilies, adjust the arrangement so that the final effect is natural-looking. Do this by gently lifting the flowers and grasses, then letting them 'fall' over the glass rim.

Clear-cut classic

RIGHT This traditionally elegant arrangement is perfect for lilies that are slightly past their best, but still with plenty of life left. A charming dinner table display, it looks equally good on a coffee table where it can be appreciated from above, as well as from the sides. Include buds as well as open flowers for a lasting display.

DAFFODILS

FOR MOST OF US THE SIGHT OF DAFFODILS IN THE SHOPS AND GARDENS IS A SURE SIGN THAT SPRING IS FINALLY HERE. MAKE AN IMPACT WITH THESE QUICK-AND-EASY, STYLISH ARRANGEMENTS.

Daffodils with their golden, trumpet-shaped flowerheads are naturally beautiful. Whether you pick up a bunch at the florist or grow them in the garden, bring their brilliant yellow colour into your home and show them off to their best advantage by trying one of our three simple arrangements.

Daffodil is the common name for a member of the family of bulbs known botanically as narcissus. There are many different kinds of daffodils on sale for just a few pence a bunch; popular varieties include: yellow with orange centres (such as 'Fortune' and 'Hollywood'), white with orange centres (such as 'Sempre Avanti'), but the traditional daffodil is yellow (such as 'Dutch Master' and 'Golden Harvest').

Daffodils once they have been properly conditioned (see 'Quick tip'), combine beautifully with other spring flowers. We have combined them with mimosa to create a perfect combination of delicious scents. As with the majority of bulb flowers, daffodil stems are soft and 'heavy drinkers' and therefore unsuitable in foam-based designs. Economy foam has been used in our spring basket design. This is less dense than other types of foam and allows narcissi to take up water more effectively.

QUICK TIP — BUYING AND CONDITIONING

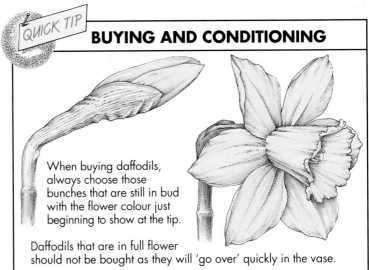

When buying daffodils, always choose those bunches that are still in bud with the flower colour just beginning to show at the tip.

Daffodils that are in full flower should not be bought as they will 'go over' quickly in the vase.

Daffodils exude latex which is harmful to other cut flowers. When conditioning daffodils, cut and slit their stems and stand them on their own, in water, for approximately 24 hours. Before arranging in a display rinse the stems in fresh water.

1 Fill a round, glass bowl two thirds full with water and add cut-flower food. Cut the stems to roughly the same length, about 30cm (12in) long. Remove the daffodil foliage and place each stem at an angle. Place the first stem to the right and the second stem to the left, one in front and one behind so that they cross one another in the middle of the vase. As well as holding the stems together, this network of stems looks attractive under water in the clear vase.

2 Continue adding the daffodils to the vase in the same way, placing one to the right and one to the left of the glass bowl, and some to the centre of the display, to build up a criss-cross network of stems that support one another. Place the flowerheads facing outwards, leaning over the rim of the bowl, resulting in a posy-shaped array of daffodil heads.

3 Remove the bottom leaves from the mimosa stems and a few leaves from the top of the stems, to thin out the foliage. Cut ten stems of mimosa to a length of 30cm(12in). Insert the mimosa stems in between the daffodils to add variety of texture and scent to the display. In our arrangement the yellow, bobbly flowers are not fully open at the top of the mimosa stems, but they will blossom over the next few days to give the design a slightly fuller effect.

Scented yellows

1 Fill the vase two thirds full with water, cut about 2.5cm (1in) off the first daffodil stem, so that you keep the stem as long as possible. Place the stem in the centre of the vase, facing forwards. Make sure that your glass vase is not too tall, the daffodil head should sit about 12.5cm (5in) above the rim of the vase so that it is clearly visible.

2 Select two tall daffodil stems and keeping their leaves, cut about 5cm (2in) from one stem and 7cm (3in) from the other stem, both at an angle. Position the two flower stems with their foliage in the vase, placing one facing to the right and one to the left of the central daffodil. If you have a ceramic rather than clear glass vase and your flowers are not quite tall enough, you can always cheat. Pack out the bottom of the container with tissue paper or small pebbles to raise the base and increase the flower height.

3 Remove the brown stem ends from the bear grass, by cutting off 2.5cm (1in) of the stem end. They do not look very attractive under water in a transparent glass vase. Add about ten single stems of bear grass. Allow these to fan out around the flowers – their arching forms trail down the edge of vase and help break up the rigid verticality of the display.

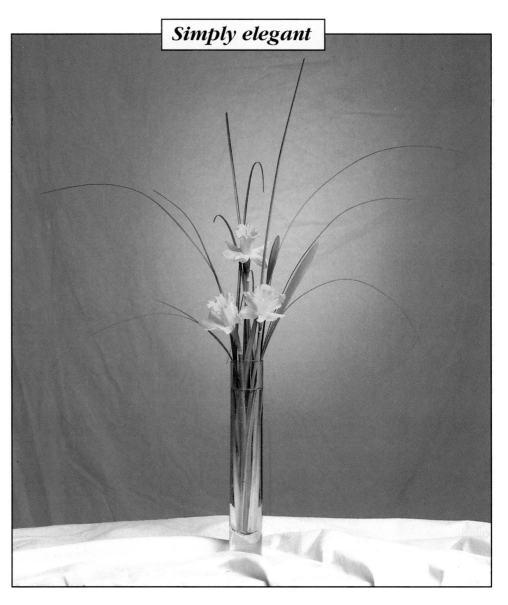

Simply elegant

1 Secure a block of wet florist's foam into a plastic lined basket. Cut three daffodil stems at an angle to a length of about 18-20cm (7-8in). Position them together in the centre of the foam to determine the basic shape and height of this front-facing, fan-shaped arrangement. Place one daffodil low down, horizontally on either side of the foam block to set the width of the display.

2 Begin filling in this basic framework with flowers. All the daffodils should be placed at an angle so that their stems radiate out from the central point. Insert 18-20 cm (7-8in) long stems, low over the rim of the basket and 10-12cm (4-5in) stems at a steeper angle towards the centre, making sure all the trumpet-shaped flowers face outwards. Use the more open flowerheads in the centre to hide the foam block.

3 Continue building up the fan shape of the arrangement by following the shape of the basket handle, adding flowers to create a generous, bushy display which conceals the foam base. Finally, frame the flowers with about fifteen daffodil leaves. Insert these into the back of the foam behind the basket handle and over the rim of the basket in the front. Top up the foam frequently with water.

Spring basket

STOCKS

USED ON THEIR OWN, OR MIXED WITH OTHER SPRING GARDEN FLOWERS AND FOLIAGE, THE TALL COLUMNS OF FRAGRANT WHITE STOCKS LEND THEMSELVES TO A STRIKING RANGE OF NATURAL AND FORMAL DISPLAYS.

Tall and stately with pastel-coloured fragrant flowers, stocks are one of the most appealing of old-fashioned English blooms. Grow your own in the garden for spring arranging or buy them from the florist at a reasonable price and discover their flower-arranging possibilities.

Stocks or *Matthiola incana*, have characteristic 3cm (1¼ in) wide double flowers arranged in close clusters about 15-20cm (6-8in) long at the top of their stems. Their average stem height when cut is 30-70cm (12-28in) which makes them ideal ingredients for tall displays. For flower arranging it is best to grow Ten Week Stocks, All Year Round Stocks and Brompton Stocks. Garden stocks are perfect for natural, country-look displays but for more formal, large-scale church or hall displays, the uniform shape, height and colour of florist flowers are more suitable.

In single-flower arrangements, use either stocks of one colour or a mixture of white, mauve, pink, cream and salmon red varieties; add a little foliage to the flowers to enhance their shape and colour. Alternatively, stocks combine well with summer herbaceous border flowers. Mix them with pink phlox, which are similar in height, to create deliciously-scented bouquets of flowers or combine them with blue or white Canterbury bells, roses, and lilies. Stocks look particularly stunning in all-white wedding bouquets or pedestal arrangements where their long stems provide strong line and shape.

QUICK TIP

BUYING AND CONDITIONING

Shop-bought bunches of stocks normally contain a mixture of pastel-coloured flowers. Their season is from late spring through to early summer, but they are increasingly available out of season. Buy stocks when about half of the flowers are open.

Stocks can be difficult flowers to use in arrangements, as they tend to have a short vase life, have weak stems and contaminate water quickly. Careful conditioning can overcome these problems. Remove the lower white section of the stems, along with the excess lower foliage. Once arranged, the stem ends should be re-cut frequently. It is important to add cut-flower food to the water to prevent contamination. Position the finished arrangement away from direct sunlight, heat and draughts. With proper care stocks will live up to seven days in the vase.

1 Fill a tall, black cylindrical vase two-thirds full with water. Trim the stem ends off three large sprigs of fresh sea lavender so that they are about 40cm (16in) tall. Position one lavender stem in the centre of the vase, one stem to the left and one to the right. These delicate flowers will form a light feathery background to the stocks.

2 Remove the lower leaves from the bottom 15cm (6in) of nine stems of white stocks so that no foliage falls below the water-level in the vase. Trim off the lower white section from each stem, about 5cm (2.5in) and cut each stem to varying lengths so that the flowerheads will

appear at slightly different heights in the display. No supporting mechanics are needed as the thick stock stems, with their bushy foliage, should support one another in this narrow-necked vase.

3 Begin the arrangement by placing one stem about 60cm (24in) tall to the right of the vase. Add two more white stocks of similar length to the middle and to the left of the vase. Arrange a further six shorter flower stems to the front and the back of the vase to build up an all-round display. Allow several leaves of the stock stems at the front of the display to cascade over the rim of the vase to break up its solid black line.

Scented elegance

Soft, frothy, fragrant flowerheads of white stocks appear refreshingly bright against vivid green leaves and a dramatic black vase. Place this tall, elegant display on a living room or hall table and allow the delicious scent of the flowers to fill your home.

1 Line a tall-handled wicker basket with plastic and, using a prong and adhesive clay, insert a block of moist florist's foam in the base. Trim ten short sprigs about 10cm (4in) long off some variegated silver pittosporum foliage. Insert the shorter stems into the florist's foam at the front of the basket and progressively longer stems towards the back. Allow the foliage to extend above the basket handle to give the display the required height.

2 Remove the leaves from the bottom 10cm (4in) of five stock stems, keep them to one side to use later to fill in the display. Decide where you are going to position the stocks, in the basket before inserting them in the florist's foam, as their thick stems leave large holes. Place the tallest stem about 30cm (12 in) high in the middle of the basket, behind the handle and positon two stems of about 15cm (6 in), each to the left and the right in the front of the basket.

3 Place two more shorter stems about 10cm (4in) high close to the rim of the basket, position one to the right and one to the left. Fill in any gaps with a few individual stock leaves to the front of the display. Allow some of the leaves to tumble over the outer edge of the basket to create a more natural look.

Country basket

The cream tips of silver variegated pittosporum foliage combine well with radiant white stocks. The natural beauty of the display is well-suited to the woven basket container. Place this informal, front-facing display in a kitchen, or present it as a gift to a friend or relative.

1 Using florist's adhesive clay, secure a pinholder to the centre of a shallow round dish. Place a large stem, of soft asparagus densiflorus fern, about 30cm (12in) high, in the centre of the pinholder. Place a shorter bushy sprig of asparagus fern about 10cm (4in) long lower down in the design to camouflage the pinholder.

2 Cut five stems of stocks to different heights, ranging from about 30cm (12in) to 10cm (4in) tall. Place the tallest stem upright in the centre of the pinholder and progress down the display towards the front of the dish, positioning one stem to the right and one stem to the left in turn. Make sure that each flowerhead is clearly visible from the front of the display.

3 Lastly, add a few short sprigs of sea lavender near the base of the display to help disguise the pinholder and to add some variety of texture. The soft grey of the lavender combines well with the pale pink dish which we have used here.

RIGHT A variety of textures and subtle range of tints gives this display the atmosphere of an oriental miniature garden. The green foliage acts as a perfect frame to the flowers and allows the eye to follow the curving line of delicate blooms down through the whole arrangement.

Miniature garden

ANEMONES

BRING A VIVID RANGE OF HUES TO YOUR HOME THIS SPRING WITH RICH BLUE, PURPLE AND RED ANEMONES. FOLLOW ONE OF OUR THREE SIMPLE DESIGN IDEAS AND CREATE AN INEXPENSIVE DISPLAY WITH A DRAMATIC LOOK.

The season to buy anemones is spring, even though it is common to find these immensely popular flowers in florist shops all year round. During spring their jewel-like colours are then at their best and, even if you do not grow your own from tubers in the garden, they are inexpensive to buy. The two most popular varieties of anemones are 'De Caen' and 'St Bridgid' which are available in a wide range of colours.

When choosing anemones to buy from the florist, look for those with petals that are just beginning to open. Though they don't look as impressive at this stage, they will open shortly and you can be sure that they will last up to ten days in a vase, if you cut and condition the thick stems properly.

Anemones, like other tuberous flowers, absorb water very quickly so check the water level in the vase at regular intervals. Florist's foam is not a very suitable source of moisture or support for anemones. (Foam does not encourage water uptake, also it tends to break up when the thick anemone stems are inserted.) As an attractive alternative, try using colourful marbles to support the stems in glass containers.

QUICK TIP

STRAIGHTENING CURVED STEMS

1 Wrap the flowers fairly tightly in a few sheets of dampened newspaper. Place the flowers facing inwards. Secure the bunch with an elastic band.

2 Stand the bunch in a deep container of water, such as a bucket, and keep them out of the light in a cool, dark place overnight.

1 Thoroughly wash the marbles in a bleach solution to clean them of bacteria or dirt particles. Pour the purple glass marbles carefully into the bottom of a square, clear glass container until the vase is about a third full of marbles. Next fill the vase two-hirds full with water and add a few drops of bleach to prevent the water from clouding over and spoiling the effect.

2 Choose four or five purple and pink anemones with long, curving stems. Cut about 2.5cm (1in) off the thick stems at an angle and position one stem towards the back of the vase in the centre. Wedge each thick anemone stem firmly into the bed of marbles, to a depth of about 5cm (2in). Position two or three anemone stems of the same length on either side, leaning slightly outwards to the right and left of the vase. Make sure that each flowerhead is facing forward.

3 Place a row of ten purple and red shorter stemmed anemones, about 20cm (8in) long in front of this row making sure all the faces of the flowers are visible. Hold the stems just below the flowerheads when pressing them between the marbles so that they do not break. Adjust any flowers as necessary so they are held in an upright position. Keep topping up the vase with water regularly as anemones are heavy drinkers.

Marble magic

Purple marbles are used as an attractive support for anemone stems in this glass container. Alternatively, you could use pebbles, shells or shattered glass to support the stems for an equally effective result. All these materials will catch the light and add interest to the bottom of the vase.

1 Fill a frosted-blue glass vase two-thirds full with water. Cut three stems of eucalyptus to a length of about 40cm (18in). Remove the lower leaves so that they do not fall below the water level. Position each long stem of eucalyptus around the rim of the vase. The neck of the vase is fairly narrow so no holding tricks are needed. Place one stem to the left and one to the right and one in the centre of the display, to form the basic height and width of the arrangement.

2 Cut about 2.5cm (1in) off the anemone stems but keep the stems long so that they are a similar height to the eucalyptus. Use only deep red and purple anemones. Position about ten anemones in this range of colours at random around the edge of the vase and amongst the eucalyptus leaves. Follow the direction they naturally lean towards: if the flowerhead leans to the right place it on the right; if to the left position it on the left.

3 Cut down the stems of anemones with more open flowerheads to about 20cm (8in). Place them towards the front of the vase so they appear to be just peeping over the rim of the vase. These will form the focal point in the centre front of the arrangement.

Midnight blue

Deep purple, red and pink anemones in a frosted-blue glass vase create a strikingly dramatic feature. Trailing branches of soft, green eucalyptus act as a frame to the full flowerheads. This modern, all-round arrangement would create an impact in a simple monochromatic room.

1 To create a small, posy-shaped arrangement, fill a plain blue mug two-thirds full with water. Cut off about five or six side stems of ming fern and arrange them around the rim of the mug. Intertwine the stem ends so that they support each other in the container. The foliage will create a light, feathery effect and form a soft frame for the flowers.

2 In this case red anemones are used in a blue mug. You will need about one bunch of anemones per mug. Cut down the stems of the red anemones to about 10cm (4in). Arrange a mixture of open and closed flowers around the rim of the mug. Position the more open flowerheads in the centre of the mug about 2.5cm (1in) higher than those around the edge.

3 Lastly, fill in any gaps with three or four more flowers of the same length to create a fuller effect. This type of arrangement is highly economical as well as attractive, as you can use flowers from an earlier arrangement. You will prolong their life by cutting the stems right down to fit into smaller displays such as the featured blue mug.

Flower cups

RIGHT A duo of bright blue and red china mugs is a simple, attractive way to liven up traditional posies of anemones. This arrangement would be ideal for a dressing table in a guest room or on a window-sill in a kitchen. Such displays are a practical way of re-using anemones from more elaborate arrangements. Cutting the flower stems short will ensure that they live for another few days.

CONTAINER CREATIVITY

Resourceful flower arrangers never run out of containers. Even the most unlikely-looking household objects have potential and can be transformed into attractive – if unusual – flower holders.

 t those times when all your usual vases are in use or you simply feel like something different, it's fun to explore the possibilities of all kinds of articles around the home that can be used to hold an arrangement of fresh or dried flowers. There's hidden potential in even the most basic kitchen equipment, and all it takes is a little imagination to turn everyday implements into attractive containers.

To hold fresh flowers, a container simply needs to be able to conceal a small holder of water – and the water-carrier can be as slender and unobtrusive as an orchid phial or a piece of soaked stem-holding foam.

The improvised container does not even have to have an opening, as several of our colour photographs demonstrate. The foam (suitably covered, to avoid moisture seepage) can be fixed on top of a box, to a basket handle, onto a figurine or other ornament, and them completely concealed by judiciously placed leaves and short-stemmed flowers.

It is even easier to convert unusual containers for use with dried flowers. A water holder isn't necessary – a piece of

florist's adhesive clay is often all that is needed to secure the stems – and there is no problem with dampness from soaked foam. The special clay (it is usually grey or brown and slightly shiny) for use with dried flowers holds stems firmly in place.

The search begins

The hunt for containers with a difference begins at home – though junk shops, jumble sales, garden centres and supermarkets all have valuable and inexpensive contributions to make.

Tableware of all kinds makes perfect flower holders. Cups and saucers, with a posy of flowers in the cup and a single tiny flower floating in the saucer; tea and coffee pots, jugs in all shapes and sizes, from romantically flowery to angular modern styles, offer inspiration for the colour and shape of your different flower designs.

Saucers and plates make flat and spacious, versatile flower holders. All they need is a block of foam held firmly in place to secure flowers in triangular, L-shaped or random designs. Elegant china might seem best suited to formal designs outlined with slender leaves, while chunky pottery plates look just right with more lush sprays of foliage, clusters of shiny berries and a more informal approach.

Kitchen classics

Saucepans, casseroles, lemon squeezers and storage jars – all of these items and any others with an aperture deep or spacious enough to hold water or conceal a piece of foam can be used for displaying flowers.

If you have a metal vegetable or herb mill that is only in occasional use, it could become the centre of attention at your next informal party. Line the bowl of the vessel with foil (since it isn't watertight), and wedge in a block of soaked foam (for fresh flowers) to extend above the rim. The kitchen has all kinds of flat containers to offer: shiny-bright baking pans, cake tins, confectionery moulds, wire cooling racks – the list is enormous.

Take, for example, a black four-hole Yorkshire pudding pan. Attach a block of foam to one of the indentations, top up with water and style an arrangement of brightly coloured flowers, leaves or berries that will be vividly displayed against the dense, matt surface.

To use a flat container that has no convenient indentation, wedge the foam into an unobtrusive container of its own – an up-turned coffee jar lid is ideal – and tape it to the (absolutely dry) surface, using florist's tape.

Novel containers

Much modern packaging has great style, so don't overlook the potential value of old food, drink and cosmetic containers; tins, jars, bottles and packets as unusual, yet striking flower containers. A collection of cola cans turned flower containers would be eye-catching and appropriate in the centre of a teenage party table; stylish cosmetic jars are at home with a posy of tiny flowers on a dressing-table; and wine bottles make tall and practical 'vases' for long-stemmed material such as hippeastrum or alstroemeria.

Food packets as flower containers are not as impractical as they might seem. Partly fill them with dried beans or tiny pebbles as ballast, line the top with a double layer of foil and insert a piece of soaked foam. After that, use them as normal containers.

RIGHT An old box Brownie camera snaps into action for a monochromatic masterpiece. Any similarly-shaped box would be suitable. Fix a holder of foam on top and arrange the flowers to extend well to the back, avoiding a top-heavy look.

BELOW A bright and breezy design on this packaging inspires a simple arrangement of flat-faced blooms.

Practically any foodstuff that has a firm, outer shell or can be hollowed out to leave firm, sturdy walls, will hold a display of flowers.

A cottage loaf is a splendid example of such an unconventional container. Scrape out the centre and put the shell in a cool oven to dry thoroughly (the bread shell will keep, in a dry place, for weeks). For an extra-shiny finish, paint the crust with clear varnish.

Insert a waterproof container (if using fresh flowers) into the loaf cavity. Fill it with water or wedge it in with soaked foam and treat it as any other flower container.

Scoop out your fruit

Pineapples and pumpkins, melons, marrows and citrus fruits of all kinds can be treated in a similar way. Cut a slice from the top, scoop out the flesh and wash and dry the shell. Check that it will stand firm, and cut a slice from the base if necessary. It is possible to dry out pineapple shells in the oven, but others tend to crack, wither and otherwise lose their natural sparkle, so its best to regard these as only short-term flower holders.

Line the fruit or vegetable shells with a layer of kitchen plastic wrap if you wish and insert a container for the water or foam. A pineapple fitted with a high-rise block of foam looks good enough to eat spilling over with a cascade of lesser fruits and brilliant flowers; orange shells lined with egg cups make neat little vases for posies of violets, forget-me-nots, snowdrops and other miniature flowers; a dark green melon shell would look dramatic with russetty leaves and glowing berries.

A sentimental journey

Children's toys, a wooden truck or bus, a small dolls' pram or cradle, can be just the shape to inspire a floral creation – big, bold and beautiful for a bus, dainty and feminine for a cradle. And outgrown, leather-look boots, polished till they gleam, look just the thing in a corner, resplendent with an array of twigs and seedheads.

Many old family favourite articles that are broken or no longer in use, such as cameras and radios make surprisingly attractive, unique containers for flowers.

ABOVE This hollowed-out (and oven-dried) cottage loaf makes a crisp and shiny container for sprays of eucalyptus and gerberas, spray chrysanthemums and a carnation in marmalade shades.

ABOVE Putting on the style with mahonia leaves, freesia and clusters of wired-on fruits cascading from a scooped-out pineapple shell.

BOTTLES

DON'T THROW AWAY OLD WINE BOTTLES AND CARAFES. PUT THEM TO GOOD USE AS APPEALING CONTAINERS FOR FOLIAGE AND FLOWERS.

Undecorated glass carafes and bottles make striking containers for foliage and flowers, providing height and form to displays in much the same way as a candlestick or pedestal vase.

Don't be put off by glass bottles with narrow necks. As long as their overall shape is attractive, they are ideal for displaying single stems of flowers or berries – especially for Oriental-style displays. Narrow-necked bottles can be converted quite simply into a more useful flower holder with the help of a candlecup that allows you to insert plant material at any angle for a generously-full overall effect.

Collecting glass containers

You can recycle old wine bottles for displaying foliage and flowers. Alternatively, kitchen shops or kitchen sections of department stores usually have a selection of inexpensive glass carafes and storage jars. There is nothing fresher-looking than clear glass, but, unfortunately, it allows any fixing mechanics to be seen. Textured or tinted glass helps camouflage the contents of the container, but the darker and more opaque the glass, the heavier the overall effect.

Some speciality foods, such as olive oils, walnut oils, flavoured vinegars and stem ginger in syrup, also come in

LEFT A candlecup, concealed by fern, eucalyptus and laurustinus foliage, allows a more generous, graceful display than if the stems were placed directly into the neck of the bottle.

1 1 branch of laurustinus
2 6 stems of eucalyptus
3 7 stems of fern
4 bottle
5 candlecup
6 florist's adhesive tape
7 florist's adhesive clay
8 florist's foam
9 scissors

1 Ensure that the bottle is clean and dry so that the florist's adhesive clay will stick to the inside of the bottle neck. Soak the florist's foam until it is saturated with water. Shape to fit the candlecup. Cut a piece of adhesive clay the same length as the circumference of the bottle neck. Press the clay onto the inside of the bottle neck.

2 Place the candlecup into the bottle neck and anchor it to the clay. Attach a length of tape to the side of the candlecup and pull it over the foam. Cross this with a second piece of tape. The tape should not cross in the very centre of the foam as this makes it difficult to insert the foliage stems that will create the focal point of the display.

3 Cut the fern into sections, the tallest of which should be one and a half times the height of the container. Place this at the centre back of the foam. Position more fern stems either side of the central stem so that they lean away from it naturally. Angle shorter stems downwards around the foam base to form a collar.

4 Soften the line of the display with stems of eucalyptus. Cut them slightly longer than the fern, but follow the same basic shape. Place one stem at the centre back of the foam and allow others to fan out as if growing from the same central spot. Insert small eucalyptus sprigs throughout the display.

5 Fill in any bare patches in the centre of the display with small sprigs of laurustinus. Allow some of the sprigs to trail and soften the vertical line of the bottle. Make sure the candlecup is completely disguised. The laurustinus flowers add colour contrast to this front-facing arrangement.

attractive bottles which you can use. Alternatively, antique bottles make pretty containers.

Using candlecups

Candlecups are small, shallow, watertight bowls made of plastic or metal. The base is shaped like a funnel so that it fits tightly into the narrow neck of a container. Originally used for arranging flowers on top of candelabra and candlesticks, candlecups are equally useful for narrow-necked bottles, vases or jugs. Candlecups are held in place with florist's adhesive clay or, more permanently, with glue.

Candlecups can be filled with water and crumpled wire mesh or saturated florist's foam block. Flower and foliage stems are inserted directly into the candlecup but, because it is hidden by the flowers and foliage, the arrangement appears to be springing directly from the container.

You can make your own candlecups by glueing small, lightweight plastic bowls, such as empty ice-cream tubs, onto suitably sized bottle corks, but there is always a risk of the two parts coming unstuck at a crucial moment. Fortunately, manufactured candlecups are inexpensive and your florist should stock them or order some for you.

Choosing the flowers and foliage

You can use whatever foliage and flowers you like in a bottle display as long as you judge the proportions correctly. The plant material should be large enough to make an impact and conceal the candlecup, but not so large that it upsets the container. The narrower and taller the bottle, the more critical this is.

In the green bottle, an all-foliage combination of evergreen laurustinus, eucalyptus and fern is used to create a cool, all-green look. Alternatively, try using cotoneaster, berberis or camellia foliage instead. If you want a trailing effect, include stems of ivy, or introduce variegated holly or elaeagnus for colour.

In the clear-glass carafe, eucalyptus and laurustinus leaves are combined with broom, *Euphorbia fulgens* and solidaster, for a cheerful, yellow display. The naturally-arching broom and *E. fulgens* add a width and grace that counteracts the potentially 'pinched' look of flowers and foliage arranged in a narrow-necked container. Flowering spiraea, philadelphus branches or arching sprays of ceanothus in flower could be used instead.

Caring for the display

If you use a candlecup with florist's foam, keep it topped up with water. On the other hand, if you place the stems directly into a clear glass container, you will probably have to change the water every two to three days.

A clear-glass carafe is wide enough not to need a candlecup. Here, eucalyptus, laurustinus, broom, solidaster and Euphorbia fulgens are combined for an informal, yellow and green display.

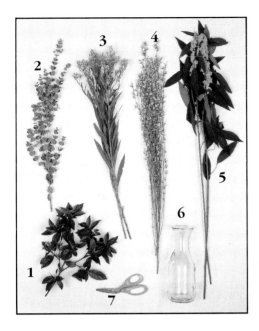

1 *small branch of laurustinus*
2 *7 stems of eucalyptus*
3 *3 stems of solidaster*
4 *5 stems of broom*
5 *7 stems of* Euphorbia fulgens
6 *carafe*
7 *scissors*

1 Fill a carafe two-thirds full of water and add some cut-flower food. Trim away the ends of the eucalyptus so that the stems are two and a half times the height of the carafe. Strip off any leaves that come below the water-line. Cross the stems of the eucalyptus as you insert them to form a framework that will hold the other foliage in positon.

2 Trim the ends of the solidaster so that it is slightly shorter than the eucalyptus. Again, remove any leaves below the water-line to avoid discolouration of the water. Insert the solidaster between the eucalyptus foliage so that its flowerheads form a colourful posy shape as a focal point in the centre of the display.

3 Trim seven stems of *Euphorbia fulgens* so that they are about twice the height of the container. Strip off the lower leaves if necessary. Place the *Euphorbia fulgens* in the carafe so that it arches gracefully over the top of the other plant material. Allow the stems to follow their natural line.

4 Group the broom into small, loose clusters. Separate the stems if too bulky. Gently bend the broom in your hand to exaggerate its natural curve. Place the broom at the base of the display to form a collar around the carafe rim. Balance the display with some taller stems placed at the centre back.

5 Cut off small sprigs of laurustinus flowers and foliage and place them at the base of the display so that they are just peeping over the rim of the carafe. Examine the arrangement critically from the front and the sides and make any final adjustments. Finally, top up the water level if necessary.

This elegant dinner party display combines flowers, foliage and candles in a cluster of chunky blue glass tumblers. The glasses can be arranged in various attractive patterns, depending on the shape of the table and according to your taste.

CANDLES AND TUMBLERS

A few charming variations on the miniature vase theme.

FLICKERING CANDLES AND A CLUSTER OF DEEP-BLUE TUMBLERS FILLED WITH DIFFERENT FLOWERS MAKE AN ENCHANTING DISPLAY, IDEAL FOR AN INFORMAL DINNER PARTY. THE WARM GLOW OF LIGHT ADDS A ROMANTIC TOUCH.

This floral display is foolproof, takes only minutes to arrange and is bound to be a conversation piece. When arranging flowers, it's always satisfying to produce an effect that is both interesting and different.

Most flowers are suitable, so the choice depends on your taste, budget and colour scheme. Even huge flower spikes, such as gladioli or delphinium, which initially seem too big, can be separated and the individual florets used. The green, flower-like bracts of fresh bells of Ireland (*Molucella laevis*) used here, have been cut into sections with the bracts forming a ruffle around the base of a group of candles.

Mixing sizes and shapes

Try to have a mixture of delicate, medium-sized and large flowers, with some foliage for contrast. Ideally, the medium-sized flowers should be suitable for tight clusters – like the small rose-buds and spray chrysanthemums here. The large flowers should be sculptural – trumpets and outsized daisies such as the lilies and gerberas pictured here.

For total elegance, alternate large orchids, such as cattleyas, with medium-sized orchids, like cymbidiums, and small spray orchids, such as Singapore orchids. For an informal summer lunch, alternate wild flowers – buttercups, cow parsley and wild daisies – for a country feel.

Foliage plays a minor role in this display, but still needs careful selection. Some flowers, such as the irises and lilies shown here, come complete with foliage. Bear grass is featured in one of the miniatures. A member of the lily family, its narrow, graceful leaves can be up to 1m (3ft) long. Bear grass is sold in single bunches or in mixed foliage bouquets with ferns. The quantity of foliage needed is only small, so you may be able to find what you are after in your own or a friend's garden, or take a leaf from a house plant, such as a spider plant or *Dracaena marginata*.

Any colour scheme can be adapted to this display, but it is sensible to choose one relating to your china and table linen or whole room scheme. Here, irises and blue-dyed gypsophila repeat the blue of the glasses and the plaid table-cloth. You will probably need to order dyed gypsophila in advance, and it is expensive, but white gypsophila can be substituted. In spring and early summer, sprays of pale-blue forget-me-nots, fresh from your own or a friend's garden, would be a lovely alternative.

Yellow roses, pink lilies, pink ger-beras and pink chrysanthemums add a soft, pastel touch. Each of these flowers comes in a wide range of colours, from white through cream and yellow to orange and rich red.

Choosing containers

Seven blue glass tumblers are used here, but choose more or less as the set-ting requires. Odd numbers tend to be more interesting than even numbers. Clear or pale-tinted glasses could be used, but the flower stems would be visible, and would need careful arrang-ing. Ruby-red glass, called cranberry glass in the United States, could set the tone for pink-dyed gypsophila and wine-red roses and lilies. Stemmed glasses are a more formal alternative; ornately cut crystal would help conceal the stems and add their own sparkle.

You could feature different but related containers – perhaps a collection of attractive hand-painted porcelain cups – each holding identical flowers.

Featuring candles

Candles always add a romantic touch, and can add height to a dinner table arrangement without creating a barrier between guests. White candles are very elegant, but you could choose pale or brightly-coloured candles to tone with the flowers. Try an interesting range of sizes. Used here are a short, stubby, candle, five tall, thin, candles and two medium-sized candles.

Choosing the setting

A long dining table is perfect for this display of glasses set out in a row, or place them in a circle in the middle of a round table, or in a square pattern on a square table. Lined up, the glasses look lovely on a mantelpiece or windowsill.

WHAT TO DO
WHAT YOU NEED

Creating a multi-vase arrangement

1 7 blue glass tumblers
2 5 long, thin candles
3 2 medium candles
4 1 short, fat candle
5 3 irises
6 8 roses
7 small spray of bear grass
8 2 gerberas
9 small spray of blue-dyed gypsophila
10 2 spikes of bells of Ireland
11 4 sprays of chrysanthemums
12 1 lily stem
floristry scissors

1 Cut two medium-size candles to different lengths. Fix them in a glass with melted wax, and fill each glass with water. Cut three irises to leave 5cm (2in) stems and add to the candles. Cut and curl the iris foliage round your finger and rest the leaves on the rim of the glass. Arrange the other leaves vertically.

2 Cut two gerbera stems to 5cm (2in) and rest the flowerheads on the rim of a water-filled glass. (Any left-over gerberas with bent or damaged stems can be used in this glass.) Don't worry if they overlap, but try to get them facing upwards like flat discs, in contrast to the round and spiky iris flowers in the display.

3 Surround the short, stubby candle with short sprigs of blue-dyed gypsophila. Ensure the gypsophila is positioned well away from the burning wick. Cut a lily stem down to 5cm (2in), and position the blooms together with some of their foliage in another glass. Add a strand of arching bear grass.

FIXING CANDLES IN AN IRIS VASE

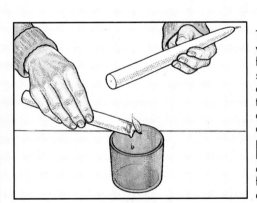

To fix a candle in a glass, simply melt some wax into the bottom, and press the candle firmly down. You can splay the candles out slightly, or have them vertical. To check the candles are vertical, use your eye to align them with a door or window frame, double-check them against each other and adjust as necessary, while the waxy base is still pliable. Cut the candles to different lengths but don't place them too close together in one glass as they will melt each other. Try floating candles or long-lasting nightlights as interesting alternatives.

4 Cut five tall, thin candles to different lengths and fix into a glass. Make a ruffled collar around their base with cut sections of bells of Ireland. Fill two more glasses with water. Pack one with eight short rose stems; place the central rose a little higher than the others. Pack the other with four short sprays of chrysanthemums – arranging them to spill over the rim.

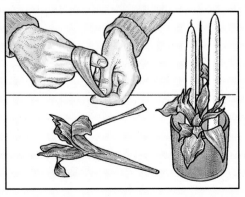

Make use of the leaves as well as the flowerheads for this arrangement. To make some of the iris foliage bend decoratively over the lip of the glass, curl individual leaves around your finger to give them a definite shape before inserting into the display. Arrange the remaining straight, spiky leaves so that they splay out slightly to the left and right of the vertical candles.

A PLAIN VASE

DECORATE AN EARTHENWARE
POT WITH NATURAL FOLIAGE
STEMS AND TURN THE
PLAINEST OF CONTAINERS
INTO AN ATTRACTIVE VASE.

Any kind of plain vase or cooking container will take on a completely new look once you have bound it with branches of ivy, pussy willow, clematis, vine cuttings or other supple foliage. Inexpensive containers are available from cook shops, junk shops and jumble or car boot sales. An earthenware or terracotta pot looks especially good when wrapped with foliage because it presents a neutral background against which the foliage can be seen.

Using storage jars

Other containers that lend themselves to being wrapped with foliage include brown and beige partly glazed storage jars, sometimes called pickling jars. These are available in a wide range of shapes and sizes. A small storage jar makes an attractive table decoration for an informal meal when wrapped with broom and filled with a handful of barren twigs and colourful flowers. Similarly, try making an interesting, floor-standing arrangement by decorating an earthenware jar with coarse, knobbly clematis stems and then filling it with white hawthorn blossom, golden forsythia or laburnum branches. It will brighten any dark room corner or wall recess. Alternatively, try placing the display at the turn on a staircase or at the end of a long passage.

**LEFT Trails of pussy willow break
up the line of the earthenware
pot in a surprisingly delicate
display of *Viburnum opulus*
'Snowball', yellow and white
feverfew and delicate arching
leaves of bear grass.**

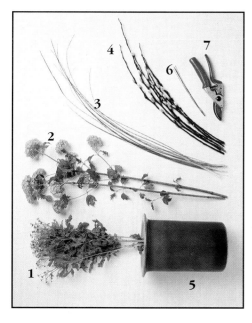

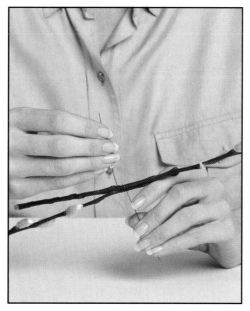

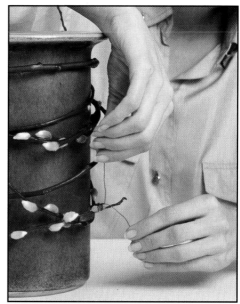

1 *10 stems of yellow and white feverfew*
(Matricaria)
2 *4 stems of* Viburnum opulus *'Snowball'*
3 *half a bunch of bear grass*
4 *8 stems of pussy willow*
5 *earthenware pot*
6 *stub wires*
7 *secateurs*

1 If necessary, join two short pieces of pussy willow together to make a length sufficient to circle the container. Place two stems side by side so that their ends overlap. Bind these ends securely together with stub wire. If the stems are not supple enough to use, bend them gently into curves in your hand.

2 Wrap the pussy willow stems around the container. Secure it with stub wire at the point where the stems overlap. Tuck in any loose stem ends or secure them firmly with stub wire. The pussy willow does not need to be flush with the container – a loose coil will give added width to the display.

3 Cut the white end section from half a bunch of bear grass. This will allow the stems to take up water. Group the bear grass into small bunches of about 10-20 stems and curve them very gently in your hand. Avoid running your hand along the sharp under–side of the bear grass. Place the bunches loosely in the pot so that they trail over the rim.

4 Trim the bottom off about ten stems of feverfew so that they stand about double the height of the container. Position the feverfew stems around the edge of the container allowing the flowerheads to form a posy shape in the centre and give body to the arrangement. The tiny feverfew flowerheads add a lacy touch to the display.

5 Remove the unsightly brown centre from the *Viburnum opulus 'Snowball'* and strip off any leaves that come below the water-line. Re-cut the stems ensuring that the *Viburnum opulus 'Snowball'* is taller than the feverfew so that all the flowerheads are visible. Place the *Viburnum opulus 'Snowball'* in the centre of the container.

You can translate the basic idea of wrapping a container with foliage to a smaller scale. For example, small, brown pottery ink pots make delightful specimen vases when they are bound with stems of dried grasses. Try grouping these composite vases together and filling them with small garden flowers such as forget-me-nots. They make a pleasant group on a kitchen shelf or a small dining table.

Inexpensive containers

Cheap glass containers including old ginger beer bottles, toughened glass preserving jars and ordinary wine bottles also can be decorated with foliage to good effect. The resulting combination of smooth, shiny glass and rough, natural stems is especially interesting for contrast of texture.

A 'bottling' jar would look just right filled with a handful of mop-topped onion seedheads and a few mauve flowering stems of sage or marjoram. Similarly, try adding a bright mixture of marigolds and cornflowers. Even ordinary brown or green glass wine bottles wrapped with willow stems become unusual specimen vases for displaying a single, perfect rose.

Natural resources

Gardens and hedgerows are full of ideal natural materials for winding around your chosen container. Just ensure that you select stems long enough to wrap around the container at least once, although you can always join shorter pieces if necessary.

Try to select foliage for its colour as well as its texture. For example, using the woody stems of ivy from well-established plants adds a deep green colour to a container. Similarly, yew stems, with their spiky evergreen leaves, have a 'green fishbone' look that is particularly attractive against a pale-coloured container. Be sure to pick off any berries from the yew since they are poisonous. Rosemary stems have a similar appearance to yew, plus the added bonus of a refreshing fragrance.

Weeping willow foliage provides the flower arranger with the choice of two contrasting looks. If you want to wrap a container with a glossy, golden foliage, use bare weeping willow. On the other hand, if you want the decorated pot to

appear wild, choose weeping willow in full leaf. However, whichever you select, the leaves will only stay on the stems for a few days because the weeping willow tree is deciduous.

The velvety 'cushions' of pussy willow stems have an irresistible textural appeal, and are especially long-lasting. However, over a long period of time the appearance of pussy willow stems will alter as the buds gradually dry and darken in colour.

ABOVE The tall container wrapped with ivy bursts forth with branches of catkins and golden elaeagnus. The cascades of broom link the pot and the branches.

Give all evergreen or leafy stems a long drink of water before use and spray regularly with water once arranged. This will keep plant material looking fresh for as long as possible.

1 *4 trails of ivy*
2 *1 bunch of broom*
3 *1 large branch of catkins*
4 *4 stems of elaeagnus*
5 *earthenware pot*
6 *secateurs*
  stub wires

1 Choose about four pieces of ivy that are long enough to encircle the container, or bind two shorter pieces of ivy together with stub wire. Wrap the ivy around the pot and secure the stems with wire where the plant materials overlap. Ivy cut from an established plant will last longer than younger foliage.

2 Wind more foliage loosely around the container until both top and bottom of the pot are partially covered. Use additional wire to anchor any wayward ivy tendrils. Snip off any sharp or protruding wire ends. Using plastic-coated wire will stop the wire rusting and eating into the plant stems.

3 Fill the pot two-thirds full of water. Divide a large branch of catkins into three to five sections. Cut the bottom of the stems at a slant. The tallest branch should be at least two and a half times the height of the container and positioned at the back of the display. Place the shorter branches in the container to secure the stems of the other ingredients.

4 Gently bend four stems of elaeagnus in your hand to exaggerate their natural curving line. Strip the leaves that will come below the water-line and re-cut the stem ends. Place the elaeagnus in the container so that it sits below the catkins. Fan the stems out over the front rim to give a pleasing shape and to provide bulk in the heart of the display.

5 Cut the bottom off the broom stems and bend them in your hand as you did the elaeagnus. Position some broom at the base of the arrangement to arch gently over the rim. Work the rest throughout the display so that it gives colour to the whole design. The broom should appear to be growing from a single point. Top up the water if necessary.

Bountiful Baskets

Fill baskets to the brim with fresh, summery blooms and contrasting dried materials, or pile them high with displays of fruit and flowers.

 Baskets are infinitely adaptable. You can use them to create any style of arrangement, from a casual country-look composition of trailing stems and shaggy foliage to a neat floral display for a special dinner party.

Available in a huge range of shapes and sizes, there are baskets to suit any type of arrangement. They are woven from a variety of materials, either natural stems or man-made fibres, in an assortment of colours. This makes them almost indispensable to the keen arranger looking for new and inexpensive containers.

New possibilities
Not all baskets, of course, are designed to hold flowers. Much of the fun of using them as containers comes from discovering possibilities in those intended for far more practical purposes. Wastepaper baskets, cutlery trays, linen baskets, garden trugs, shopping baskets and picnic hampers can all be transformed into original containers to suit a range of flower designs.

Wastepaper baskets, whether they are woven in willow or shaped from spirals of plaited rushes, are large enough to hold a floor-standing display for a fireplace, passage, room corner or porch. Filling a wastepaper basket with dried flowers can prove expensive - any container that tapers towards the base and has sloping sides needs a substantial amount of material. Choose a good selection of 'fillers' such as dried pampas grass, cereals, ornamental grasses and the dried flowers and everlastings that are cheapest in the shops or that are grown easily at home.

Filling deep baskets
To prepare a wastepaper basket or other large container for dried flowers, pack out the base with a few clean stones to weigh down the display and then add crumpled newspaper on top. The amount of newspaper you need will depend on the length of the stems you are working with. Position one or two blocks of dry foam on top of the newspaper and secure them firmly. The usual method is to criss-cross adhesive tape over the foam in both directions and secure it to the container – in the case of large containers this requires a great deal of tape. Alternatively, you can tie the foam, parcel-fashion, with thin string, taking the string through one of the top weaves on all sides of the basket. Rock the foam before you start arranging to make sure that it is secure.

Deep basket containers look just as good with long-stemmed fresh material. Indeed, if you want to arrange a bunch of forsythia or laburnum branches, leafy foliage or fruit blossom, a wastepaper basket may be the only container you have that is deep enough.

Again, you will need to fit the basket with some kind of stem-holding

apparatus. If the stems are long enough to reach to the base of the basket and still look in proportion, you need only stand a bowl or bucket in the basket, fix a ball of crumpled wire netting in the neck and tie it firmly to the rim.

The other way – more suitable for shorter stems – is to stand a platform (such as an upturned bowl or some bricks) in the basket and position a shallow bowl on that. Stand one or two blocks of pre-soaked foam in the dish and tie them in place. Remember to keep the foam topped up each day so that it never dries out.

Low-lying flowers

Woven cutlery trays or filing baskets make interesting containers for displays of a completely different style. Their flat shapes make them ideal for low-lying, table-top designs. There is no need to fill the whole of the tray or basket with flowers, however. If you use a large, flat container with plenty of textural interest, you can give impact to a relatively small amount of material.

One unusual way to turn a cutlery tray into a flower container is to place a few herb and spice jars around the divisions. If the surface of the basket is not quite level, steady the jars with a blob of blue tacky clay underneath each one. Make up posies of unruly stems and tiny wild flowers for each jar. For a completely different look, you could conceal a cylinder of foam in a small plastic tub or container at one end of a cutlery basket and create a triangular arrangement that curves forwards. A design made up of grasses and cereals, marguerites and poppies would be in perfect harmony with a bleached willow container. For a more permanent display, blend the grasses with colourful dried flowers and a few sprays of preserved beech or oak leaves.

A natural look

Garden trugs and flower-gathering baskets look attractive with bunches of flowers or grasses arranged as if they have just been cut. You can place dried bunches of different lengths in a fan shape, one on top of the other with each row of flowerheads lying just below the next. Choose glixia or lagurus dyed red, blue, green and yellow and arrange them in rows to make dramatic stripes or create an attractive multi-coloured effect by mixing the bunches together.

Small posies of dried flowers placed in a gathering basket are another way to increase the effect of a small collection of materials. Gather the stems in one hand, arrange the flowers into an attractive shape and bind the stems with twine and then with ribbon. Tie one posy to the handle, the ribbons trailing prettily, and place the others attractively in the basket.

Flowers in shopping baskets

Narrow-woven shopping baskets of the grip-handle or shoulder-bag type provide a wealth of possibilities for flower designs. You can hang one on the back of a door or in a hall-way and arrange a sheaf of dried flowers to spill over one edge. Fluffy, lacy shapes like pale-pink silene, silvery acacia and green chenopodium seedheads suit this shape well. Or you could opt for a more symmetrical shape and arrange a fanburst of flowers to come over the rim of the basket.

RIGHT A large shopping basket doubles as an outdoor flower container. There is plenty of depth for a bowl and a block of foam to hold the cascade of chrysanthemums, wallflowers, freesias and bear grass.

To arrange fresh flowers in a shoulder basket you simply have to conceal inside it a block of soaked foam set into a plastic box or tub. Position the foam so that it extends a little above the rim. This enables you to angle and slant stems sideways and downwards. Yellow spray chrysanthemums alternating with warm russet wallflowers and cool cream freesias make a lovely combination for a design that would look equally at home hanging alongside a fireplace or on a balcony.

Weaving your way

Whether they are woven of natural willow, craggy vine twigs, hazel or mountain ash stems, reeds, rushes or bamboo, most baskets are fine examples of craftsmanship. Sometimes, though,

you may come across one which is old and worn or just too plain to be used as an attractive container for flowers. If this is the case you can decorate the basket yourself in a number of ways.

If you have a basket with widely spaced vertical slats, a very open weave or a gap in the weave pattern, you can thread fresh or dried stems in and out to add texture and colour. There is no need to fix the stems in any way. The basket uprights will hold them firmly in place. Simply thread one after another, slightly overlapping the stems where they join.

Rosemary stems will make a thick, green basket wall and retain their refreshing fragrance as they dry; thyme stems give a woody and straggly appearance and santolina stems stay a

LEFT Spray-painted pastel blue and pink, the basket suggests the tonal theme for a summer garden selection including phlox, geranium mallow, stock, scabious and scented pelargonium leaves.

BELOW A mouth-watering display of fruit one side and a mass of carnations, green orchids and freesias on the other add up to a party design perfect for a buffet table or sideboard.

pretty, silvery-grey colour as they dry. All will contrast well with dark-brown basket weaves. Dried hops – which you can buy in bunches from the florist – give an appealing wild look to a basket arrangement and the pale-green, papery flowers contrast effectively with a dark basket. Lavender stems can be woven four or five at a time to make a sweet-scented basket that, whatever its shape or size, will look lovely with a casual arrangement of roses.

Decorate a broad-rimmed basket by sticking flowerheads all along it. Helichrysum flowers are particularly suitable and give a bright and colourful ribbon effect. A small basket decorated in this way, packed with crumpled newspaper and then filled with pot pourri makes a lovely dressing-table accessory.

Decorating the handle

Much of the charm and character of some baskets is in the shape of the handle, whether it is a tall hoop or a pair of small hand-grips at the sides. Emphasise the elegant curve of a handle by following the line with arched stems such as broom, artemesia and ivy.

To incorporate a high handle into your flower design, you can bind it with an evergreen such as ivy or wire on a small block of pre-soaked foam wrapped in foil. This provides a source of water for trails of leaves and flowers to arch around the curve of the handle. Conceal the foam with closely-arranged, short-stemmed flowers.

DECORATING BASKETS

• To make a basket of summery flowers look even brighter, create a pretty, scalloped effect by decorating the front with a paper doily. Cut a doily in half, wrap the two cut edges, side by side, over the basket rim and hold in place with a length of adhesive tape.

• You can trim a basket in a similar way with paper napkins – choose from designs such as checked gingham or polka dot.

• Give a basket a new lease of life with a coat of paint; spray-paints are the easiest to use. Paint stripes by masking the basket in strips with wide bands of adhesive tape and then spraying different colours.

LIDDED BOXES

BOXES MAY SEEM UNPROMISING CONTAINERS FOR FLOWER
ARRANGING, BUT THEY OFFER POTENTIAL FOR LARGE AND
SMALL-SCALE DISPLAYS OF EVERY SHAPE AND STYLE.

Think twice before throwing away an attractive box. Non-waterproof and fragile boxes can be lined easily, and even a modest-looking box can be decorated. Boxes range in size from matchbox miniatures to huge wicker laundry baskets and wooden linen chests, and a box filled with a florist's foam block can hold flowers many times its own width and height.

Some boxes are horizontal, that is, wider than they are tall; some are square and a few are more upright or tall and narrow. Flower arrangements can either repeat the proportions of the box, as the horizontal layer of flowers does in the wood box on page 76, or contrast with them, as in the tall vertical flower arrangement placed on the horizontal picnic basket on page 77.

Fruit boxes and biscuit tins

Many foods traditionally come in attractive boxes; for example, chocolates, tea, shortbread and, on a miniature scale, stock cubes. Look out for attractive boxes at a top-quality grocers or large supermarket. It can be worth the extra money for luxury food items if you get a box you can re-use for flower displays. Old-fashioned, slatted-wood strawberry boxes, lined with plastic wrap make lovely containers for informal summer floral bunches; ask if there are any to spare at your local greengrocer's.

Festive packaging

Nowadays, chemists, chain stores and shops specialising in cosmetics, hair and body care products often present their goods in attractive packaging and boxes, especially at Christmas. Around Valentine's Day, heart-shaped wicker boxes are often available.

A wide range of wicker, wooden, earthenware and china boxes can be found at gift shops, oriental shops, and basket shops that carry wicker and woven goods of all description. Modern plastic boxes in bright, primary colours or plain black and boxes with interior mirrors would all suit displays to match a modern decor.

Antique boxes

P re-wrapped gift boxes, with attractive paper laminated onto the cardboard, can be used as containers for cut-flower displays. Although they don't last as long as china, you should be able to re-use them at least three or four times.

Many antique collectables, such as Victorian work boxes, candle boxes and

LEFT A large-scale display, this wooden storage chest overflows with masses of summer flowers. The flowers are arranged informally in florist's foam, set in a waterproof container, which is placed on a low stool concealed inside the chest.

1 Use two or three stems each of escallonia, privet and elaeagnus to form a large triangle that reaches the floor and to just above lid height. Make an inner triangle with four stems of gladioli with four golden rod stems covering half of the triangle. Drape one viburnum stem over the edge of the box and insert one in the centre.

2 Fill out the arrangement with five long stems of white campanula to make a fan shape. Cut four stems of orange alstroemeria to graduated heights and insert them in a diagonal line across the display. Place the stems of four or five yellow lilies in the centre of the arrangement, the flowers facing forwards.

3 Strip the lower leaves from five stems of white antirrhinum and insert them centrally. Make a star shape from five stems of pink stocks. Cut short three stems of pink phlox and insert them lower in the display. Intersperse five stems of white allium among the other flowers for an informal profusion of summer blooms.

jewellery boxes of carved wood, ivory, papier maché, metal, or tooled leather make interesting box containers. Only use dried or artificial flowers in expensive antique boxes, however, as the water in a fresh display could damage them irreparably.

Lining boxes

If used for fresh-flower displays, porous boxes need to be lined to prevent discolouration, as do waterproof metal and alabaster boxes. Inexpensive plastic florist's trays made to hold single blocks of florist's foam can be placed inside the container, but a plastic soft cheese or margarine tray or tub from the supermarket can be used instead. Otherwise use inexpensive aluminium or plastic freezer containers, or a double thickness of aluminium foil

shaped to fit the inside of the box. For small boxes, kitchen plastic wrap works just as well. It helps if you put a few pieces of adhesive clay in the box to secure the plastic wrap in place.

Choosing the flowers

As with any container, the size of the flowers should relate to the size of the box. Use tiny forget-me-nots and sprigs of heather or gypsophila for a miniature box; huge branches of foliage, large lilies and gladioli for a trunk-sized display.

The flowers can also match the mood of the box – a traditional tea caddy filled with old-fashioned paeonies, roses and lilacs, for example. Alternatively, fill the same tea caddy with curly willow and echinops.

It would spoil the finished effect to obscure an attractive box with too many

flowers. However, one or two sprigs or stems trailing over the box can make a pleasing transition between the container and the flowers, unifying the two elements of the display.

Experimenting with lids

The three featured arrangements show the lids of each box or basket closed, slightly open and fully open. If you want to display the box with its lid partly open, support it on a toothpick, dowel or a twig from the garden. Affix the support to the base of the box with adhesive clay so the lid rests on the support and not on the flowers. Experiment with the angle of the lid to get the best effect. Try to prevent the flowers from looking uncomfortably crushed, as sometimes happens with a partly-closed lid display.

1 Trim a small piece of pre-soaked florist's foam into a cylindrical shape. Place the soaked foam inside a 'well' pinholder, which is a hollow cylinder with pins set into the base. Attach a small stick to the base of the box with a piece of adhesive clay so the base of the box lid rests on the stick rather than the flowers. Insert three stems of variegated ivy, *Hedera canariensis*, in the middle of the foam. Insert two stems of honeysuckle, angled forward, on one side of the display, three on the other. Drape a wooden necklace over the side of the box.

2 Cut three stems of greenish-white trollius to even lengths. Choose open flowerheads and position them in the foam so that two flowers face forwards and one flower turns out to the side. Insert one tightly budded stem on one side of the foam, sloping downwards. Frame the trollius flowers with eight to ten stems of golden rod, above and alongside the flowers. When cutting the stems of golden rod, leave them slightly longer than the trollius stems for width variation, and insert them horizontally, following the line of the honeysuckle.

3 Cut the ends of three to four stems of *Euphorbia marginata*, 'Snow on the mountain'. Be careful when cutting the stems, as euphorbia sap is a very strong irritant. Wash your hands thoroughly after handling the stems. Insert four or five euphorbia stems evenly at intervals among the other flowers. Lift the box lid slightly and insert a few short stems in the foam at the back. Snip the ends of three or four stems of pink spray roses and intersperse them among the other flowers to give small pockets of colour and to cover any exposed patches of foam.

Perfect for a dining or coffee table display, this partly-open wooden chest reveals its treasure of roses, golden rod, *Euphorbia marginata*, trollius, ivy and shrubby honeysuckle. A wooden necklace makes an unusual decorative addition.

1 Tape half a block of pre-soaked florist's foam securely to a small plastic tray with florist's adhesive tape. Place the tray on the lid of a picnic hamper. Insert one tall straight stem of escallonia into the middle of the foam to set the height. Make an uneven triangle shape using two or three straight stems of privet. Insert large elaeagnus leaves close to the base of the foam.

2 Cut the ends of seven larkspur stems at a slant. Place them vertically in the foam, three leaning out to the left, three to the right, following the triangular line set by the stems of foliage. Cut four allium stems to graduated lengths. Insert some vertically and others at a slight angle, following the upright line set by the larkspur.

3 Cut five stems of pink phlox to graduated lengths. Place them in a line across the arrangement to cut the triangle in half visually. Cut the ends of six *Viburnum opulus* 'Sterile' stems. Position them centrally so that the lime-green flowerheads hang loosely in the centre to form a focal point. Fill in any gaps with more large-leaved elaeagnus foliage.

RIGHT A closed wicker picnic hamper is the base for this formal, upright triangular display of larkspur, phlox, *Viburnum opulus* 'Sterile' and allium flowers; escallonia, privet and elaeagnus provide the foliage foundations.

ORIENTAL
ARRANGEMENTS

These arrangements with an eastern flair will stimulate your creative talents. Many of them use a minimum of material to create maximum impact and offer the opportunity to experiment with unusual blooms and containers. You can explore traditional techniques from the Orient to create simple, yet stunning displays.

Combine the best of eastern and western flower arranging techniques to create a distinctive display with exotic influences.

The different styles of eastern and western flower arranging are mixed together in our featured display with striking results. The mechanics and decorative techniques of oriental ikebana displays – the use of a bamboo foundation and floating flowerheads in water – are combined with an informal grouping of English garden flowers, Australian and African florist's blooms. The result is an asymmetrical display with a distinctly modern appeal.

The fresh colour scheme of yellow, green and white flowers is simple yet effective. For a different colour scheme, omit the yellow flowers and create a sophisticated look in green and white. Alternatively, substitute pink, red, mauve or blue flowers for the yellow blooms to produce a riotous effect.

Choosing the flowers and foliage

Try to include frothy, daisy-shaped and bell-shaped blooms in a range of sizes to add shape and textural interest to the display. Flowers with tall, strong, foliage-free stems, or with stems branching at the top of the plant are most suitable for this arrangement. However, if the flowers of your choice have abundant foliage and side shoots, remove these from the lower stems, otherwise they will become trapped in a bamboo tube and will rot, shortening the vase life of the material.

Kangaroo paw (anigozanthus), is the most unusual flower featured. This Australian herbaceous perennial requires greenhouse conditions in cooler, northern climates. The paw-shaped flowers, with their claw-like lower petals, are available in green, scarlet and yellow; some species have stems covered in brightly coloured, velvety down. Kangaroo paw is some-times sold in mixed bunches with other Australian flowers; however, single kangaroo paw stems can be ordered from florists. Use leafless stems of curly willow or gypsophila for a similar branched effect.

African beauty

Ixias, or African corn lilies, are half-hardy corms that belong to the iris family. The wild species, *I. viridiflora*, has long-lasting, star-shaped green

Assembling a bamboo and fresh-flower display

1 1 bunch of lady's mantle
2 9 yellow doronicums
3 2 bunches of white ixia stems
4 3 stems of feverfew
5 11 stems of trachelium
6 3 stems of kangaroo paw
7 1 plait of dried bear grass 40cm (16in) long
8 reel wire
9 6 hollow bamboo tubes
10 scissors
11 round glass bowl 20cm (8in) in diameter

1 Construct the bamboo stem-holder (see 'How-to' box for details). Fill a clear glass bowl about 20cm (8in) in diameter a third full with water. Cut 30-35 feverfew flowerhead stems at the base of the calyx. Make sure no stalk remains or the flowers will capsize in the water. Pick up each flowerhead between thumb and forefinger and position them around the outer edge of the clear glass bowl.

2 Trim off the bottom 5-7.5cm (2-3in) of three stems of kangaroo paw and remove any side branches that will be trapped inside the bamboo tube. Make sure the stems are slightly different heights. Position the bamboo stem-holder in the middle of the bowl. Arrange the kangaroo paw in the tallest 35cm (14in) bamboo tuber. The stems should be twice the height of the bamboo tube.

3 Next, add the light-green lady's mantle for textural variety. Cut about ten stems to graduated heights, the tallest stem should be approximately 25cm (10in) long. Position the lady's mantle in the 15cm (6in) bamboo tube to the right of the display. Insert the tallest stems towards the back and the shorter stems to the front of the bamboo tube. Fan out the stems slightly.

4 Cut the bottom 2.5-5cm (1-2in) from the stems of two bunches of white ixia,or African corn lilies, making sure that their heights vary slightly. Do not remove their long, slender leaves, but tidy up any ragged edges by trimming the leaf tips. Arrange the straight ixia stems in one of the 20cm (8in) tube to the back of the display. Position them so that all the flowerheads are visible.

5 Continue filling out the display with trachelium florets. Remove the side branches from the lower section of the stems so the trachelium will fit comfortably into the bamboo tubes. Trim five stems to lengths varying between 30cm (12in) and 25cm (10in). Place the trachelium in the 20cm (8in) high bamboo tube to the left of the display. Place six stems of varying lengths in the 15cm (6in) bamboo tube.

6 Lastly, trim nine yellow doronicum stems to varying heights; the tallest stem should be about 50cm (16in) long. Use these to create a colourful focal point in the front of the arrangement by placing five stems in the 25cm (10in) hollow tube. Next, place the four remaining stems in the 15cm (6in) bamboo tube with the lady's mantle. Gently bend the stems for a more natural look.

flowers carried on slender stems. The hybrids, sold commercially, come in a variety of colours usually with a contrasting central eye. The best time to buy ixias is when the buds are just showing colour. Ixias are vulnerable to ethylene gas which shortens their vase life, so keep them away from ripening fruit and vegetables, and flowers that are past their best, as these give off ethylene gas as well. You could substitute long-stemmed freesias, schizostylis or species gladioli, although avoid large-flowered, hybrid gladioli as these would be too bulky. Montbretias from the garden are also suitable.

Country-garden flowers

Doronicum or leopard's bane is a cottage-garden spring flower valued by flower arrangers for its bright-yellow daisies. Doronicums are available throughout the summer from florist shops. Use single or double gazanias, daisy-flowered spray chrysanthemums, iris or large single or spray carnations as suitable alternatives.

Trachelium belongs to the campanula family. The white form is used in our featured display although the blue-variety is more common. Alternatively, you could try using cow parsley, white valerian or scabious.

Lady's mantle is a hardy perennial garden flower with tiny, star-shaped flowers that add a frothy texture to the arrangement. If you cannot obtain lady's mantle buy short sprigs of gypsophila or pick a mass of London pride (*Saxifraga umbrosa*) from the garden.

The tiny, daisy-like flowers of feverfew, or matricaria, have been cut just below the calyx and floated on the water in the clear glass bowl to give the display an oriental touch. Any small, flat or broad cup-shaped flower that can float could be substituted, for example, you could use violets, periwinkles, flax, polyanthus, geraniums or chicory. Alternatively, floating rose or paeony petals instead of whole flowers would look just as good.

The only foliage used in this display is plaited, dried bear grass. This forms a decorative band around the bamboo to hide the reel wire that holds the bamboo tubes in position. Create a similar effect by plaiting natural garden twine or raffia; both can be bought from a craft shop or garden centre.

Choosing the foundation

In most fresh and dried-flower displays, the florist's foam or wire-mesh netting foundation is well hidden. In our featured display, hollow bamboo tubes

of varying lengths are tied tightly together to form an attractive group of stem-holders that fits comfortably inside the container. Bamboo stakes are sold in garden centres but they are too thin to be used as multiple-stem flower supports. Alternatively, try using the wide, hollow stems of angelica, if you cultivate it in your herb garden. Otherwise, buy an inexpensive bamboo curtain rod, and saw it into six sections of varying lengths (see 'How-to' box for details on constructing the hollow bamboo stem-holder).

Choosing the container

A clear glass bowl is an ideal container for this arrangement as it shows off the innovative bamboo support. If you do not already possess one, they are inexpensive to buy and available from department stores, interior design and pet shops. You could use a transparent glass storage jar or a cylindrical or cube glass vase instead. Slightly tinted glass is also effective. In particular, pale-green glass would give water a beautiful cool tinge. Opaque-coloured glass is unsuitable, as it would obscure the floating feverfew flowerheads.

Choosing the setting

As this display contains references to both eastern and western styles of flower arranging, it would be appropriate in a modern European or oriental setting. A summer room decorated with cane furnishings would be an ideal location. Above all, this display requires space. Its height makes it unsuitable for the centre of a room where it may interrupt people's line of vision. However, this display would make an imposing display in an otherwise unfurnished corner area.

Looking after the display

Do not allow the vase water to become cloudy or dirty and spoil the look in the glass bowl. As soon as the water loses its clarity, lift the bamboo unit holding the flowers stems out of the bowl and place it carefully to one side. Clean the glass thoroughly and re-fill it with fresh water. Remove any dead floating flowerheads and replace them with fresh feverfew flowerheads. Lastly, re-cutting the flower stems will help to extend their vase life.

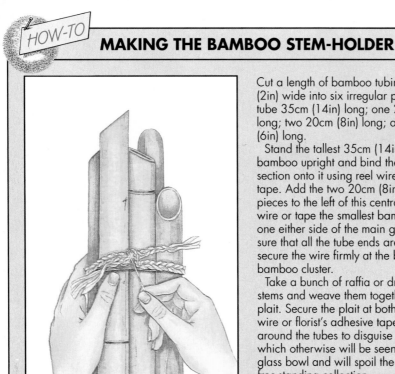

HOW-TO

MAKING THE BAMBOO STEM-HOLDER

Cut a length of bamboo tubing about 5cm (2in) wide into six irregular pieces. Cut one tube 35cm (14in) long; one 25cm (10in) long; two 20cm (8in) long; and two 15cm (6in) long.

Stand the tallest 35cm (14in) piece of bamboo upright and bind the 25cm (10in) section onto it using reel wire or florist's tape. Add the two 20cm (8in) bamboo pieces to the left of this central pair. Lastly, wire or tape the smallest bamboo sections, one either side of the main grouping. Make sure that all the tube ends are flush and secure the wire firmly at the back of the bamboo cluster.

Take a bunch of raffia or dried bear grass stems and weave them together to form a plait. Secure the plait at both ends with reel wire or florist's adhesive tape. Tie the plait around the tubes to disguise the reel wire which otherwise will be seen in the clear glass bowl and will spoil the effect of the free-standing collection.

The ORIENTAL TOUCH

Capture the stark simplicity of oriental design with a few carefully chosen flowers. We draw inspiration from the ancient art of ikebana to give you the first steps towards adding a hint of the East to your arrangements.

he understated flower designs of China and Japan look good in both stylishly modern or more traditional settings. The formal study of these spiritually-based art forms takes years to master completely, but it is easy to adapt oriental ideas and arrange your own flowers with an eastern flavour.

Flower arranging originated in China and spread to Japan in the sixth century AD when a Japanese emissary returned home and introduced the Chinese custom of offering flowers as a religious tribute. The flowers had to be arranged in the purest form and the ike-no-bo (temple by the river) school of ikebana floral art dates from early Buddhist temple offerings.

The art of ikebana

Today, the two cultures have distinctly different ways of interpreting flower arrangement. The Japanese tradition of Ikebana, which means 'beautiful flower arrangement', has had a stronger influence in the West than the Chinese school and is widely practised in floral art clubs.

Each arrangement tries to interpret nature at a symbolic level, creating graceful lines and harmonious proportion. Inspired by literature and paintings, floral artists incorporate many natural and man-made objects into their designs. Bleached driftwood, gnarled twigs, spirals of wood shavings, stones, rocks, sculpture, wooden balls and iron and metal wires can all be used in Japanese-inspired displays. Often the flowers, if any are included, play only a small part in the overall design, while shapes and spaces are equally important. This has an added cash bonus for the arranger in that few flowers are needed to complete an arrangement.

Arrangers use twigs, stems, wires or pointed leaves to symbolise the three elements of heaven, man and earth. In an upright design, the 'heaven' line (shin) is placed at ten degrees from the vertical, the 'man' line (soe) at 45 degrees and the 'earth' line (hikae) at 75 degrees. This imparts a feeling of gradual movement to a display and the elements serve to eliminate the dangers in 'hit and miss' free-style floral arrangements.

The choice of container is crucial for Ikebana arrangements. Artistic designs are created on flat dishes, plates and boards; in shallow pottery, bronze, or brass bowls; in pottery troughs of water; and on cane, bamboo or wooden woven slats. Upright containers are elegant, simple and often austere. The container must suggest the design's line and movement, but never distract from its form.

The Chinese art

The Chinese approach centres on the intrinsic qualities of the flowers, and their designs highlight the natural beauty of the single bloom rather than the arrangement itself. Both intense and subtle colours are used skilfully and fragrance is very important. Ideally,

LEFT A pagoda-shaped bird-cage makes a spectacular container for a handful of rose-pink spray chrysanthemums and a few stems of toning alstroemeria. A block of soaked foam in the bird bath (concealed with foliage) holds the stems.

RIGHT The flowing lines of the painted flowers are echoed in the full outline of the flower composition, a blend of white spray chrysanthemums, dried chamomile and silken petunias.

flowers are only used in arrangements when they are in season.

The figure three is also deeply significant in Chinese floral art. One line is held to be symbolic, two lines to be harmonious, and three to represent fulfilment. Many flower arrangers, unaware of this formula, discover for themselves that three branches, three arched leaves, or three key flowers make a successful combination.

Containers also play a central role in Chinese floral design and are frequently highly decorated works of art. Hand-painted porcelain pots, vases and jugs and plain glass pots in black, brilliant red, sharp blue or rich imperial yellow reflect the Chinese reverence for flowers.

Oriental containers

Most people have some object with an oriental flavour to provide a springboard for design ideas. You may have an old Chinese teapot, a jug or painted vase suitable for a cluster of white spray chrysanthemums, cerise Doris pinks or full-blown roses. Hothouse roses, such as the shell-pink Oceania, are available all year round but look and smell as if they were picked in summer. White chrysanthemums are often used in

IKEBANA TOOLS

• The Japanese use pinholders in their flower arrangements, which are more appropriate to their sparse designs than the florist's foam used in the West. These pinholders are fixed to the container with adhesive clay and are weighted in order to prevent the design overturning. If you have trouble balancing your materials try securing the pinholder with pebbles.

• The ikebana school often uses woody stems against which florist's scissors may prove ineffective. The Japanese have developed special scissors called hasami to cope with this problem. However, you will find a good pair of secateurs will serve just as well.

ABOVE A Chinese hand-painted panel inspires a floral design of oriental simplicity. Three pieces of bamboo (fitted with plastic pill bottles containing water) display two-toned red and cream carnations alongside wispy stems of broom.

Chinese floral art, because the pure colour symbolises innocence, truth and serenity and the flowers are long-lasting. Float one or two flowers in a clear glass bowl or in individual glass dishes, or even scatter a few petals on a salad, soup or stir-fry for another distinctly Chinese touch. Traditionally, chrysanthemums were eaten in the belief they would prevent old age.

Alternatively, you could create a design to complement a Chinese print. A painting of a windswept tree may inspire an arrangement of twigs arched in a similar direction, with a trio of flowers nestled against them.

Free interpretation

Anyone can draw inspiration from oriental art, and interpret the styles individually. Ikebana continues to inspire floral artists and can spark ideas for simple, untraditional designs for your home.

Bamboo instantly evokes images of the East, so use a piece of bamboo screening as a background, a split bamboo mat as a base, or sawn bamboo poles as containers to capture an oriental spirit. Saw a wide bamboo pole into 20cm (8in) lengths, with the tops steeply angled to act as a frame, and you have natural, vertical vases. A cluster of five can be used to display three single blooms – carnations, dahlias, chrysanthemums, roses or lilies, according to the season.

Your own Japanese style

If you design a Japanese-style arrangement, first decide upon the perfect place to display it. Japanese designs rely on simple lines for visual impact and need light, air and space to be displayed to advantage. A design with pure and symbolic lines would be ruined if displayed in cramped surroundings or against a confusing background.

Perhaps strip three arched holly branches of their leaves to accentuate the berries and compose them in a boat-shaped dish with a single red gerbera. An appropriate surrounding would be an alcove with a plain painted wall, a lightly-textured wall covering, a large piece of white wood furniture or a wide stretch of plain curtain fabric. If there is no single-coloured space available to you, simply hang a textured rug, silk or woollen shawl, or a linen panel to serve as a backdrop to your design.

Tricks with lighting

Lighting is also important. Back lighting can show off a floral display in a way that would otherwise be impossible to achieve. In sparse compositions, ensure that every component is shown to the best effect.

Placing a design in front of a window by day and in front of a spotlight by night can highlight it dramatically. The light will emphasise leaves which are heavily patterned with veins, or intricately cut ferns, and will define the line of twigs, feathers and seedheads.

These points on displaying arrangements to advantage apply not only to oriental designs, but to all your flower arrangements.

SPOTLIGHT

MIRRORS

A vase of flowers set in front of a mirror was a favourite subject for Dutch flower painters. Positioning an arrangement in front of a mirror doubles the visual impact of your flowers and gives added depth to an arrangement. Even simple bunches of flowers in a cylindrical vase or domes of flowerheads in a shallow bowl can be shown off to best effect with the benefit of mirrors.

To provide added interest to a dinner table, try placing your clear glass bowl of floating flowerheads on top of a mirror. The reflection from beneath will double the size and impact of your simple arrangement and create the illusion that the blooms are floating in a pond. Alternatively, try anchoring your flowerheads by short stems in a few marbles or polished pebbles.

In the hallway, where space is often minimal, hang a round display of dried flowers in front of the mirror to give the illusion of an abundant display without taking up too much room.

A row of miniature arrangements placed on a shelf in front of the mirror in the bathroom looks delightful and fills the room with a luxurious fragrance.

The dressing table is an ideal spot for your flower arrangement, especially if you have a hinged mirror which will reflect the your display in several different directions to fill your bedroom with images of flowers.

A jug of bright orange Chinese lanterns, the most cheerful of all seed carriers, has twice the colour impact when it is placed in front of a mirror.

To get the best out of the reflected image, treat an arrangement that is destined to be seen through the looking-glass as an all-round design, making sure that the back looks as pretty as the front. Cover any unsightly mechanics with foliage or save a few flowers for the back of the design.

ABOVE Twice the impact – the bright orange Chinese lanterns placed in front of the mirror perfectly complement the modern Oriental pottery vase and the warm colour of the upholstery seen in the reflection.

RIGHT Two rosebuds, and a few well-chosen pot plants, are all it takes to turn an eye-catching and colourful mirror into a floral picture with strong Oriental connections.

IKEBANA

LINE AND FORM PREDOMINATE TO
CREATE SPACE IN THESE BOLD AND DRAMATIC
JAPANESE FLOWER DISPLAYS.

Some of the main characteristics of Japanese flower arranging are shown in these three designs. Line is of crucial importance. Most ikebana displays have three main lines with branches used generally for the longest two lines and a flower for the shortest.

Formal Japanese flower arrangements usually are made to a precise 'recipe' which has its own name. This gives details of the type of material and container to use, the angle at which to place the stems and the lengths of the stems relative to the size of the container. Each 'recipe' varies according to the type of arrangement and the 'school' of arranging to which it belongs.

Asymmetric balance represents harmony rising from balancing opposite elements, such as emptiness and fullness, rather than similar elements. As a result, whichever way you divide an ikebana arrangement, the two halves are completely different.

Space forms an integral part of the design, unlike the western tendency to fill all the gaps, and arrangements are three-dimensional. Branches and flowers lean forward giving ikebana much greater depth than western-style displays.

Selecting ingredients

When composing Japanese designs, always use seasonal material as far as possible. Heed the characteristics of the plants and display them to full advantage – flowers and branches follow their natural line of growth with their tips reaching up to the sun. Select strong, clear branches for the first two lines. Cut away side branches which complicate the line and trim leaves, aiming to clarify the line and create interesting spaces. Usually few flowers are used but summer arrangements tend to be fuller and richer.

Resist the temptation to put a flower or branch in the heart of the arrangement. This immediately makes it a western-style display.

Moribana and nageire

The first two arrangements featured use a kenzan (pinholder) to support material. A kenzan needs a container with a flat bottom. This type of arrangement is called moribana, literally 'piled up with flowers'. Both displays featured are upright styles.

The third design is a simple chabana – literally 'tea flowers' or flowers arranged for the tea ceremony. The material leans to one side in a slanting or flowing nageire style. In nageire, or 'thrown in' arrangements, no kenzan is

needed. Instead, the material is balanced in the vase, a skill acquired with patience and practice.

Each style has a right and left-hand version, therefore where you place your arrangement is very important. The two moribana arrangements featured are both left-hand versions which need space to their right side. Place them to the left-of the surface they stand on.

The flowing nageire arrangement should sit on the right-hand side of a surface, with space to its left. Always have a simple, neutral background to display to advantage the pure and uncluttered lines of Japanese designs.

Choosing a container

For the first moribana arrangement, you need a flat-bottomed container 25-30cm (10-12in) wide and 4-5cm (1½-2in) deep. It can be round, oval, rectangular or square and preferably a plain, dark colour. You may find something suitable in your kitchen. The second moribana arrangement uses a compote-style vase with four legs and deeper than the first – about 8cm (3in) – but not as wide – 17-20cm (6½-8in). You could use a casserole or paté dish. The third nageire design is created in a black woven bamboo basket.

The container is an integral part of the overall design and its size indicates how long to cut your branches and flowers. Add together the width and depth of the container. The line-one branch is cut one and a half to two and a half times this measurement, the line-two branch two-thirds as long as the first branch and the flower for line-three half to two-thirds as long as the second branch.

Additional plant material should support one of the three main lines but should be shorter and subordinate to it.

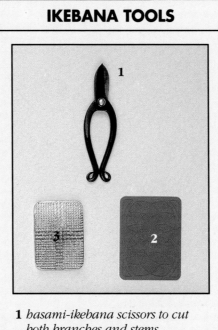

IKEBANA TOOLS

1 *hasami-ikebana scissors to cut both branches and stems*
2 *Japanese kenzan (pinholder)*
3 *plastic mat to protect the inside of the container from the kenzan*

1 Position the kenzan on the plastic mat in the front right of the container; fill two-thirds full with water. Insert the line-one stem of *Gaultheria shallon* into the centre of the pinholder so it curves out and upwards. Place the line-two stem 1cm ($^1/_2$in) to the left, leaning forwards, again curving out and upwards.

2 Cut an orange lily stem to two-thirds the height of the line-two stem and place it 1cm ($^1/_2$in) to the right of the main stem, angling the lily well forward so it leans out over the container rim. Trim off one of the four orange flowers to make an asymmetrical arrangement and thin out the leaves on the lower part of the stem.

3 Next, add the companion material. Remove the foliage from two guelder roses and trim to different lengths. Twine the longer around the main gaultheria branch and the shorter around the line-two stem. Fill out the lower right side of the display to disguise the pinholder. Trim one stem of leather leaf to half the length of the lily stem and place at right angles to it. Add another branch of gaultheria foliage.

RIGHT Minimum of material gives maximum impact in this design. Branches and flowers reach out and upward, leaving most of the container free. Place it in a low position to enjoy the reflections in the water.

1 Position a kenzan in the middle of the container on a plastic mat. Strip most of the leaves off two stems of bottle-brush and position the main stem towards the left of the pinholder. The stem should be about 1½ times the height of the container so trim it down slightly once it is in position. Make sure the stem curves out and upwards. The second stem should be about two-thirds the height of the first and positioned to the right of the display, leaning forwards. The two stems create a 'V' shape with a space between them.

2 Cluster the three pink stock flowers in the front centre of the container. Allow them to lean forward over the rim. The flowers should be about a third of the height of the second bottle-brush stem.

3 Next, add the companion material: pink thistles, purple wax flowers and white spiraea. Arrange the six pink thistles, three each on the right and on the left of the display. Make sure they stand at different heights and do not intrude on the central space. Place three sprigs of wax flowers of different heights on the left of the display. Add highlights with the white spiraea, short sprigs in the front of the display and longer stems as companion pieces to the bottle-brush.

BELOW This soft, delicate display is more intimate. The main lines reach forward and up like the arms of a dancer. Place it at eye level or lower.

1 Place a block of wet florist's foam 5cm (2in) in diameter into a cylindrical container and place this inside a bamboo basket. Position the main line of privet stem so that it leans left and forward. Thin out the leaves on the branch. Add a second stem about two-thirds the length of the first and place this further to the right and forward. This forms a very delicate asymmetrical balance.

2 Take one large, lime-green spider chrysanthemum stem and position it to the right of the golden privet branches. The stem should be about 8cm (3in) long and angled forward. The traditional ikebana method would be to keep the stem long and to achieve the forward angle by bending the stem forward – this way it would be weighted properly, but this takes a lot of practice.

3 Next, two stems of feathery astilbe are included to add softer lines to the design. Ease one stem of white astilbe forward gently, positioning it behind the spider chrysanthemum flowerhead to give a completely contrasting shape. Place the second astilbe stem behind the first stem to soften and fill out the composition, but trim the stem down by snipping off the top 2cm (1in).

Simple and natural, but perhaps the hardest design to create. The branches and flowers are bent and balanced in position. Place it at eye level or lower and where it will be safe from accidental knocks.

A *precious* FEW

*Even a handful of simple flowers
can look sensational if they are stylishly
displayed. Here we show how to make
a big impact on a small budget.*

hen budgets are low
and the cost of flowers
is soaring, a few
blooms can seem like
an expensive luxury
and one you may be tempted to forgo.
But there are ways to reconcile both
your hobby and your purse. With a
clever choice of containers, the judi-
cious blending of inexpensive and readily available plant materials, and even
by the siting of the arrangement, the
eye can be deceived. If you think that's
difficult, remember that Oriental floral
artists have been making the most from
the minimum for centuries.

All eyes on the container
One good trick is to use the showiest
container you can find, one that is so
eye-catching and attractive in its own
right that the flowers tend to take second place. This is not to belittle the
flowers; it simply shifts the emphasis.

Look around your home for container
inspiration. A highly-decorated jug containing a trio of chrysanthemums; a floral-
patterned teapot with a posy of small
flowers instead of the lid; an engraved
glass wine carafe with a single red rose
or a spray of freesias – designs like
these have style and make an impact.

Another good trick is to select the
container as much for its size and shape
as for its purely decorative quality. Tall,
slender vases add height; long, flat dishes
and troughs, with a design arranged on a
pinholder at one end, add width while
bulbous containers look substantial.

Seeing double
It is not necessary just to stick to one
container – another way of boosting
your blooms is to assemble several
identical or complementary containers
to form a still-life group. A few old-
fashioned medicine bottles, scent bottles or milky-white ginger-beer bottles;
a blue anemone in one, a pink anemone
in another, a purple flower in a third,
can be spread over a wide surface area
or grouped in a cluster. Either way the
visual effect is striking.

The effect would work equally well
with other containers: with a handful of

**RIGHT A trio of striking brick-
red gerberas. The unusual
container, a cluster of cut
bamboo poles tied around
with seagrass, grabs the
attention, and is reminiscent
of the Orient in its simplicity.**

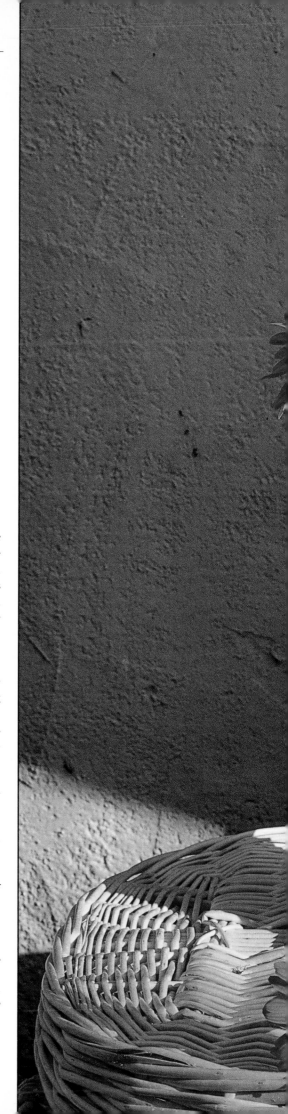

colourful dried flowers; a collection of small coffee cups or sake cups with a single flower floating in each; a few straight-sided drinking glasses with one long-stemmed flower apiece.

Sort out a collection of herb and spice jars and place one flower in each, the heads just resting on the rim. Arrange the pots in a line, a circle or block; whatever suits the shape of your table.

Looking down on them

Multi-container displays work well because they allow single flowers to be seen in splendid isolation. Devise ways of arranging the flowers in the shallowest of containers so that you can – literally – look down on them, and you maximise the effect. Float a few flowerheads in a shallow bowl of water – this always looks pretty – or, more unusually, in a glass container with a piece of mirror-glass in the base. The undersides of some flowers make intriguing viewing.

Displaying flowers with little or no stems saves money from your flower budget and has another cost-saving advantage. Very often the stem is the weakest part of the flower and disintegrates while the bloom is still in perfect condition. Snip it off and you've doubled the life of your display.

Filling in with foliage

Add evergreen leaves to enhance a display for which only a few flowers are available. Don't use so much foliage that the flowers are hidden. It is better instead, to create a framework of foliage, whether a full, flowing and casual shape in a waterjug or a more contrived and specific shape on a flat dish. Then place the flowers in a cluster or a unified group – a slight zig-zag or a curve – so that they become the focal points in your arrangements.

BAMBOO CONTAINERS

Bamboo poles are hollow between 'knots' and, unless they are cracked, can be filled with water. Before adding a flower, test the bamboo to make sure it is watertight. If it is not, insert a water-holding tube such as a plastic orchid phial to hold the stem.

FLOATING FLOWERHEADS

A COMBINATION OF SPARKLING GLASS, CLEAR WATER AND
FLOATING FLOWERS WILL BRING A SPECIAL MAGIC TO YOUR DINNER TABLE.
MARBLES, FLOATING CANDLES AND MIRRORED GLASS CREATE EYE-CATCHING
DISPLAYS TO IMPRESS YOUR GUESTS.

Floating flowerheads in a bowl has its origins in the floral art of China, where white chrysanthemum blooms and flower petals were favourite water-borne decorations. The simplicity of a single perfect bloom floating in clear water makes a most compelling table arrangement. Your guests will enjoy watching the gentle movements of the floating flowers and foliage.

Flowers to float

As you only need a few flowers for this type of display you can choose slightly more expensive, exquisitely-coloured and patterned flowerheads. A single, creamy-white and fully-opened parrot tulip, cymbidium orchid, gladiolus flower, camellia, begonia or ranunculus will each look stunning. Or use single spray white chrysanthemums, which are inexpensive and available all year.

We have used chrysanthemums in one of our featured designs to create an elegant and sophisticated look for a candle-lit dinner party indoors or on the terrace. For a special party you could float three or four flowers and a spray of variegated ivy leaves in a large bowl, and arrange individual glasses each with a single floating flower around the central container.

Later in the season, you could use white marguerites with golden centres, or for a dainty display in smaller glasses, a handful of lawn daisies with deep–pink petal edges.

Foliage also has a role to play in floating arrangements, either as a frame for the flowers or on its own. Create an attractive display from a variety of light, interestingly-shaped foliage such as cypress leaves, maidenhair fern, rose leaves and cyclamen leaves. These designs are easy to make and create an impressive table centre-piece.

Suitable containers

You can use all kinds of decorative or household containers. For individual floating flower designs, at dinner table settings use wine or brandy glasses, sturdy tumblers or small dessert bowls. For a table centre-piece featuring two or three flower types use a shallow glass bowl, baking dish, goldfish bowl, fruit bowl or even an old-fashioned jelly mould. For a more ornate look try pressed and embossed glass plates and dishes with colourful designs.

Special effects

Update this simple idea and give extra sparkle to the water by placing a handful of clear or coloured glass marbles or even shattered glass into the base of a transparent container. Magnified by the water, the marbles or glass will reflect the light. For other colourful effects, add food colouring to the water to match the flowers or use coloured-glass containers.

Mirror images

If you don't wish to place objects actually inside your flower bowl you could always lay a piece of mirrored glass underneath your display to create a modern dramatic look. It is possible to have a sheet of mirrored glass cut to a round, rectangular or asymmetrical shape at a good hardware shop or builders merchant and use it as a reflective stand for the floating flowers and their containers.

Alternatively, use a sheet of coloured card mounted under a piece of plain glass. Choose the card to complement the colour of your flowers. For example, vivid red to flatter old-fashioned roses or a bright, light green to give a fresh look to yellow enchantment lilies. To capture the oriental feel of floating flowers you could place your display on a piece of handmade Japanese paper under glass.

You can enhance your floating flower designs by adding individual floating candles amongst your flowers to add interest and light to an evening dinner table. These candles, made specially for this purpose, have light plastic bases so that they don't capsize in water. You can purchase them from kitchen shops or department stores.

FLOATING WATCHPOINTS

• Floating flowerheads draws attention to an individual bloom. Make sure that each is in perfect condition as any blemish would spoil the effect. Pick off any outer petals that may be slightly discoloured or damaged.

• If the display is to be viewed from above, choose fully-blown flowers rather than those in bud. Stand buds in warm water to encourage them to open. Once open, ease back the outer petals gently with your fingertips.

1 Position a coloured plate in its intended location and fill the central, slightly deeper recess with water. Select an unblemished, fully-open, yellow garden rose and cut it directly below the calyx, removing the stem. Keep this to one side. Carefully place the bloom in the centre of the bowl.

2 From the reserved flower stem, cut off three side stems which have good quality, shiny leaves. If the leaves are not in very good condition substitute large, individual ivy leaves or castor oil plant leaves. Keep the rose leaves together in their natural groups. Don't separate them or they will float around the dish.

3 Position the three groups of leaves around the central flower to form a frame for the rose. Hold the leaves gently by their stems to avoid damage. Spray mist the flower periodically to keep it looking fresh. If you don't have a perfect rose, float rose petals in the bowl to create an equally attractive design.

Flower platter

RIGHT Add a floral touch to your table when you make an oriental meal or decorate the dressing table in a lady's bedroom. Viewed from above this delicate, sweet-scented bloom has a very Eastern feel especially when displayed on handmade Japanese paper.

1 You can use something from your kitchenware for this design. Fill a shallow clear glass bowl half full with water and carefully position three floating candles at three points around the circle to form a triangular design. Make sure that the candle wicks are standing upright so you will be able to light them.

2 Choose three good-quality, open lily flowerheads from the main stem of a single spray, cutting just below the calyx. Position in a cluster in the centre of the floating candles. If you find that he flowers won't stay in position, remove some of the water so that the flower stems rest on the bottom of the dish.

3 Cut off about ten 2.5cm (1in) pieces of conifer foliage from a single stem. Float each piece of conifer foliage around the outer edge of the bowl so that they form a continuous line. Spray mist the lilies and light the candles just before your guests arrive. The candles should last for up to two to three hours.

Water lilies

LEFT Add candlelit romance to your evening by creating this captivating dinner table display. In this feature we have chosen exotic, bright orange lilies. To complement the blooms, you will find that the warmth from the candles will enhance their delicious fragrance.

1 Place a round, tray-sized mirror in its intended location. Fill four glass dessert bowls two-thirds full with water and place about four frosted marbles and four clear marbles in each. Position the bowls in a square about 10cm (4in) from the outer edge of the mirror and place more marbles in between the bowls.

2 Cut four white chrysanthemum blooms off a single spray just below the calyx. Pick up each bloom between thumb and forefinger and position one flower in the centre of each bowl. Make sure the flower floats the right way up. As this is a fairly delicate operation, try using tweezers to place the flower in position.

3 Finally, select eight variegated ivy leaves and cut off just under the leaf, removing the stem. Place two leaves on either side of the central chrysanthemum flowerhead. As the leaves are very light they are likely to float around the bowl but you can gently nudge them back into position with your fingertips.

Pearly reflections

RIGHT For a candle-lit dinner party this simple floating display would look particularly striking with the flickering flames reflecting in the mirrored glass. For extra interest use coloured marbles or water. Be careful not to disturb this design or the effect will be spoiled.

WILD
— and —
GARDEN FLOWERS

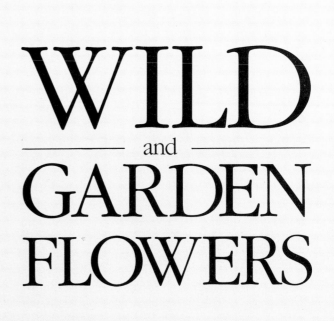

Wild flowers in their natural beauty lend themselves to informal airy displays, while garden flowers inspire a fresh country look. Many of these lighthearted arrangements look unstructured, but they are carefully planned, while at the same time offering scope for your imagination. Try some of the original ideas for outdoor displays.

With imagination and a gentle touch, wild flowers from your garden and the countryside can be used to create a charming display, such as this basket arrangement.

ny wild-flower arrangement – from an array of forget-me-nots to a basket of buttercups – adds a special atmosphere to a room and can match any occasion with style. Primroses, field poppies, meadow daisies and a host of heather stems; the possibilities are enchanting.

Try arranging a small nosegay of tiny wild flowers – violets and windflowers, for example – and position it where it can attract attention and be admired at close quarters. On your dressing table or beside a favourite chair would be a perfect setting.

Conserving our heritage

We cannot, however, rush out into the countryside and pick wild flowers indiscriminately. Native flowers paint our meadows, waysides, woodlands and wasteland with seasonal splashes of colour, and governments impose heavy fines to deter the picking of protected wild flowers which should be left for others to enjoy.

If you come across a field splashed yellow and white with buttercups and ox-eye daisies, or a woodland path being colonised by a mist of tiny blue

speedwell – and if the plant is plentiful in that area – it is acceptable to pick a few stems to bring indoors. Make sure you only cut one or two stems from each plant to avoid sapping its strength.

For the most part, we should be content to enjoy wild flowers in their natural habitat and then look them up in a specialist seed catalogue at home. You can buy seeds of most well-known wild flower species and, providing you choose those which grow well in your locality, you can easily create your own wild-flower garden display.

Beauty in miniature

Many native wild flowers seem almost too frail to survive in their natural habitat. Allow for this in your arrangement and never let hefty blooms overshadow the delicacy of these wild beauties. Dainty flowers, such as sweet violets and primroses, snowdrops, wood-sorrel, aconites and star-of-Bethlehem, are best arranged in bunches by themselves or mixed with each other, and ringed by a protective collar of leaves.

Choose the prettiest, daintiest containers you can find – egg cups, perfume bottles or pearly seashells, they all look delightful when brimming over

ABOVE Match a small bunch of delicate flowers to food and a table setting and they soon take pride of place. Primroses picked from the garden look prettiest when they are arranged simply and with their own foliage.

with springtime posies. To heighten the impact of these small displays, use your posy as the focal point in a larger group of flower arrangements.

Hidden assets

Many wild flowers have a high leaf-to-flower ratio – lots of vigorous and showy leaves and small, almost imperceptible flowers. It is a characteristic that some people find disappointing. Forget-me-nots, with their minute blue and pink flowers protected by long, pointed, oval leaves; germander speedwell, with their fragile, four-petalled sky-blue flowers and yellow and white eyes; soft comfrey with its clusters of milky-cream, bell-shaped flowers, the palest of pale against the thick, hairy leaves. You can use this ratio between foliage and colour to your advantage, however. Try clustering these modest

LEFT A simple rustic basket is perfect for showing off wild flowers. Here, pink campion is combined with violet-blue hardy geranium.

BELOW Mauve scabious, pink and blue geranium, yellow verbascum and lacy stems of cow parsley and may weed make a bold display of contrasting shapes and colours in a large blue-black container.

flowers into a mass of stems, using them as a background for toning complementary, but more decorative flowers.

Whether you have gathered enough wild forget-me-nots, or perhaps speed-well, to trail over the rim of a wide, shallow pottery bowl, or just enough to spill out of a small, white jug, adding a few flowers of a different species enhances the delicate blue of the arrangement. A few stems of grape hyacinths or bluebells, one or two small blue anemones, or a handful of mead-daisies or ox-eye daisies – you will be amazed at the difference they make.

Ground ivy (*Alechoma hederacea*) can also be used to great effect. The minute, purple flowers nestling close to the stem are almost hidden from view. Some purple freesias, a few purple anemones or a cluster of violets will pick out the colour of the ivy flowers to create a colourful and complementary display.

Sweet perfume

Soft comfrey (*Symphytum orientale*) is another plant that tends to hide its most attractive feature, concealing its pale lemon flowers under a bushel of deep purplish-green leaves. For a simple but stunning effect, highlight the comfrey by adding a few stems of cream and yel-low freesias which echo both the colour and the shape and have a sweet perfume.

When planning an arrangement that combines the best of both worlds – the countryside and the florist – garlic mus-tard (*Alliaria petiolata*) is an ideal choice. The brilliant-green leaves, though more than a match for the small, modest cluster of white flowers perched at the tip of the stems, can be used to create an original and striking backdrop for more traditional flowers.

First pick off any garlic mustard leaves that would come below the water-line, and then place a handful of the stems in a sparkling glass vase. Finally, add a few florist's flowers – some red spray carnations, a trio of scarlet carnations or a bunch of bright Doris pinks, for example. These will strike a dramatic contrast and provide a delightful breath of country air.

When enhancing shy-violet flowers in the same way, avoid the temptation to add crowds of large and perfect cultivated specimens; the contrast will be lost and the wild flowers will pale by compari-

son. To ensure both species complement one another, add between two and five cultivated flowers depending on the size and scale of the group.

A taste of the country

Deadnettles are another candidate for inclusion in an imaginative wild-flower arrangement. You can find them both in the wild and as garden weeds, with white, cream, purple and pretty pink flowers. Strip off a few of the leaves to spotlight the rings of snap-dragons clustered around the stems, and they

take on a new and altogether brighter complexion. Don't stop there – young deadnettle leaves have a light, sharp, vivid green colour that adds a real lift to mixed arrangements. Group a few of the leafy stems around the rim of a bowl, and position two or three day lilies, a luxurious orchid or a handful of freesias to tower over them and provide a stately feel. Alternatively, try blending the leafy deadnettle stems with a nosegay of garden flowers such marigolds, cornflowers or marguerites.

Cloud effects

Some wayside flowers have a pretty cloud-like feel that softens the outline of both casual and more contrived arrangements. Shepherd's Purse, cow parsley, chervil, yarrow, wild carrot – all those white umbrella-shaped flower heads, known as umbellifers – can be used to draw a delicate veil over other more distinctive shapes.

Try arranging an unruly mound of Shepherd's purse in a large white jug, adding a few white highlights in the form of some stems of mock orange blossom, some white tulips, or a bunch of ox-eye daisies. Clippings of these massed white flowerheads can provide a very attractive effect when mingled with wild and garden flowers. A pot of

ABOVE A bunch of wild forget-me-nots fanning out across the window creates a pretty veiled effect that would improve many a city view. The flowers are arranged in crumpled wire netting in a shallow, lidded box.

bright orange marigolds and nasturtiums looks much brighter with a thin white blanket of wild carrot flowerheads.

Show-offs

For a wild flower capable of an almost virtuoso performance, the poppy is ideal. Poppies have milky, sappy stems that need to be sealed and then put in water as soon as they are cut. Otherwise, the flowers will fold up almost immediately. Burn the stem ends with a small flame and put them into a little water straight away. When you re-cut the stems to arrange them, make sure that you burn them again. Poppies look spectacular when arranged with perhaps a stem or two of deep blue larkspur, or some purple or midnight-blue anemones to form a contrast.

Wild flowers cover the whole spectrum, from dainty primroses to poppies that splash meadows with their bright scarlet. With imagination and a little work, they add the perfect touch to any arrangement.

SPOTLIGHT

SUMMER FIREPLACES

An empty fireplace is the ideal location to display flowers. A generously-rounded fire surround such as an arch or alcove makes a natural frame for a tall arrangement and an open fireplace with an iron grate is a perfect platform for a low, wide design. A small Victorian grate can double as a base for a cornucopia display of dried flowers which spills forwards into the hearth. A walk-in fireplace of the ingle-nook type is perfect for a large country-style basket, filled to overflowing with fresh or dried flowers.

Size up the fireplace – whether it is an upright or landscape shape – and design the arrangement accordingly. Fill a basket or casserole, an earthenware jug or flowerpot with dry florist's foam and outline the shape with delicate stems such as grasses. If the fireplace calls for a large design, position some flowers in groups or clusters to give strong patches of colour.

To turn a small fire grate into a floral cornucopia, tape a block of dry foam inside a cardboard box and wire it securely, foam facing forward, to the fire basket. Position the flower stems so they seem to fall outwards. Cut short the stems of the topmost materials, and the heads will cover the stems of those below them and give an easy, graduated look. Alternatively, place a block of dry foam into a basket to create a more portable display.

Maximise the effect of the fire surround as a background. Black is a dramatic backdrop to pale materials from parchment-coloured grasses and seedheads to pastel-pink paeonies and old-fashioned roses. Beige and grey marble and tiles project dark colours well. Nut-brown seedheads; preserved leaves and cones; deep blue and mauve, warm red and pink, firelight bronze and orange flowers make a perfect picture against a neutral background.

ABOVE and BELOW Brighten a dark fireplace. with white marguerites, red campion and yellow buttercups, or cool marble with a display of lilac, wild carrot and mock orange blossom.

FIREPLACE FLOWERS

*Transform an empty fireplace hearth into a radiant celebration
of summer with a basket full of seasonal garden blooms.*

A fireplace is nearly always the focal point of a room and in summer it provides the perfect setting for a cut-flower display. Our choice of arrangement aims to capture the spirit of a herbaceous border in full bloom, using massed foliage and flowers in warm shades.

You can vary the style and colour of the arrangement. Pale and white flowers look especially dramatic against a dark background, but dark colours, such as deep blue, crimson or violet, are less suitable as they tend to recede into the shadows and lack the warmth needed to bring an empty fireplace to life. Rather than mixing flowers randomly, group them loosely, creating an informal design to contrast with the strict geometric lines of the fireplace frame.

Choosing the flowers

Our display features white, yellow and blue herbaceous perennials but white, pink and blue would be an equally attractive colour scheme. You also can try a single, clear pastel shade.

The branching stems, foliage and flat, yellow-green flowerheads of fennel create a fine backdrop to the display. There is a particularly beautiful bronze-leaved form you may like to experiment with. Always condition these plants by dipping cut stems into boiling water for a few seconds before arranging.

Echinops, the globe thistle, is rarely stocked by florists so you may have to order it in advance. The soft metallic colour and perfect shape of the thistle-heads are difficult to match, but you can try using sea holly, another thistle, such as knapweed, or large poppy seedheads in their natural silver-grey colour, as interesting variations.

Achillea, or yarrow, is one of the few flowers that is more commonly featured dried in arrangements. We have chosen to use it fresh for its soft-rounded shape and bright, clear colour. There are white, pink and rose varieties that you can use in a different colour scheme. As a substitute, use yellow tansy which provides a similar effect to achillea.

Flame-yellow rudbeckias, or coneflowers, are widely available in both annual and perennial forms. There are striking red and purple varieties to keep in mind for a richly coloured display. Heleniums and coreopsis are similar in shape to rudbeckias and may take their place; alternatively, you can use single yellow chrysanthemums.

The showy panicles of phlox make a handsome filler and come in white, pink, salmon and lavender shades. The white variety is used here in striking contrast to the subtler shades of the other flowers in the display. Blue polemonium, or Jacob's ladder, is a possible variation, or you can experiment with Brompton stocks or colourful antirrhinums.

White agapanthus, or African lily, is the most unusual flower featured in our display, and, unless you grow your own or are able to take a few sprigs from a neighbour's garden, you'll have to order

DISPLAY CARE

Soaking the florist's foam regularly with warm water will prolong the life of your arrangement. Insert a watering can spout into the back of the display where the foam block is exposed, rather than trying to water through the stem-packed front and risk disturbing the flowers.

it in advance. Pale blue agapanthus is more commonly grown and may be substituted; alternatively use pale blue brodiaeas, or pale cream alstroemerias.

Choosing the foliage

The background foliage is a feature in its own right in this display, so try to combine an interesting range of leaf shapes and sizes with curling or arching branches. Avoid anything too exotic looking that would detract from the country-garden appeal.

Golden privet, a popular hedging plant, adds a warm glow to the arrangement. Green or variegated privet or golden-leaved varieties of laurel, pittosporum and shrubby honeysuckle will create their own subtle variations.

Rosemary spikes create a contrast with the rounded forms of the other leaves. You can substitute a small-leaved variety of hebe or a conifer, such as pine or podocarpus, with spiky needles.

Aucuba, or spotted laurel, adds mass and bright colour. There are more subtle varieties, with all-green leaves, as well as ones with almost entirely yellow leaves. If you prefer more subdued foliage shades, use ordinary laurel, Portugese laurel or laurustinus.

Variegated Canary Island ivy is a common house and garden plant and you should have little difficulty getting hold of the few sprigs needed for this display. Other varieties of variegated ivy will do equally well or you can try a variegated elaeagnus.

Choosing the container

The display needs to fill the fireplace to be effective, so select a basket large enough to support and contain a great quantity of flowers and foliage. Ideally, it should be just over half the width of the fireplace opening, and about a third of its height. Often florists sell wicker baskets lined with plastic, but here a plastic bowl is used. Make sure the bowl is hidden completely and stable.

Adding drama

Spotlight the display at night to bring the bright warm colours to life and to accentuate the contrast of the shadowy backdrop. A spotlight from a ceiling track, or a fluorescent light, which gives out little heat, are both ideal.

Assembling a fireplace flower and foliage display

1 *2 stems of variegated Canary Island ivy*
2 *3 stems of aucuba*
3 *2 stems of rosemary*
4 *4-6 stems of golden privet*
5 *4 white phlox flowerheads*
6 *10-12 stems of yellow achillea*
7 *14 globe thistleheads*
8 *10 stems of yellow rudbeckia*
9 *3 tall, branching stems of fennel*
10 *3 stems of white agapanthus*
11 *oval wicker basket with handle*
12 *plastic waterproof bowl*
13 *2 blocks of fresh florist's foam*
14 *floristry scissors*

1 Soak both pieces of florist's foam. Trim the outer edges of each block to a rounded shape so that together they fit snugly into the plastic bowl. Place the bowl when pressed in the centre of the wicker basket, wedging it firmly into position with florist's foam or crumpled newspaper. Insert the largest branch of fennel to one side of the handle at the back of the arrangement.

2 Position the privet stems at intervals around the back and sides of the basket so they give a soft background shape to the arrangement. Add a second branch of fennel horizontally to the left of the display to give it an asymmetrical look. Trim the bottom leaves from the rosemary stems and place them at opposite sides of the basket so they curve round and downward.

3 Use the large, solid leaves of aucuba to give weight to the middle of the arrangement. Trim the stems and insert them in the front of the display in a fan shape. Take five to six globe thistleheads and position them, slanting vertically, towards the top right-hand corner. Angle the remaining stems horizontally in the lower left-hand corner, allowing some to hang over the edge of the basket.

4 Add bulk to the display with the soft, rounded heads of achillea. Cut the stems to varying lengths and intersperse them naturally around the display. Concentrate the flowerheads particularly in the middle area between the thistleheads and the aucuba leaves on the right of the display, and use them to fill the empty area below the branching fennel in the top left-hand corner.

5 With both sides of the arrangement now complete, add the daisy-like rudbeckia flowerheads, using them to fill the upper middle area and to complete the basic fan-shaped outline of the display. Insert at varying heights at a slightly higher level than the achillea. Leave the drooping lower leaves on the lower end of each stem so that they hang down and cover the basket handle.

6 The white phlox and agapanthus are used in striking contrast to the subtler shades of the other flowers. Add the heavy phlox panicles in the front of the display, arranged in a circular shape. Insert the agapanthus at varying heights, using them to build up a swathe of pure white colour. Fill any remaining gaps around the base of the display with the variegated Canary Island ivy.

BERRY BONANZA

Evergreen foliage, branches and a wealth of colourful berries make an impressive floor display in this large, earthenware jar. Adapt the arrangement to suit the season and the materials you have to hand.

vergreen leaves, branches, berries and seed pods are as ornamental, and every bit as colourful as flowers in a decorative display. Whether or not flowers are included, the same design points should be taken into consideration when creating an attractive arrangement. A display should include contrasts of form, colour, texture and visual balance, and it should be suitable for its intended location.

Colourful berries, a seasonal bonus of autumn and winter, feature prominently in this display. Berries are at their best at this time of year and provide a good supply of colourful materials when floral colour in the garden is starting to fade. But if the birds have eaten all the berries you could substitute winter catkins, such as hazel, alder and *Garrya elliptica*; and dried seed pods, such as teasel. In a mild winter, ornamental berries may remain on the trees and shrubs until well past Christmas.

Sources of material

You could make this display with material ordered through your florist, but if you have your own garden or access to the countryside you could gather your own materials. An ordinary-sized gar-

den, (provided it is well established), should have more than enough material, especially as only a small amount is used of each for the display.

Foliage and berried branches are usually sold in large bundles from the florist. Since at least a dozen different plants are used in this arrangement, it's worth asking your florist to put aside a branch or two from each bundle. If not, a good compromise is to combine ordinary florist's foliage – eucalyptus, for example, and broom – with the best from your garden or the wild.

Choosing the foliage

The bulk of the display is made up of evergreen foliage which is available throughout the winter: rhododendron, elaeagnus, laurel, eucalyptus, cupressus, camellia, holly, ivy and pyracantha. Plain leaves are chosen so that the various shades of green, different textures and shapes can be appreciated to the full.

In this arrangement, variegated ivy is confined to the lower part of the display. The key to success is to use variegated foliage with restraint; combining several different types can lead to a confused effect.

Try to follow the spirit of the display, it does not matter if you do not have the exact foliage and berries featured here.

Most of the material comes from ordinary, hardy trees and shrubs, and other, similar material can easily be substituted. There are lovely evergreen viburnums, skimmias, pittosporums, cotoneasters, senecios and sweet bays that would be equally effective. Alternative conifer foliage, such as pine or cryptomeria, could also be substituted for the cupressus.

Choosing the berries

Three types of colourful berries are used: holly, pyracantha and euonymus (spindle). Both holly and pyracantha berries are available in a range of colours: red and yellow for holly; and orange, red, yellow and creamy-white for pyracantha.

Cotoneaster berries could be substituted for the pyracantha, and there is the added bonus of not having to deal with the pyracantha's fierce thorns. Though less densely packed, you could also use rose hips; the apple-shaped hips of *Rosa pomifera*, for example, or the slender scarlet, bottle-shaped hips of *R. moyesi*.

Spindle, a hedgerow plant, is grown in gardens largely for its bright, scarlet seed capsules containing fleshy orange seeds. The variety 'Red Cascade' is especially beautiful, with its arching stems weighed down by berries. With spindle, plant more than one shrub and you will get an abundant crop of berries.

Choosing the container

For this impressive floor-level display a hand-made earthenware pot is used. You can buy similar pots from garden centres or you may prefer an Oriental glazed tub or a large terracotta pot. Kitchen shops sell huge ceramic bread crocks, which would be equally suitable. Antique shops occasionally have old-fashioned glass battery jars, and modern reproductions are starting to appear in fashionable gift shops. Whatever you use, make sure it's waterproof, wide-necked and broad-based, for stability.

Choosing the setting

This display is too heavy for anywhere but a floor setting. Make sure there's plenty of 'walking' space around it, to prevent accidental damage. Keep it away

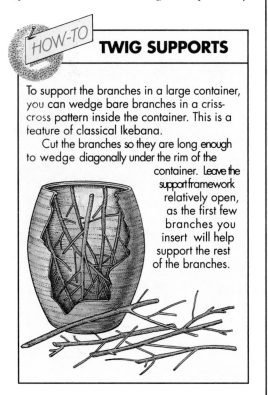

HOW-TO

TWIG SUPPORTS

To support the branches in a large container, you can wedge bare branches in a criss-cross pattern inside the container. This is a feature of classical Ikebana.

Cut the branches so they are long enough to wedge diagonally under the rim of the container. Leave the support framework relatively open, as the first few branches you insert will help support the rest of the branches.

from radiators or draughts, which would shorten the life of the foliage. If the display is placed on a carpet, make sure the base of the container is scrupulously clean and beware of dropping berries!

If your front door opens onto a patio or urban courtyard, consider displaying the arrangement outdoors. Cool weather would keep it fresh for weeks.

WHAT TO DO WHAT YOU NEED

Making a grand-scale foliage and berry arrangement

1 *2-4 large branches of holly with berries*
2 *stem of camellia*
3 *1m (3ft) branch of broom*
4 *3-4 trailing ivy stems*
5 *1m (3ft) branch of laurel*
6 *2 large branches of spindle*
7 *10 stems of eucalyptus*
8 *6 stems of cupressus*
9 *2 branches of rhododendron*
10 *4 stems of elaeagnus*
11 *6 stems silvery-grey santolina*
12 *2-4 stems of pyracantha*
13 *secateurs*
large earthenware pot; 6-8 garden twigs

1 Place the container in its final position; filled with water, it is too heavy to move. Make a twiggy support (see 'How-to' box) or insert crumpled wire mesh, then ⅔ fill with water. Remove the lower leaves from the rhododendron branch, and insert it in the centre, to help set the height. Insert a multi-branched laurel to the left, to set the width.

2 Check that the first two branches are stable before proceeding. Next, begin adding colour to the display. Remove the lower leaves from two large branches of holly. (Holly berries drop off at the slightest touch, so handle with care.) Insert them on the right of the display, opposite the laurel. Let the stems overhang the rim of the container.

3 Remove the lower leaves from the elaeagnus branches. The species used has silvery leaf undersides, which contrast effectively with the dark green foliage. Insert the elaeagnus with its silvery undersides showing, creating a 'thicket' towards the back of the display. Next, insert several long stems of ivy to drape over the front and sides of the rim.

4 Add a long, slender branch of broom next to the rhododendron, to reinforce the vertical line. Begin increasing the density and focus towards the middle of the display, filling in the central recesses. Insert a tight bunch of cupressus branches, to form a green 'flower'. Under the holly, create a cascade of eucalyptus.

5 Remove the lower leaves of about six stems of silvery-grey santolina. The pale, silvery foliage forms a contrast with the abundance of green. Insert the stems in a loose cluster, in the centre of the display. Use a multi-branched stem of camellia to continue building up the centre. If it has its fat, glossy seed pods, use these as well.

6 Lastly, add the bulk of the coloured berries. Insert two large branches of spindle in the front, angled outwards and downwards, so the seed pods hang attractively. Check the branches are secure, then insert the pyracantha branches. Use trimmed stems to build up a concentration of berries in the centre. Check the display, re-adjusting as necessary.

GOLDEN ROD

OUR ARRANGEMENTS SHOW YOU HOW EASY IT IS TO MAKE AN IMPACT WITH THIS RADIANT FLOWER. DISPLAYED ON ITS OWN OR MIXED WITH FOLIAGE, GOLDEN ROD LENDS ITSELF WELL TO BOTH MODERN AND TRADITIONAL ARRANGEMENTS.

Golden rod (or *Solidago*) is a traditional cottage garden flower that adds a vivid splash of colour to any autumnal display. Tall spires of feathery, lemon-gold flowerheads sit elegantly on 75-150cm (2-4ft) high stems depending on variety, making this one of the showier flowers around; all the more so at the time of year when the garden is changing from summer to autumn livery and there are fewer really dazzling flowers to pick.

A popular herbaceaus species, golden rod is an easy (and worthwhile) plant to grow in the garden. Its dramatic appearance makes it economical to use in flower displays; just one stem is needed to create a stunning design – as shown in the following arrangements. Several longer stems need only a spray of greenery to give a softer effect – use bear grass instead of asparagus fern, or experiment with variegated green and yellow holly or ivy to contrast with and complement the flower. With golden rod you can bring a touch of sunshine into your home on even the darkest of autumn days.

QUICK TIP | BUYING AND CONDITIONING

Buy golden rod from the florist when a few tiny yellow florets are beginning to open but the overall colour of the flower is green. If you buy golden rod at this stage, the flowers will last for up to ten days in the vase.

Before using golden rod in arrangements, remove the lower leaves that will fall below the water line and cut away the bottom of the thick stems with a sharp knife in a long slanting slice – this will help the stems to take up water.

1 You will need six stems of golden rod and a spray of asparagus fern. Trim the stems of golden rod so that they are one and a half times the height of the vase. Stand the stems in the vase to see how much foliage needs to be removed. Strip off any leaves that will come below the rim of the vase. (If left on the stem, the leaves will rot under water.) Fill the container two thirds full of water. Place the first two stems in the centre of the vase. The other flower stems will be added later, also grouped in pairs, but with shorter stem lengths. Pairing stems of golden rod makes a stronger colour impact.

2 Trim several pieces of asparagus fern to the same height as the first pair of golden rod stems and place them at a slight angle, to one side of the vase. The fern adds textural contrast and frames the flowers.

3 Continue adding pairs of flowers to the vase but make each successive pair of stems slightly shorter so that all the flowerheads can be seen. A strong line of colour runs down the arrangement; the larger flowerheads in the centre provide the focal point. This distribution of flowers and foliage prevents the arrangement appearing top-heavy. Lastly, add shorter pieces of asparagus fern to make a collar around the rim of the vase.

Tall, dark and modern

A tall, black, streamlined vase that says 'sophisticated', lends itself perfectly to this modern vertical arrangement. The narrow neck gives proper support to the tall stems, holding them securely in an upright position. The foliage is placed so that a 'clean line' extends from the bottom of the vase to the top of the arrangement creating a strong diagonal of yellow which is softened slightly by the feathery asparagus fern.

1 You will need seven *Alchemilla mollis* leaves (four of the leaves should have long stems attached), and one stem of golden rod. Place three of the alchemilla leaves around the lip of a round vase.

2 Break off individual florets from the golden rod stem. Add them to the leaves in the vase so that they form a mass of colourful sprays.

3 Place the four alchemilla leaves on long stems in the centre of the vase above the golden rod to form a green-canopy. Not only do the leaves add an unusual touch, they also create a new higher focus for the arrangement.

A shade different

Just one stem of golden rod is used in this unusual display. The unique design is achieved by using long-stemmed alchemilla leaves to form a green canopy over the golden flowers. This novel touch livens up a traditional posy style and gives a higher focus to the small arrangement. The leaves will last in an upright position for up to two weeks without wilting.

1 You will need eight stems of golden rod. Fill the container two thirds full of water. Cut the stems so that the flowers stand about 20cm (8in) above the rim of the container. Place two of them in the container and let them fall naturally into place.

2 Add three more stems, but cut them slightly shorter in order to form a round domed shape.

3 Add the last three stems to the arrangement. Place them close to the rim of the container, so that they just hang over the edges. Bend the flowerheads slightly to keep the rounded shape.

A golden glow

This golden rod arrangement would be perfect to brighten up a dark hallway. Here the slightly unconventional use of a white plant-pot holder emphasises the yellow flowers' vibrant impact. Alternatively you could use a sturdy terracotta or earthenware pot to complement the cottage-garden appeal of these autumn flowers.

HYACINTHS

IDEAL FOR ARRANGING, YET OFTEN OVERLOOKED, HYACINTHS ARE LONG LASTING, VIVID AND WONDERFULLY FRAGRANT. DON'T LEAVE THEM OUT IN THE COLD, BRING THEM INDOORS AND ENJOY CREATING ONE OF THESE EYE-CATCHING DISPLAYS.

Hyacinths are one of our more traditional spring flowers and we have become accustomed to growing them indoors from bulbs or planting them in the garden. But as the Dutch have discovered, hyacinths make beautiful, easy-to-use cut flowers and contrary to popular belief they will last over a week in the vase. Grow a few extra hyacinths yourself for arranging purposes, or buy them from the florist in single or mixed-colour bunches, and discover why hyacinths are one of the top spring cut-flowers in Europe.

The variety of hyacinths used as cut flowers are known as 'Dutch hyacinths'. They are a hybrid of the common hyacinth, *H. orientalis*. Each hyacinth stem consists of a compact spike 10-15cm (4-6in) long, of bell-shaped flowers. They come in a range of colours, blue, white, pink, purple and, more unusually, yellow and red. Their stem length when cut is about 20-30cm (8-12in).

Combined with other spring flowers, or displayed on their own with a small amount of foliage for contrast, the vibrant colour and delicious fragrance of hyacinths will enhance your spring arrangements. Group them together with other scented spring flowers such as lilacs, mimosa and narcissi, or try one of our three ideas using just one bunch of mixed hyacinths and a little foliage to create a striking, informal display.

QUICK TIP

BUYING AND CONDITIONING

Buy hyacinths as cut flowers from the florist in single or mixed-colour bunches. Alternatively grow your own hyacinths from bulbs. Plant hyacinth bulbs in the autumn for flowers in the following spring. Hyacinths should be bought from the florist when a few of the lower florets are just open, and all the unopened florets are showing their true colour. Make sure the flowers are well wrapped to protect them from the cold and the wind on your journey home.

Condition both bought and home-grown hyacinths by recut-ting each stem and remove about 2.5cm (1in) from the stem end. Stand them in tepid water, half way up their stems, for a few hours before arranging. Always use the special cut-flower food sold for tulips or bulb flowers. The flowers should last up to a week in the vase.

1 Choose a basket that echoes the pastel pinks and blues of the hyacinths. Line your basket with a waterproof material and insert a block of wet florist's foam. Use economy foam for these thick-stemmed bulb flowers. Cut off the bottom 10cm (4in) off five blue and pink hyacinth stems and remove their leaves. Insert the hyacinth stems firmly into the florist's foam in a circle around the rim of the wicker basket.

2 Fill in the centre of the basket with a further five slightly longer blue and pink hyacinth stems. Remove the leaves as the bell-shaped flowers will hide the foam. Arrange in a domed shape that repeats the curve of the basket handle. Trim about eight small sprigs of *Asparagus densiflorus* fern from the side branches.

3 Place four or five fern stems into the florist's foam around the rim of the basket to create a light, fluffy collar and to add some contrast of colour and texture to the hyacinth blooms.

RIGHT An array of pink and blue hyacinths creates a fragrant posy in this original woven basket. Ideal as an informal country kitchen or bathroom arrangement, this basket can also serve as an attractive container for potted by hyacinth bulbs.

Fragrant flower basket

1 Attach a pinholder to the centre of a round, shallow white dish. Trim two large and one slightly smaller green leaves from an indoor house plant or a garden shrub and polish them up with plant leaf-shine spray or wipes. Insert each leaf stem at an angle between the prongs in the pinholder. Place the two larger leaves to the left and right respectively, so that they cover most of the outer edge of the container hiding all of the mechanics. Place the third leaf slightly higher at the back of the display.

2 Rinse the hyacinth stems under cold water if they are slightly dirty and cut each stem away from its leaves. Cut a pink hyacinth stem to a length of about 20cm (8in) and insert it upright in the centre of the display. Next cut a white hyacinth stem 8-10cm (3-4in) long and place it directly in front of the pink hyacinth. Position a blue hyacinth with the same stem length as the white hyacinth to the left of these central flowers.

3 Lastly, place a white hyacinth stem 8-10cm (3-4in) long to the left of the blue hyacinth. Cut a further blue hyacinth stem just below its flowerhead and place this close to the pinholder directly below the taller blue hyacinth. Frequently top up the shallow dish with water.

Hyacinth oasis

Castor oil leaves fan out gracefully over a low level container to create a dark, shiny green background for a vibrant cluster of hyacinths. Place this all-round arrangement on a low coffee table where it can be viewed from above and allow the delicious spring fragrance of the hyacinths to fill the room.

1 Fill a large frosted coupé glass two-thirds full with water and wash any dirt off the hyacinth stems. Cut off the bottom 8cm (3in) from the thick white stem ends but keep the leaves on the stems. Place a mixture of eight hyacinths around the rim of the vase. Allow the flowerheads to lean outwards and let the stem ends cross one another for support.

2 Once you have formed the base of the display, begin inserting six stems of pink, blue and white hyacinths about 15cm (6in) tall into the centre of the coupé glass. Wedge the thick hyacinth stems between the network of stems already built up so that they stand vertical in the display. Add more flowers if necessary to create a full, all-round look.

3 To add interest to the display, cut off 5cm (2in) from about 20 stems of bear grass. Place four groups of stems of bear grass to the left, right, front and back of the display. Wedge the stem ends deep down into the glass bowl for maximum support. The arching sprays of bear grass lighten up the arrangement and soften the lines of the container.

Brimming glass

A frosted coupé glass brimming with blue, pink and white hyacinths will add a touch of sophistication to a hallway table and give a fragrant welcome to your guests.

COTTAGE GARDEN

*An enchanting cut-flower display that is as
beautiful and realistic-looking as a country-
cottage herbaceous border.*

The fresh, unsophisticated charm of this cut-flower garden arrangement makes a pleasant change from more formal, stylized displays. For those who love gardening but have no garden, making this arrangement is doubly enjoyable: you can imagine that you are designing a garden as well as arranging cut flowers.

Technically, this type of display is called 'vegetative', since it's meant to look as if it's growing naturally from the ground. However, 'vegetative' sounds more like a description of items on sale in a greengrocers than a flower arrangement, and so some people prefer

the term 'cut-flower garden'. The basic construction consists of a horizontal base layer of overlapping leaves from which a dense mass of vertical flowers and foliage emerges in straight rows and definite groupings, but with each group gradually intermingling as it would in an informal garden.

Setting the mood

The more home-grown material you use, the cheaper the arrangement will be and the better it is for re-creating the look of a garden. At this time of year, florists have a good range of material such as feverfew, spray roses and astilbe that looks home grown. Avoid sophisticated or exotic flowers, such as bird of paradise or orchids, and all-year-round types, such as double chrysanthemums and large, single carnations, which lack seasonal identity.

If you want to cut down on expense, use branches from garden shrubs or trees to accentuate the vertical lines.

Flowering branches are best, but foliage branches can still create an attractive, shrubby setting enlivened with sprigs and clumps of flowers.

The soft pastel colour scheme, containing pinks, blues, creams and white, with bright dots of yellow provided by daisy-like feverfew, captures the informality of a cottage garden, but you could interpret the arrangement in a more restrained way, in monochromatic tints of blue, mauve, pink or yellow, or all white.

Choosing the flowers

Pink Canterbury bells, biennial members of the campanula family, catch the eye first. Ordinary Canterbury bells are shown, but especially lovely are the hose-in-hose types, with deep, petal-coloured calyces. As an alternative, use foxglove, mallow or tall-growing perennial campanula.

The most exotic flower used is florist's wax flower. This Australian

LEFT This cut-flower garden display is dense and brimming with brightness. Garden and florists's flowers and foliage combine to make a stunning focal point for a mantlepiece or shelf.

shrub, related to myrtle, has delicate pink or white starry flowers and needle-like, lemon-scented leaves. Garden leptospermum, escallonia or myrtle (in late summer) could be substituted. Buy cut wax flower with half the flowers open. Stephanotis and hoya also are called 'wax flower', so tell your florist which flower you want.

Hedgerow blooms

Ammi majus, similar to cow parsley in appearance, is a florist's flower that is reminiscent of hedgerows and gardens. If it is unobtainable, use angelica, dill or fennel flowers from the herb garden, or, on a smaller scale, sedum or common valerian. Florist's trachelium, or throatwort, or tall stems of alstroemeria or tiger lily could be substituted.

Astilbe, like cow parsley, looks home grown whether it comes from a garden or a florist. Creamy white astilbe is shown, but there are pink, crimson, coral, white and mauve varieties. Alternatives include lilac stripped of its leaves; goat's beard; meadowsweet; fresh sea lavender; *Celosia plumosa* or sweetly scented mignonette.

Florist's spray roses in pale and deep pink provide small-scale delicacy. Old-fashioned garden floribunda or polyanthus roses would be ideal, but avoid large hybrid tea roses as they look too formal. Tobacco plants or fresh love-in-a-mist – with its clear-blue petals intact and before the seed pods form – would make a lovely substitute. As a last resort, use spray carnations.

Spicy scents

White stocks add a spicy scent and a dense concentration of colour; they also come in pale yellow, pink, mauve and crimson. Buy them when half the flowers are open, and remember to re-cut the stems when you get them home, or they wilt quickly. You could use antirrhinum or godetia instead, or a tightly massed cluster of sweet peas in a single colour.

Matricaria, or feverfew, carries masses of small white daisies on sturdy, well-branched stems, and there is a lovely, golden-leaved variety, more often seen in gardens than in florist shops. Anthemis or Michaelmas daisies could be used instead, or the

WHAT TO DO
WHAT YOU NEED

Making a cut-flower garden

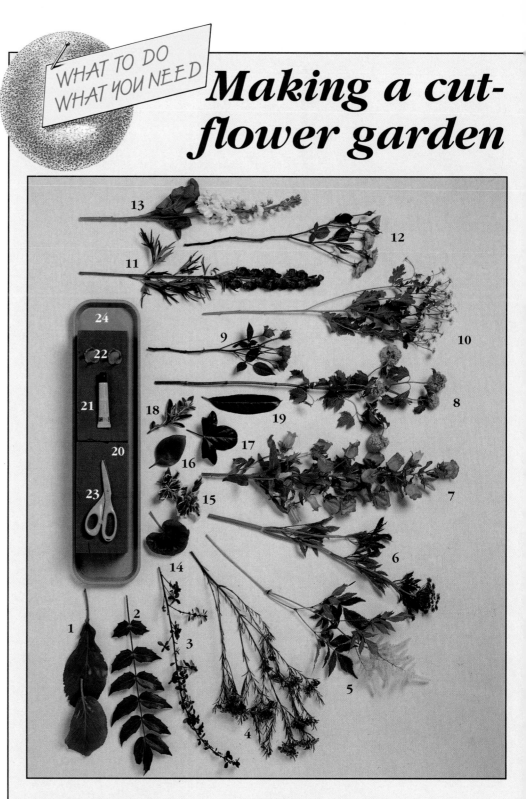

1 *2-3 bergenia leaves*
2 *2-3 stems of mahonia foliage*
3 *2-3 stems of cotoneaster foliage*
4 *6 stems of pink wax flower*
5 *8 stems of white astilbe*
6 *5-6 stems of* Ammi majus
7 *3-4 stems of pink campanula*
8 *5-6 stems of* Viburnum opulus
9 *1 bunch of red spray roses*
10 *1 bunch of matricaria*
11 *4 stems of blue aconitum*
12 *1 bunch of pale pink spray roses*
13 *8 stems of stock*
14 *geranium leaves*
15 *euonymus leaves*
16 *griselinia leaves*
17 *ivy leaves*
18 *senecio leaves*
19 *laurel leaves*
20 *2 blocks of florist's foam*
21 *glue or florist's adhesive clay*
22 *2 prongs*
23 *scissors*
24 *spray-painted plant tray*

1 Trim away the foam block corners to give a rounded edge. Group the leaves around the foam to form a collar (see 'How-to' box). Position the leaves to achieve optimum contrast of colour and texture, placing most at the front if you intend the display to be front-facing. Insert a few short, upright stems of foliage at one end of the foam, a selection of low-lying leaves in the centre and one stem at an angle at the opposite end.

2 Cut three stems of cotoneaster foliage, the tallest to a length of 30cm (12in), the other two stems slightly shorter and insert to one side of the foam. Strip the lower leaves from three stems of campanula. Cut the stem ends at a slant for easy insertion into the foam. Leave the campanula stems long, the tallest approximately 40cm (16in). The pale-pink campanula grouping marks the central point of the display.

3 Cut four stems of white stock to a length of 30cm (12in) and insert them at one end of the display. Insert six *Viburnum opulus* stems, the same height as the campanula, at the opposite end. Cut four stems of blue aconitum slightly shorter than the campanula. Place them amongst the campanula stems. Strip most of the leaves from about ten stems of matricaria. Insert them in a bushy group alongside the white stock.

4 Strip the lower leaves from eight stems of white astilbe, cut to graduated lengths. Group them in the middle of the display between the campanula and the *Viburnum opulus* to bring a splash of white and contrast of texture. Cut five stems of *Ammi majus*, one stem taller than the other flowers, three at graduated heights and one low-lying. The feathery flowerheads contrast with the other, more compact, flowers.

5 Begin inserting the low-lying stems. Cut some wax flower stems to stand vertically, half as tall as the existing stems, the others to lie horizontally against the foam. Make small low-lying groups from the tops of *Viburnum opulus*, campanula and stocks and insert them into the foam in clusters. This fills out the base with colour to make a hedgerow effect and covers any remaining patches of exposed foam.

6 Finish off with the spray roses. Strip the leaves from the stems of one bunch of pale and one bunch of dark-pink spray roses. Cut the stems to graduated lengths, but no longer than 18cm (7in). Place the most open flowers in the centre of the display, facing forwards. Fill in any gaps at the back with short lengths of left-over foliage. Take care not to obscure any low-lying flowers.

gypsophila-like saponaria with large, starry pink or white flowers.

Blue spikes of monkshood, or aconite, accentuate the vertical line of the display. Delphinium, larkspur or herbaceous veronica could be used – a good idea if you have children, as monkshood is highly poisonous.

Finally, the round greenish white flowerheads of the snowball tree, *Viburnum opulus*, can look highly sophisticated in certain displays, but here they play an informal, almost semi-wild role. Green-white mophead hydrangeas could be substituted but try to use small flowerheads rather than the very large ones.

Choosing the foliage

Nine different types of foliage are shown, although three or four would suffice as long as they include a good range of leaf form, size and colour. If you're dependent on your florist for foliage, ask for a large mixed bunch.

If you're taking foliage from the garden, mature leaves last longer than new, soft growth; leathery evergreen leaves last longest of all. Before cutting off leaves, check whether the stalks are tough enough to insert in the foam block, otherwise keep a small length of branch attached.

Bergenia is the most solid-looking foliage used. It is also known as

FIGURINE INTEREST

Many people feel a garden isn't complete without a garden statue. This opinion often extends to include indoor cut-flower garden displays. The addition of a figurine or ornament can transform a simple arrangement into a stunning still-life composition. This cut-flower garden could easily accommodate a small, glazed china animal for example. Tiny rabbits, squirrels, birds or even frogs, in white-glazed or realistically painted china or wood, could be included to give the impression of a real-life hedgerow.

Decide where you want to situate the ornament before you start and leave room to position it alongside the display.

elephant's ears because of its huge, round, glossy evergreen leaves. You could use a broad-leaved hosta instead, but submerge it overnight in water to condition it before arranging.

Glossy, evergreen, pinnate mahonia leaves provide bold, contrasting form. Large-leaved berberry could be substituted, or the elegant pinnate foliage of the sacred bamboo (*Nandina domestica*) which, despite its name, is nothing like bamboo in appearance.

A small-leaved cotoneaster is used here but large-leaved varieties, box or privet could be selected instead. Pyracantha, with its fresh green leaves

is ideal but be careful of its sharp thorns when handling the stems.

Fragrant foliage

It's easy to snip a few leaves from zonal pelargonium house plants or bedding plants. Some varieties have bold leaf markings, or zones, of yellow, white or scarlet. For a more subtle, fragrant effect, choose one of the scented-leaved pelargoniums, such as the lemon or peppermint-scented varieties.

Ivy is even easier to get hold of than pelargonium, but you could use ivy-leaved pelargonium instead. Both come in plain and variegated-leaved varieties, but too many different variegations in one display will result in the finished arrangement looking confused.

Yellow-variegated euonymus leaves add a splash of bright colour, but there are also plain green types. Finally, plain green laurel, griselinia and silver-grey *Senecio greyi* 'Sunshine' complete the foliage list. If you are short of foliage, snip a few leaves from a good sized weeping fig, kangaroo vine or sweetheart vine house plant, but only if the plant is strong and healthy.

Choosing the container

A shallow plastic plant tray, spray-painted to match the flowers, holds two adjacent florist's foam blocks. If you use a plastic or wooden window box, the

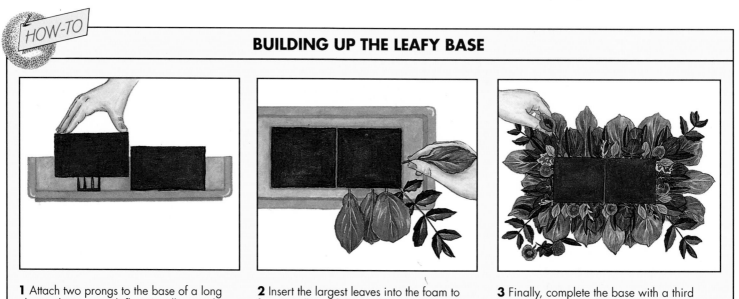

HOW-TO

BUILDING UP THE LEAFY BASE

1 Attach two prongs to the base of a long plastic plant tray with florist's adhesive clay. Press a block of pre-soaked florist's foam firmly onto each prong. Trim away the block corners to give a rounded edge.

2 Insert the largest leaves into the foam to form a collar of foliage, disguising the tray base. Continue with slightly smaller leaves, pushed into the foam so that they form a step up from the bottom layer.

3 Finally, complete the base with a third layer of the smallest leaves. This dark green leafy foundation also will cover the base of the foam blocks and form a strong support for the lighter summer flowers.

collar of foliage will be narrower, so angle the leaves downwards to conceal the sides. Avoid containers that are much deeper or wider than the florist's foam block.

A shallow rectangular china dish from a Victorian dressing table set would make a pretty base for a smaller display using one block of foam. Another alternative is to use a celery or canapé dish, but remember that the horizontal band of foliage virtually hides the base.

If you don't have a container of a suitable shape, attach the foam blocks to a plank of wood or large piece of bark, cut to fit the dimensions of the display; both have garden overtones. Take care with water spills when topping up the foam block if you choose to use such a base. As a last-minute option, use a wooden bread board or carving board – impale the florist's foam blocks directly on the meat spikes. Whatever you choose, make sure it fits the display space available before you start,

remembering to allow room for the broad, leafy extension. If need be, trim the florist's foam blocks to fit the base.

Choosing the setting

The long, narrow dimensions of this arrangement make it ideal for a shelf or mantelpiece, especially one backed by a mirror. Displayed on a windowsill, it would pleasantly confuse the division between indoors and out and would be especially welcome if the view out is uninspiring. A north or east-facing window is cooler and therefore kinder to the cut flowers than a hot, sunny south or west-facing one. Stocks, especially, don't like exposure to direct sunlight or excessive heat.

Decide on the setting before you start. If the arrangement is intended to be front-facing, as shown, you can concentrate your best flowers and foliage towards the front. If it is to be viewed from all sides, on a low coffee table for example, distribute the

ABOVE Roses, delphiniums, feverfew, masterwort, yarrow, shasta and Michaelmas daisies are mixed with exotic flowers and foliage to create a sophisticated table display.

material evenly all the way round. The display is too tall to go on a dining room table, since it would make meal-time conversation almost impossible.

Looking after the display

Spray-mist the arrangement regularly, especially the leaves, which otherwise will droop quickly. It would be too fiddly to re-cut the stems every few days but, once the display looks past its best, be ruthless. Discard any flowers and foliage that are past saving and re-cut the stems of material that still has some life in it. Then make up a scaled down version or simply arrange the blooms in a pretty glass vase.

SPOTLIGHT

LIVING ROOMS

Whatever your choice of flowers for the living room, think in terms of bringing the beauty of the summer garden indoors. Display a basket of leafy branches on the windowsill, a bowl of flowering plants in the hearth or a bunch of scented blooms on an occasional table by your favourite chair.

You may not want to spend much time on a lovely sunny day composing large arrangements with armfuls of flowers. Often, several simple floral groups dotted around the room are more appropriate in the height of summer.

Make the very best of the flowers you bring indoors by positioning them where they will attract most attention. Remember that the focal point of a living room changes in summer. Sometimes the furniture is moved around to look out on the garden, or chairs repositioned to a cooler spot. If you place a lovely summery vase of flowers in a favourite place on a side table, people could have their backs to it.

A leafy look in flower arrangements helps to connect the living room with the world outside. Gather together a collection of foliage plants in a basket or bowl and use them as a background to a jug of flowers, such as pink paeonies, Canterbury bells, roses or marigolds. Flowers seen against a cluster of leaves look as if they're growing in the garden.

Plan your arrangements to include more leaves than usual. Outline the height of a china basket of pinks and marguerites with a handful of fern leaves and cluster a few scented leaves around the rim. It's worth noting that heavily cut and frondy leaves make interesting silhouettes when they're placed against the light. In a simple arrangement of scented freesias or stocks for the table, create the outline shape first with light, glossy leaves. This forms a natural and cool-looking background for the finishing touch of a few flowers. If you haven't got much time, simply fill one jug with leaves – lady's mantle, buttercup, privet – and another with flowers.

LEFT Tea by a window overlooking the garden. The arrangement matches the occasion – a pottery basket of pinks, single chrysanthemums and yellow heads of fennel flowers, with scented pelargonium leaves to add to the blend of aromas.

BELOW Take an old china cakestand and a piece of foam, cover it with glossy leaves, arrange a triangle of freesias and you've made a lovely link between the living room and the garden.

Conservatory Cornucopia

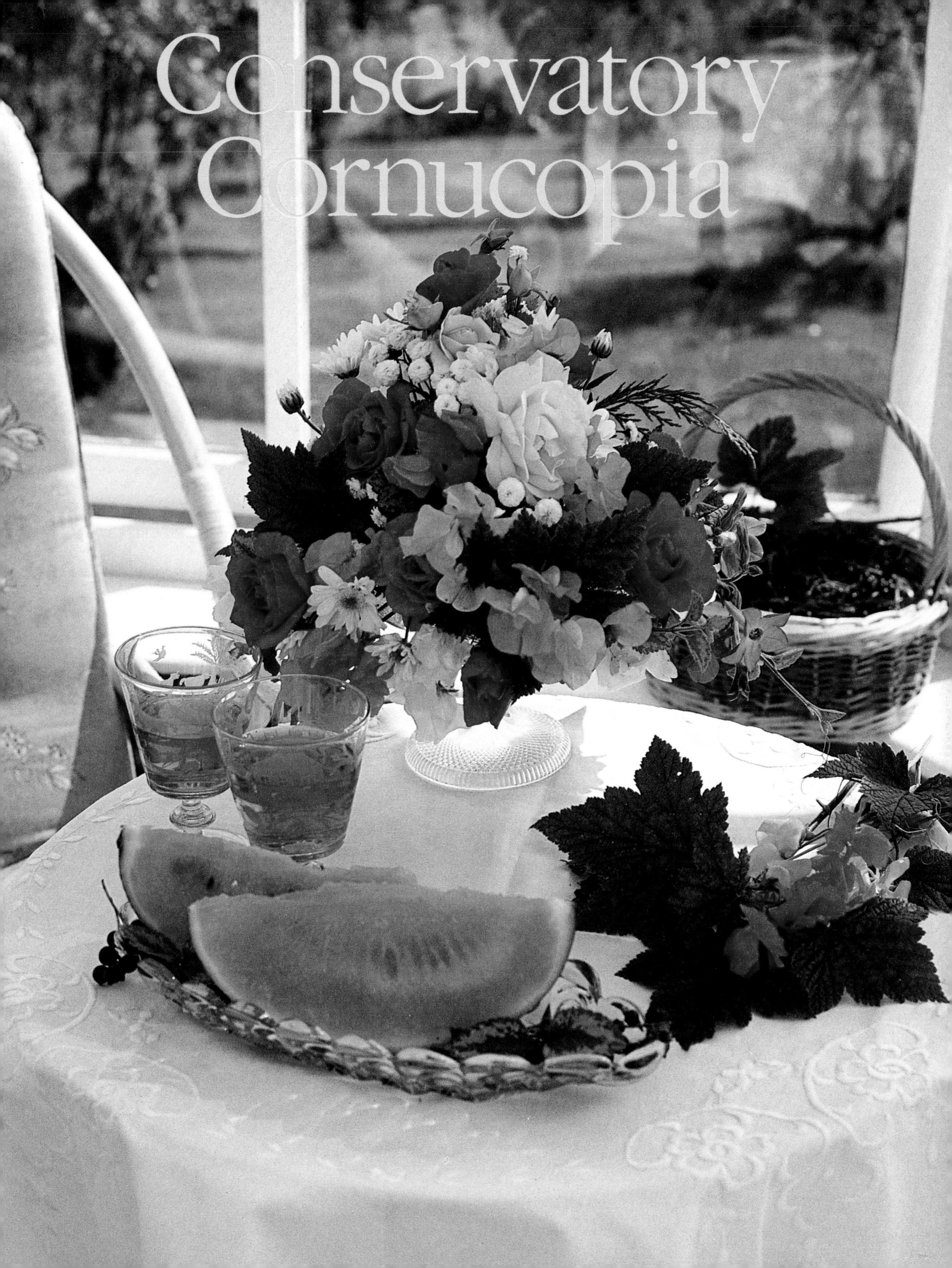

here is a luxurious air about a room, even just a small porch, that has only a pane of glass separating it from the garden beyond. It also provides a golden opportunity to grow plants and display flowers in ideal conditions. However, exactly which plants you can grow successfully all year round depends on the temperature you are prepared to maintain in winter to keep them in constant warmth.

The temperature zones

There are four 'temperature zones' for conservatory plants which apply equally to room extensions and greenhouses. It is useful to know what they are so you can understand the instruction labels given on plants in shops and garden centres. Without this information, the terms can be confusing. Once you know the recommended temperature scales and have monitored the thermometer in your own glass-covered room, you can build up a selection of indoor plants with complete confidence, knowing that they will thrive in their surroundings.

Many people who have had disappointing results with indoor plants are all too ready to blame themselves for not having green fingers, when the real problem is much more tangible. Very often, they are trying to grow plants in conditions that are too hot or too cold for them.

Starting at the exotic end of the scale, conditions that are known as a 'warm house' are similar to the tropical house at a botanical garden – and would be very expensive to maintain in winter. Plants which flourish in these conditions like to be cosseted at temperatures of 21-27C (70-80F) in summer, dropping to a minimum of 13C (65F) in winter. They include tropical orchids, the spectacular red and pink anthuriums, hibiscus and mimosa.

The temperature range for an 'intermediate house' is perhaps more affordable, from 16-21C (60-70F) in summer to a minimum of 13C (55F) in winter. A wide range of plants would flourish in these conditions, including acacia, begonia, bougainvillea, bouvardia, monstera, saintpaulia, stephanotis and even citrus fruit trees.

Simple precautions

The trick with conservatory plants is to prevent the summer temperature from rising above the maximum suggested. Glass traps and concentrates the heat which can burn foliage and wilt flowers quickly. Be sure to fit shades or sunblinds, provide adequate ventilation and keep your plants and flowers well watered. It is especially important to spray-mist them at night and in the morning during hot weather.

These precautions are even more important for plants that require the 'cool house' conditions – that is temperatures of no more than 13-18C (55-60F) in summer and no less than 7C (45F) in winter. There is a long and colourful list of plants you can select and grow in this category which includes agapanthus, azalea, cineraria, cyclamen, gerbera, mesembryanthemum and nerines.

The fourth temperature zone is only suitable for frost-resistant, or frost-free, plants. Conditions for the fourth zone arise when no artificial heat is introduced to a conservatory or sun room, so the room reflects the external temperature, irrespective of whether it is hot or well below freezing point.

LEFT A bright and casual bunch of flowers arranged in a pottery watering can stands half in and half out of the garden. Orange pansies and roses, blue scabious and cornflowers, green lady's mantle and Chinese lanterns make a delightful mixture.

Consequently, plants kept in these conditions have to be very resilient. Suitable varieties include *Fatsia japonica*, phormium, camellia and aspidistra.

Check the plant labels, or ask the advice of the grower or plant retailer before you buy, but don't be put off from growing a plant you really like for the sake of a few degrees of heat. There are a great many plants that span two (but never more) of the temperature zones. Providing they are fed and watered properly, they will thrive.

Well contained
The way you grow your plants will depend on how much room you are prepared to give them – whether you have a planthouse with just room for a table and a couple of chairs, or a living

room under glass that's only decorated with a few plants. In a cool intermediate-range room you could have a soil bed underneath the windows with a passion flower or a blue-flowering plumbago twining up and over a wall and, for contrast, a carpet of pink and red impatiens or nasturtiums.

Planting in permanent soil beds needs a long-term commitment. Planting in containers gives you the chance to move the pots around according to the temperature or weather conditions and to take them outside or into other rooms in the home when you want an extra splash of colour.

The style you set for the room will influence your choice of containers. If you want to model your glasshouse on the kind of grand conservatories and

ABOVE Space can sometimes be at a premium on a conservatory table. This tall cylindrical glass vase lifts the roses high above the place settings and allows the clematis leaves and other foliage stems to arch in natural curves.

orangeries that grace stately homes, then simulated stone or lead urns would be appropriate; both are available cheaply in plastic. In a cool room, stand a pair of cream stone-type urns on either side of a door, trail silver-leaved plants and variegated periwinkle over the edge and fill in the centre with a mound of bright-blue hydrangeas.

For a more down-to-earth look, choose large free-standing wooden containers, which are lined with plastic,

cream. A large blue and white jug, which could be anything from Chinese style to striped kitchenware, would make a perfect container. Fill it to overflowing with trailing silver-green leaves such as eucalyptus, senecio and artemisia, yellow-green fennel or dill seedheads, green tobacco plant, bells of Ireland or cool-looking spurge, blue and white campanula and long, arching stems of forget-me-nots. Repeat the theme with several blue and white jug arrangements of varying types and sizes positioned around the room.

Party-time

Conservatories make ideal party venues and if you want to set the scene with a special flower arrangement, take your cue from the food and drink on offer. Colour matching food and flowers makes a tremendous impact. If you are serving rosé wine, decorate the drinks tray with a glass bowl of soft pink roses. Match deep, coral-red sweet peas, roses or geraniums with slices of glowing watermelon. Emphasise the rich golden colour of a bowl of mangoes with an arrangement of orange and yellow marigolds or nasturtiums.

or opt for traditional tubs and barrels. To make a focal point in the room, display a dramatic house plant such as a tall rubber plant; a *Fatsia japonica* with its huge glossy leaves and white flowers in summer; a yucca with its long, sword-like leaves and tall spires of white flowers; or a miniature and wide-spreading evergreen juniper.

In keeping with this natural style, group together pots of warm brown terracotta containers which could include scented geraniums; a collection of stately crown imperial lilies and white arum lilies; a white jasmine; a deep rose-coloured oleander or red or white bouvardia. Display them on shelves, windowsills and tables or in a grouped, floor-standing arrangement.

Cut-flower displays

However many growing plants you have in a conservatory, they are no substitute for a vase of cut flowers whether from the garden or florist. Arrange fresh

flowers to suit the style or the mood of an occasion, to introduce a different splash of colour or to fill a gap where a favourite plant has finished flowering.

Take the outlook into consideration when arranging fresh flowers. If the garden is not looking its best, display flowers on the windowsill – a large jug of phlox, sweet williams, tobacco plant, sweet peas, gerberas and cornflowers will attract attention, thereby drawing the eye away from the view outside.

Casual-style arrangements are most appropriate for the informal look of outdoor rooms. Display a mass of sweet peas in crimson, pastel pink, mauve, coral, white and cream in a full, rounded container such as a jug, an old painted teapot or goldfish-style bowl. These all look good with a mound of flowers that settles naturally and attractively into a soft, easy shape.

To create a cool look in your conservatory or sunroom, choose a colour scheme in blue, green and white or

---

THE RIGHT CONDITIONS

To keep your conservatory plants bright and healthy, you must give them the best possible growing conditions. They need not only heat, light and moisture but also adequate drainage. Few plants will thrive if their roots are waterlogged.

• Cover the base of each container with shards – pieces of broken earthenware pots or tiles – and then with a layer of gravel or shingle on top to provide some drainage.

• Use peat compost for summer flowers and a soil-based compost for shrubs and perennial plants.

• Leave a gap between the soil surface and the container rim to allow space for watering. This gap can vary from 1cm (1/2 in) for small pots to 7.5cm (3in) for large tubs and urns.

The Great Outdoors

*Add to the atmosphere of an
outdoor meal or party in the garden or a picnic
with a casually placed container of flowers or medley of flowering plants.*

Almost every garden, however well-planned, has an off-peak flowering period when the borders don't look as bright and colourful as they might. For outdoor parties, when the weather is warm and sunny, there are all kinds of ways to introduce arrangements of fresh cut flowers and growing plants to compensate for this.

Flowers in pots

Some gardens are a medley of greens, with a small patch of lawn and a few dwarf evergreen trees. Potted plants are an obvious answer to the need for instant colour in such a garden. A large earthenware container of potted bright-pink mallow, larkspur and spray chrysanthemums is an ideal floral addition to this kind of setting. The flowers will shine against the green, leafy background. Take a collection of flowering plants from inside the home. The garden and patio will be transformed just by adding a few geraniums, begonias and some fuchsias.

How and where you display the plants in their temporary outdoor setting will make all the difference. If possible, hang them in pots from hooks on a trellis fence or place them in a trough and elevate them to eye level on top of a low brick wall. If there is enough room, stand a small step ladder on the terrace or close to the party area and arrange the plants on each step to make a slanting wall of colour. Add some trailing plants to stand on the top two steps so that the leaves trail down to cover the stand, mingle with the flowering plants and unify the whole arrangement. House plants such as spider plants, *Asparagus sprengeri*, tradescantia and ivy would all provide suitable trailing material.

If you don't have any trailing plants, create a more temporary effect with long shoots of garden ivy, Virginia creeper or wisteria. First condition the stems by standing them in water for several hours and then press them into the soil in the featured plant pots. Arrange them so that they tumble down the steps just like growing stems.

For a more portable grouping of indoor plants, cluster together several pots in a shallow basket or trug. Include in the plant group a large fern and a few

ABOVE A basket of cascading broom and ranunculus that looks as if it had just been picked from the garden. In fact, the stems are held in soaked foam, and the flowers will stay fresh for several days to come.

RIGHT A group of fruit and flowers makes a compelling focus of attention in a garden corner. You could follow the idea for a party table and have fruit spilling out, cornucopia style, from a wide-necked jug or vase.

LEFT A tall and narrow arrangement in a stoneware pot provides eye-catching brightness. Position the design against a fence or shed wall.

BELOW A picnic by the river can be enhanced with bunches of large, leafy flower stems arranged informally in a jug or country-style basket. White flowers set against the water provide an attractive reflection.

brilliantly coloured pelargoniums. Place the basket in an appropriate spot – the corner of the patio, on a large flower pot at the edge of a flower border or on a kitchen stool against a wall.

Remember that not all indoor plants can stand the sharp temperature drop at night. If your indoor plant selection falls into the hothouse or delicate plant category, take them inside at the end of the evening's festivites.

Brilliant bedding plants

Another way to brighten up the garden is with flowering bedding plants. At this time of year, garden centres and local markets have an extensive and varied collection. Look out for boxes of bright yellow and purple pansies, pink and mauve petunias and pink and red impatiens.

Make a prominent splash of colour by setting all the plants in a large flower-pot, or divide them between several small pots and group them on a wall or table. Look around the home for other suitable containers. Fill a large plastic waste-paper bin with red impatiens that spill out over the side or pack a lined wastepaper basket or a shopping basket with bright pansy plants.

There's no need to fill a container to the brim with soil, especially if it is tall and deep. Trays of bedding plants haven't had the chance to develop a deep root system and they won't need much more depth of soil. Pack out a deep container with a few stones to act as a ballast. Make sure the top is level, then position an old baking tin or similar shallow container with plants on top to fit inside the rim. It's quick and easy to do, especially if you buy plants that have been grown in small fibre pots. These are readily available throughout the year from garden centres.

The just-picked look

It is easier to achieve a casual look with flower arrangements for the garden and patio than with indoor displays. To arrange a basket of flowers that look as if they have just been picked from the garden, use a large shallow basket or trug and a collection of colourful and cascading stems. Place a shower of pink, yellow and orange broom to spill over the sides and a cluster of tightly furled and brilliantly coloured ranunculus in

LEFT A portable display of flowers, this woven lavender basket is filled to overflowing with a fern at one end and a burst of golden gerberas and lilies, pink nerines at the other.

colour choice for an evening party as the flowers go on glowing long after dusk when darker colours have faded into obscurity. Position a few stems of blue flowers such as irises, borage or forget-me-nots to distribute the colour evenly. Finally, pierce a few strawberries on wooden cocktail sticks and place among the flowers as highlights.

For a much 'warmer' colour scheme, fill the container with deep-pink and coral-red sweet peas and a few apricot-coloured flowers, such as godetia or eschscholzia.

Shades of evening

When the scene is set for an evening party in the garden, with pots of plants and jugs of flowers displayed on the patio and buffet table, don't forget to include candles in your arrangements. As the evening draws in, the flicker of candlelight really contributes to a party atmosphere. Beat the breeze by placing candles or nightlights in jam jars to protect the flame, or float special lightweight candles and flowerheads in deep bowls to create pools of light.

If there is no wind, push large candles into the top of plant pots to cast a soft light on the flowers. Use bright-red candles with yellow pansies and golden ones with scarlet geraniums. Alternatively, decorate candles with a wired hoop of flowers. Use short stems of sweet peas, small roses, side shoots of larkspur and buttercups – but not daisies as they close up at night-time.

exactly toning shades. All you need to compose this effective, horizontal arrangement is a large block of soaked florist's foam placed towards one end of the container. Position the basket or trug on a garden seat, a low wall or a pillar on the patio.

Baskets look completely at home outdoors and suit most combinations of plants and cut flowers. Any bright foliage plant such as a lettuce-green fern or a sunset-pink coleus makes a natural background at one end of the basket. Place a shower of golden gerberas and lilies, pink nerines, spray chrysanthemums and annual dahlias in a block of foam at the other end.

Using different fruits

For casual get-togethers such as a barbecue, arrange a basket of fruit as part of the meal and decorate it with a few choice flowers. Cornflowers look good with red fruits, such as cherries or strawberries, and marigolds contrast well with green apples.

Place a pile of fruit on the table, as if it is tumbling from the mouth of a wide-necked jar, lain on its side, cornucopia style. A large stone pot of stocks, golden rod, antirrhinums and Canterbury bells makes a bright decoration for the garden or patio. Add a similar vessel placed on its side and spilling over with a pineapple, bananas and polished apples and the whole group multiplies in colour and visual appeal.

Red, white and blue

For a really striking effect, choose a red, white and blue colour theme. Place a piece of soaked foam in a lined basket or other container and cover it with a handful of strawberry leaves or aquilegia foliage. Arrange a mass of casually placed white flowers. White is a good

SPOTLIGHT

PORCHES AND BALCONIES

If you think of porches and balconies as a halfway point between the home and the garden, they seem a natural situation for a floral decoration.

If the area is open to the elements, choose containers that can stand up to strong gusts of wind. For table-top arrangements, use rugged-looking, wide-based containers. Sturdy glass is highly suitable for this situation and looks refreshingly cool in warmer weather. For balcony displays, use a rectangular glass trough filled with an armful of garden flowers standing up to their necks in cool, clear water; or a collection of decorative preserve jars or tumblers brimming over with a mixture of flowers, red in one, yellow in another; or a shallow glass bowl with floating pansies, stocks and roses.

If you are intending to fill some tubs with flowering plants but haven't done so, a floor-standing flower arrangement can serve as a temporary alternative. Choose a rugged container such as a large jug, stone jar or flowerpot fitted with a watertight holder. Select large or brightly coloured plant materials. A mixture of leafy branches and deep-pink pyrethrum, red and gold gaillardia, scarlet penstemon and orange marigolds will catch the eye of passing visitors.

Dried-flower arrangements made up and ready to take outside for an impromptu party or a sunny evening on the balcony can be just as showy. Baskets look good and are easily transportable – just be sure the container is heavy enough to be stable. If not, a few stones tucked around or under the foam or crushed wire will keep it in place.

Go for a selection of dried materials that is packed with colour and texture. Strawflowers and statice in primary colours; cones wrapped with wire and pushed into the holding material; exotics such as dried protea flowers from the florist; teasels sprayed with bright paints; globe artichoke heads – all would combine to give your arrangement a natural outdoor look.

LEFT Summer flowers signal a cheerful welcome beside a cottage doorway. Geraniums, marigolds, roses, single chrysanthemums, delphinium florets – the stems are all cut short and pressed into a pre-formed plastic ring of soaked foam.

BELOW A weather-beaten wooden background and a sturdy garden table call for a floral style that captures the outdoor mood – an unusual petal-shaped vase holds an informal display of valerian, larkspur and mallow.

BACK TO NATURE

For most of us, the patio is used most frequently during the summer months, so this is the time to decorate it with flowers. In the colourful display featured, the flowers are arranged in a loose, casual style, entirely in keeping with the informal atmosphere of a patio living area. The scale of the display is large, reflecting the sense of spaciousness outdoors, whatever the actual size of the patio or garden.

Choosing the flowers
Delphinium, monkswood, solidaster, astilbe and nerine are typical summer garden flowers; together they create a multi-coloured display based on yellow, blue and pink. All are available from florists and alternative flowers and colours can be substituted easily.

If you have a big garden with plenty of flowers grown for arranging, try using flowers cut from borders next to, or visible from, the patio. For example, a huge arrangement of red-hot pokers set against the same flowers growing in a border; or a display featuring dahlias placed in front of a formal bedding-out scheme of dahlias would create a pleasing sense of visual continuity.

In general, garden delphiniums are at their most abundant in early summer but, if the first flower spikes are cut to ground level as soon as the flowers fade, they often flower again in late summer or early autumn. Florist's delphiniums have an extended season so you should be able to obtain them throughout most of the summer months. There are white, mauve, yellow and even pink delphiniums, as well as the more popular blue forms. You could use mullein or mallow from the garden as an alternative; both are late-flowering summer blooms.

Monkshood, or aconitum, is a close relative of delphinium; both are members of the Ranunculaceae, or buttercup, family. Often florists do not carry monkswood as part of their ordinary stock. However, you may well have it growing in your garden, If you have problems obtaining either delphiniums and monkswood, you could substitute one with more of the other, or incorporate tall spikes of gladioli.

Yellow border flowers
Solidaster, a complex hybrid cross between solidago and aster, is featured here, but the similar-looking golden rod is equally suitable. It is a typical late-summer border flower and so tough that it is sometimes a nuisance, overwhelming weaker neighbours in the garden. Yellow tansy or yarrow could be used instead, or the fluffy heads of Michaelmas daisies.

Astilbe adds a feathery touch; it comes in shades of pink, mauve and rich red as well as creamy white. Goat's beard, meadowsweet, meadow rue, bugbane or big plumes of pampas grass could be substituted from the garden. If none of these is available, use masses of florist's gypsophila or sea lavender.

Spiky nerine
The spiky flowerheads of nerine, or Guernsey lily, provide strong pink highlights in the display. The similar-shaped agapanthus would provide touches of blue, or use one of the ornamental alliums or brodaiea instead. Another alternative would be to use florist's alstroemeria, in as bright a shade of pink as possible.

Late summer is a good time for fresh foliage as well as for flowers, and by now the foliage should be hardened growth, which is easier to condition and longer lasting than spring or early summer material.

Variegated elaeagnus is available in several combinations of yellow, creamy white and dark green. All-green types could be used, or the lovely silver grey of *Elaeagnus x ebbingei*. If you prefer, try using stems of variegated holly.

The purple beech stems featured in this arrangement are supple and can be coaxed into loosely flowing or arching shapes. Copper beech or plain green beech foliage also can be used. Beech is sold commercially for floristry work, but may have to be ordered in advance. Other suitable display foliage includes hornbeam, hazel or birch.

Choosing the container
A hollow section of log, 45cm (18in) high and 30cm (12in) wide, has been used as an attractive display base, concealing a tall, plastic container which holds the water. If you live in the country, you are more likely to come across a hollow log than if you live in an urban area, but it is relatively easy to hollow out a section of a complete wooden log. Simply use a power drill or brace to drill a series of adjoining holes in the central core using extra-long drill bits. Chip away any loose wood with a chisel to create a cavity deep enough to hold the plastic container.

LEFT A crab apple tree stump makes an unusual container for this display of delphinium, aconite, astilbe, solidaster and nerine flowers, with beech and elaeagnus foliage.

HOW-TO
WEATHERING A LOG

An outdoor display in a log should look as if it is growing naturally. As well as arranging the flowers in a loose, casual style, add to the authenticity of the display by making the log itself look weathered. Stick small clumps of fresh or dried moss or lichen and small plates of fungi to the log surface and in the holes and indentations of the bark.

Alternatively, if you cannot obtain any of the above, blend together live natural yoghurt and a little milk and, using a brush, paint this mixture onto the log. Leave it outside, exposed to the elements. Over a period of a few weeks, the yoghurt mixture will encourage lichen to grow on the bark surface, thus lending the log a weathered appearance.

You could use an old, woven wicker basket of a similar size instead of the log, or large terracotta flower pot. If you have a formal patio with stone balustrades, urns and steps down to the garden, use an empty stone urn as the basis of your display, since the natural log base would look out of place in such a setting.

Choosing the setting

Whether indoors or out, cut flowers last longer in cool shady conditions than exposed to direct sunlight. If your patio has an overhang or sheltered corner, the flowers will benefit from being positioned in the shade. However, if your patio is south or west-facing and in full sun, it is sensible to keep the flowers inside until late afternoon when the sun is not too fierce and the temperature begins to drop.

If you have a similar-sized glazed vase in your home, you can transfer the display in its plastic cylinder, so that you can both enjoy the flowers, even when you are not using the patio, and protect them at the same time. Obviously, if you're giving a luncheon party on a sunny patio, shortening the display's life is worth the pleasure the flowers give you and your guests.

For the most natural effect, avoid placing the log on a paved surface, where it may look unnatural. Instead, position it on a lawn or on low-growing ground cover, such as ivy; the display would seem to emerge naturally from the ground, as if it were still growing.

If you don't have a patio, place the display in a bright breakfast or dining room, positioned just to one side of sliding or French doors so that the flowers are shaded and people can get in and out easily. If the floor is carpeted in a pale colour, glue felt to the base of the log, to help prevent stains.

Looking after the flowers

In hot, dry weather, spray-mist the display occasionally, and remember to keep the water topped up. Pick off the lower florets of the spiky flowers as they fade and re-cut the stems every few days. The nerines are likely to last longer than the other flowers; when you take the display apart, re-use them in a smaller vase, perhaps with a few elaeagnus leaves.

WHAT TO DO
WHAT YOU NEED

Making your own patio display in a hollow log

1 *2 stems of beech leaves*
2 *2 stems of variegated elaeagnus*
3 *6 stems of solidaster*
4 *8 stems of astilbe*
5 *3 stems of delphinium*
6 *5 stems of monkshood*
7 *10 stems of nerine*
8 *30 x 60cm (1 x 2ft) chicken wire*
9 *scissors*
10 *crab apple tree stump*
11 *plastic container*

1 Clean the inside of the log, removing any moss or flaking wood. Push the plastic container inside the log so that it stands straight; prop it up or pad the hole with newspaper if necessary. Crumple a 30 x 60cm (1 x 2ft) piece of chicken wire and place it inside the container to hold the flowers. Half-fill with water. Cut the ends of five monkshood stems and group in the centre of the container.

2 Trim the ends of six stems of yellow solidaster at an angle so that they are about twice the height of the wood stump. Remove the lower foliage from the stems to avoid it rotting and fouling the water. Place them in a fan shape in front of the monkswood. Solidaster will last over a week in water and so can be used in another arrangement if it outlasts the other plant material.

3 Select three blue-purple delphiniums on which most of the lower flowers on the spike are already open. Cut the stem ends and strip the lower leaves as before. Position the delphinium in front of the solidaster so that the flowerheads fan out and appear to be growing from a central point. Always wash your hands thoroughly after handling delphiniums as the sap they exude is poisonous.

4 Trim eight astilbe stems so that they are about half the height of the other flowers. Astilbe stems will 'bleed' when cut so sear the ends with a naked flame or immerse in boiling water as a preventive measure. Remove any foliage on the stems as the leaves tend to wither before the flowers. Place the treated stems in a delicate, feathery circle around the edge of the log.

5 Cut ten nerine stems to graduated lengths. Remove the unattractive papery brown outer petals underneath the flowerheads. Intersperse the nerines with the other flowers so that the heads form a pink arch. Place one stem slightly lower to the front of the display. Only include in the arrangement flowers that are beginning to open; buds that are not already well developed will not open out in water.

6 Bend the supple beech foliage gently in your hand to exaggerate its natural curve. Position one stem at the front, trailing over the edge of the log and one tall, straight piece upright at the back of the display. Add two more stems on either side. Divide two long stems of elaeagnus into smaller sprays. Place these to form a foliage collar around the edge of the log. Top up the water level.

ENTERTAINING
and
CELEBRATIONS

You can create stunning arrangements for special occasions and celebrations, from weddings to Christmas and Valentine's Day. More extravagant floral displays are highlighted here, appropriate for parties and special get-togethers. Bring your own touch to these occasions with flowers to evoke a festive mood.

A domed display of yellow, cream and white flowers is an ideal arrangement for a special celebration, such as a christening. The elegant silver punch bowl used to hold the flowers also adds to the sense of festivity.

STYLISH SUMMER ENTERTAINING

Experiment with flower displays of different styles to set the mood for every kind of occasion, from a relaxing picnic to an impromptu summer party.

ummer is the ideal time for renewed inspiration and thinking afresh about the way you arrange flowers. It provides the perfect opportunity to try out different design styles, to mix the latest colours and shapes in exciting ways, or to bring a tropical touch to your flower displays.

Eating out of doors is the perfect cue for a flourish of flowers, whether the meal in prospect is a grassy picnic or a stylish buffet. The mood may differ but flowers can play an important role on both occasions.

Picnic flowers

Taking flowers along with the food for a picnic in the garden or in the country may seem unnecessary, but in fact there are many garden and idyllic country spots without a flower in sight. Choose only long-lasting flowers for your picnic display, for example, carnations, roses, lilies, single chrysanthemums, marigolds, pinks, cornflowers, and spray carnations. Give them a long drink before arranging as they will dry out quickly outside and in the heat.

Place a piece of soaked foam in a small unbreakable container, for example, a margarine tub or plastic sandwich box, and secure the foam with one or two lengths of florist's adhesive tape. Arrange the flowers just before you are ready to leave, and don't forget to add a few sturdy foliage sprays or individual leaves, such as ivy, to conceal the foam and holder. A simple, compact design like a fan shape or a low dome of pretty pink and cream roses would make a lovely finishing touch for a summer picnic on the grass.

The most practical way to carry flowers is in soaked foam. The foam holds the flowers firmly in place so that they won't move about too much during the journey and also provides a constant source of moisture.

ABOVE Take flowers on a picnic in the garden or the countryside to add to the occasion. Arrange roses in an unbreakable container and soaked foam. RIGHT Arrange exotic strelitzia and daisy-shaped golden gerberas in a shiny watering can. The fruit is supported on canes pushed into the foam.

LEFT Add floral elegance to an outdoor picnic table by wiring together groups of flowerheads, such as marguerites, broom, marigolds and alstroemeria, and foliage and pin them to the sides of a snow-white table-cloth.

brighten up a small table by pinning dainty posies to the front of the table-cloth. A colourful mixture – marigold, some stems of love-in-a-mist, a side shoot of larkspur and a leaf or two – is all you need for each one. For added effect, tie the posy together with colourful, trailing ribbons.

A larger table looks best with a garland of leaves and flowers looped across the front fall of the table-cloth. For quickness and lightness, wind long leafy stems together and bind at intervals with short lengths of stub wire – much less time-consuming than binding bunches of leaves onto a cord base – until they are long enough to drape in deep, even scallops. The easiest foliage to use is smilax (*Asparagus asparagoides*) which you can buy, or order, from florists. It has long tendrils of pointed oval leaves on either side of the main stem and makes a garland that looks full but not too dense. A practical alternative is variegated ivy which is more summery-looking than its plain, dark-green counterpart.

Decorate the leafy ribbon with short-stemmed flowers in a co-ordinating colour scheme. Use snippings from large arrangements and side shoots from long stems such as clarkia, larkspur and golden rod. If you have a spare spire of delphinium or a large head of hydrangea, cut it into a dozen or so groups of florets, using each one separately to maximise the visual impact. Wire the groups of flowers to the foliage stems using short lengths of fine wire.

Fruit and flowers

When fruit is plentiful, in the middle of the strawberry or peach season for example, include a selection of fruits in your flower arrangements. If you are indulging in a strawberry cream tea in the garden, then decorate the table with a narrow basket brimming over with clusters of strawberries, roses, corn-flowers and some prize specimens of

Once you get to your picnic spot, position the flowers in partial shade – under the dappled light from a tree rather than in the full glare of the sun.

If you want to adorn your picnic with just one perfect rose, fill a plastic orchid phial, obtainable from florists, with water and push the flower stem through the hole in the lid. Wrap the flowerhead in tissue to protect it on the journey. Once at your destination, you can stand the phial in a wine bottle or similar sturdy container. Check the water level in the phial frequently and top it up whenever necessary.

Setting the table

An elegant garden buffet or tea party set on a table calls for something a little more eye-catching. Go for a traditional country-style look by decorating a small buffet table with a large-scale daisy chain. Use single spray chrysanthemums or wild marguerites as your daisy look-alikes. Give the flowers a good long drink of water and arrange them as close as possible to the time when your guests will arrive.

Cut the stems short, no longer than 5cm (2in) and make a slit close to the end of each with a narrow knife blade. Carefully push the stem of one flower through the slit in the stem of the next, and draw it through so that each flower-head rests against the stem before. Continue in this way to form a long chain. Hang a short trailing length of the daisy chain from each visible corner of the table-cloth and secure with a safety pin. Cover the corners with another flower, a neat posy or a ribbon bow. You can also hang the two lengths of daisy chain along the sides of the table to meet in a loop at the centre.

If you're putting on a special meal for an occasion such as a birthday tea, ripe berries. The kind of basket made to hold two wine bottles is ideal. It won't take up much room on the table and has enough height for the strawberry leaves to trail attractively over the sides. Line the basket with polythene, or place a water-holding container inside, and position a piece of soaked foam to extend above the rim. Arrange the strawberry stems first then fill in the design with a free-style arrangement of garden flowers. Lastly, for a really mouth-watering touch, pierce a few choice strawberries with cocktail sticks and place them as focal points, close to the basket handle.

Two or three downy peaches or blushing nectarines placed at the centre of a summer flower display of roses or lilies add another bountiful touch and transform even the most ordinary arrangement. (See tip box for details on how to fix fresh fruit in a display.)

Tropical fruits look even more enticing. Bring hot-summer style to a room

ARRANGING WITH FRUIT

Using fruit in arrangements is a quick and easy way of introducing different shapes, textures and colours, and making your designs more varied.
• Avoid using stub wires to pierce the fruit as they are corrosive. Instead, use plastic-coated wire or cocktail sticks.
• Fix heavy fruit, such as an apple, by pushing a stick through from one side to another close to the base. Twist the ends of two stub wires around the exposed ends of the stick and twist together to make a stem. Press this stem into the foam, or twist it around crushed wire netting to fix the fruit in the design.

corner by using star fruit, pomelos, guavas, lychees, passion fruit and many others with brightly coloured flowers. Any flowers look exotic if the colours are vibrant and the containers bold enough but, where possible, use bright blooms such as gerberas and

pyrethrums, geranium species and poppies, geum and penstemons. A quick and easy way to combine fruit with flowers is to pile them in a basket to display alongside a showy flower arrangement.

Traditional style

Use flowers to form part of a still-life group with a selection of favourite antique or treasured ornaments. A tall, slender, trumpet-shaped glass would be a suitable equivalent to the popular Victorian cone and horn shapes. You could fill one with a drooping fan shape of cornflowers, godetias, freesias, petunias and roses, including plenty of trailing foliage.

You may have a cone-shaped corn dolly or a brass or copper huntsman's horn which you could lie flat and fill with a cornucopia of dried flowers, arranged in dry foam, fanning out into a full shape. Place one alongside a Victorian brass clock or vase and add a twist of fabric or a piece of comtemporary lace to complete the scene.

By contrast, an Art Deco-style ornament, such as a silver mirror frame or a tall pewter candlestick, calls for fewer flowers. Place one or three arum lilies in a black-and-white striped jug or vase, or a stem of enchantment lilies or agapanthus in a specimen vase.

Special elegance

A pedestal design is a lovely way to raise flowers to new heights. For a special party, use a tall candlestick, spaghetti jar or a lily vase and a cascade of broom and carnations. Match a glass container to your chosen colour scheme by adding a few drops of food colouring to tint the water.

Pale colours in a cool-looking arrangement appear most stylish. Try filling a creamware jug and bowl with a graceful curve of green orchids, cream freesias and pale-pink roses. Form the outline of the display with naturally curved stems such as broom, clematis, honeysuckle and ivy.

LEFT A long, narrow basket looks effective and countrified, half filled with flowers. Combine marguerites and irises with luscious strawberries speared on cocktail sticks pushed into foam.

FRUIT
FLOWER

FRUITFUL FLORA

This luscious array of bright flowers, tropical fruit and foliage makes a mouth-watering buffet table display for a special occasion.

All eyes will be on this striking 'helter-skelter' of fruit and flowers so give it pride of place on the buffet table at an engagement, birthday or anniversary party. Only a few stems of each flower type are required so this splendid display can look extravagant without being expensive. Choose a range of standard, brightly coloured flowers and concentrate on an unusual collection of nuts and tropical fruit.

Selecting the shades
The colour scheme of the featured display is a vivid mixture of bright tropical fruit and flowers in all the hues of the rainbow. Warm and hot colours predominate, with sunny yellows, pinks and oranges setting the tone, and cool purple, neutral beige and white providing contrast. You could interpret the idea in a single colour scheme, but it's easier and more exciting to buy for a multi-colour display, and the finished effect looks more festive. Although some blue-dyed gypsophila is included,

blue is not a colour normally associated with food, so use it with restraint.

Make the arrangement in its finished location so that you don't risk disturbing the display by moving it around. As some of the fruit needs to be sliced for display, and fruit stains are notoriously difficult to wash out, cover the tablecloth under your cutting board with something waterproof, such as a kitchen dustbin liner. Ordinary absorbent kitchen paper does not provide enough protection. Tuck the waterproof covering underneath the base of the stand so the cut fruit does not pass over any exposed tablecloth. Have a damp sponge handy to mop up any spilt juice.

Try to make up the display as close as possible to the beginning of the party as cut fruit surfaces discolour quickly and dry up. Painting the exposed surfaces with lemon juice helps prevent discolouration, as does covering the arrangement completely with kitchen plastic wrap before it goes on display.

Choosing the flowers and foliage
A mixture of garden and florist's material is used, but the choice of flowers is flexible. If you have a garden, you could still achieve striking effects with just garden flowers and foliage. Make sure that the material to be used has rigid stems for insertion into the florist's foam foundation, and

will be resilient enough to stay fresh-looking for several hours.

Florist's yellow spray roses are featured, but they could be replaced easily with garden roses. If you are working to a budget, buy double chrysanthemums but go for clear colours, avoiding autumn russets.

Pale-pink florist's stocks and spray carnations provide both fragrance and frilly textural interest. You may have Brompton, seven-week or ten-week stocks in flower in the garden to use instead. Pink spray carnations are inexpensive, and one bunch should be enough, but garden pinks or sweet williams are possible alternatives. Avoid large, single carnations as they're out of scale with the rest of the display.

Suitable alternatives
Evergreen spurge (*Euphorbia robbiae*) is a valuable garden plant that has flower-like basal rosettes of shiny, dark-green leaves and long-lasting flower bracts. Here, it's used to give a strong vertical accent to the display. Your florist may be able to supply evergreen spurge if you order it in advance; otherwise, use caper spurge, lady's mantle, or florist's pittosporum. (See tinted box for important information on using spurge in arrangements.)

A mixed colour selection of florist's Turk's-cap ranunculus feature in the

147

display. They could be replaced with garden roses, double geums or trollius. Yellow freesias make unusual filler flowers as freesias are rarely used on such short stems in displays. You could use pink or purple freesias, or tightly packed heads of garden rhododendrons, azaleas or viburnums.

Feverfew, or matricaria, is a short-lived perennial chrysanthemum that seeds itself freely in gardens. Any similar, daisy-like flower, such as anthemis, English daisy or small, single, white florist's chrysanthemums could be substituted; later in the year, asters would be ideal. The alternative flowers must be dainty, or they'll overpower the display.

Flexible stems

Weeping willow branches are wound in ribbon-like spirals around the display. Any other malleable stem, such as honeysuckle, ivy, clematis, jasmine or ornamental or edible grape vine could be used instead. Florist's asparagus fern is another alternative, or you could cut sprigs from an *Asparagus sprengeri* house plant. As a last resort use a long, trailing stem of spider plant, complete with plantlets.

Pieris is a hardy evergreen shrub with flowers similar to lily of the valley. In fact it's a member of the Ericaceae family, and related to rhododendron and heather. Your florist may be able to order some for you, but it won't be cheap, as it's slow growing and only bears heavy crops of flowers when mature. The related arbutus, or strawberry tree, with white, bell-like flowers could be used instead. Stems of wisteria or laburnum also will create a similar weeping effect. Once cut, both last better without their foliage.

Lastly, eucalyptus provides unusual, reddish-brown flowers, as well as its familiar grey foliage; most florists carry a year-round supply. Otherwise, use the grey-leaved *Senecio greyi* 'Sunshine'.

Choosing the fruit

With today's sophisticated interest in food, and a number of television programmes on exotic cooking, many high street supermarkets stock a wide range of tropical fruits as well as more ordinary varieties. Often, too, local outdoor markets have stalls brimming with colourful exotic fruits and vegetables.

Creating a fruit and flower display

WHAT TO DO
WHAT YOU NEED

1 *2 stems of matricaria*
2 *3 stems of weeping willow*
3 *3 stems of evergreen spurge*
4 *8-10 stems of ranunculus*
5 *2-3 stems of gypsophila, blue-dyed and natural*
6 *5 stems of pinks*
7 *6-8 stems of freesia*
8 *3 stems of spray roses*
9 *3 stems of pieris*
10 *2 stems of flowering eucalyptus*
11 *2 stems of stock*

12 *strip of adhesive clay*
13 *A selection of fruits: 6 walnuts, 4 hazelnuts, 8 kumquats, 4 gooseberries, 1 lemon, 2 star fruits, 6 lychees, 6 satsumas, 6 strawberries, 6 grapes, 3 bananas and 1 aubergine*
14 *stub wires*
15 *2 prongs*
16 *adhesive tape*
17 *scissors*
18 *florist's foam*
19 *pedestal cake stand*

1 Stick two prongs to the base of the cake stand with adhesive clay. Trim the edges of a block of foam to make a pyramid shape. Criss-cross tape over the foam, bringing the two pieces over each side of the cake stand. Hook lengths of wire around three bananas and attach by pushing the wire ends into the foam. Press three or four sprigs of eucalyptus into the foam between the lower two bananas.

2 Cut the stems of eight to ten roses about 6cm (2½in) from the flowerhead and press into the foam, following the line of the top banana. Cut three long slices from an aubergine and remove the inside flesh so that the slice lies flat against the foam. Bend three lengths of stub wire into hairpin shapes. Place each aubergine slice against the foam. Attach to the foam with the wires.

3 Cut the stems from eight to ten ranunculus just underneath the flowerhead. Press each one into the foam, working upwards, filling the space between two slices of aubergine. Insert a group of six to eight slices of wired star fruit (see 'How to' box) above the ranunculus. Build up the group by overlapping the slices in an uneven vertical line alongside the aubergine.

4 Turn the arrangement slightly. Cut flowering sprigs of stocks and insert them in a tightly bunched group between the aubergine slices. Cut four or five stems of pinks underneath the flowerhead and insert in a mass above the stock. Turn the display again. Cut six to eight stems of freesias leaving a short stem. Insert them into the foam in a low-lying group with three wired lemons slices in a row above.

5 Insert eight wired kumquats above the roses, tight against the foam. Cut off sprigs of matricaria and insert into the foam above the kumquats. Make bunched florets of gypsophila and insert into the foam above the freesia. Top this with grapes, lychees and gooseberries. Insert three upright stems of evergreen spurge into the top of the foam, and walnuts and hazelnuts in a line above the kumquats.

6 Cut off three, long stems of pieris at a slant. Insert them at the top of the display. Place two or three strawberries underneath the pieris and the same number at the base of the cake stand. Cut the peel from two satsumas to make a spiral and hang it over the edge of the base. Insert one end of three long willow stems into the foam and wind them round the display in a spiral to finish.

Take your time when shopping and buy only perfect fruit. If you are not satisfied, choose a substitute fruit or even vegetable; the distinction between the two is irrelevant in this display. Unusual tropical fruit is expensive but, as with the flowers, you only need a few specimens of each type.

Grapes have long been associated with festivities, perhaps because of their alcoholic by-products. Green, or 'white', grapes are shown but a good selection of reasonably priced varieties is available now, and you could use red or black grapes instead.

The citrus family is well represented, with kumquats, lemons and satsumas. Kumquats look like miniature oranges. Sometimes they are grown as house plants for their fragrant flowers and glossy leaves, although they won't fruit indoors except under ideal conditions. Kumquats have a bitter but refreshing taste when eaten fresh. If you can't get kumquats, use grapes instead, but choose a different sort from those used already in the display.

Lemons are always available but limes look more unusual. Instead of satsumas, use tangerines and clementines; all were Christmas-time treats originally, but are widely available now from autumn through to early summer.

Cape gooseberries are related to the bright-orange Chinese lanterns used in

dried-flower displays and can be eaten fresh or preserved. Here, they are used with their papery outer coverings, or calyces, still attached.

Aubergine, or eggplant, is technically a fruit, since it contains seeds, but is cooked as a vegetable. Its glossy purple skin gives its name to a popular fashion colour, and there is also a white-skinned variety, hence the name eggplant. Aubergine is related to potato and tomato, and to Cape gooseberry; they all belong to the Solanaceae family. Only the skin is used for the display,

but you can put the scooped-out flesh to good culinary use. Buy the largest, shiniest aubergine you can find. Acceptable but less attractive alternatives are pineapple, grapefruit or melon, but make sure the skins are sliced thinly enough to be pliable.

Out of the ordinary

Star fruit, or carambola, is the most unusual ingredient. It has five distinct ribs creating star-shaped cross-sections. Its waxy flesh is bitter-sweet and is eaten fresh in fruit salads, or stewed in jams. There is no other fruit to match star fruit, but cross-sections of kiwi fruit with its bright-green flesh and central ring of black seeds would look just as attractive.

Tinned lychees are the staple dessert of Chinese restaurants, but here the tropical fruit is used fresh in its rough pink outer shell. Lychee pips germinate freely, but the young plants need high humidity to thrive. Like kumquats, lychees are sold by weight, and only a few are needed. If you can't get them, use cherries instead.

Strawberries are available all year round, thanks to modern commercial growing techniques and transport, but they are expensive out of their natural season. They get cheaper as summer progresses, and should be reasonably priced and widely available at the height

---

HANDLE WITH CARE

Evergreen spurge (*Euphorbia robbiae*) releases a sap when the stem ends are cut. This sap causes severe irritation to the skin and is especially harmful if it gets in the eyes. Always wash your hands thoroughly after handling spurge. In the featured arrangement, intended for display on a buffet table laden with food, you may prefer to use one of the suggested alternatives to spurge, such as lady's mantle or pittosporum.

If you do use spurge and want to eat some of the tempting exotic fruits used in the arrangement, be certain to wash each piece of fruit thoroughly before consumption. To be absolutely safe, only eat fruit that still has its skin on such as kumquats or gooseberries.

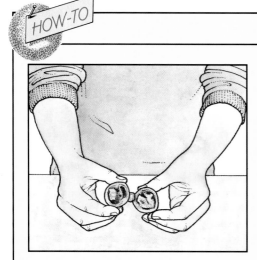

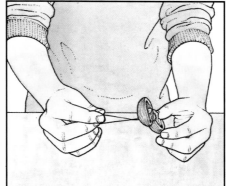

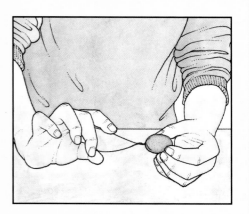

WIRING FRUIT AND NUTS

HOW-TO

1 Insert a narrow blade along the seam of a walnut to split it cleanly into two equal halves. Fix a small blob of adhesive clay on one side and push the two halves of walnut together, both sides facing in the same direction.

2 Wrap a single fine stub wire around the blob of clay in the middle, taking care not to cut through the clay as you go. Twist the wire together to make a false stem to insert into the foam.

3 Insert a length of stub wire through the fat base of a small fruit such as kumquat, lychee grape or strawberry. Pull the wire halfway through the fruit and twist the two lengths together to form a false stem.

RIGHT The 'back' view is as beautiful as the front and, ideally, the arrangement should be seen in the round to enjoy the wealth of fruit and flowers on display.

of summer. Raspberries, blackberries and similar cane fruits are too soft and small to use individually, though you could insert short lengths of cane with clusters of fruit attached at intervals.

Choosing the container

A clear glass, raised cake stand, 15cm (6in) high and 20cm (8in) across, is used as the display base. You could use a plain china cake stand but avoid those with detailed decorations that would detract from the tropical effect. The display could be built up on a flat plate, but the raised stand counteracts the visual weightiness, and the curled satsuma peels would have to be left out.

Choosing the setting

The centre of a buffet table is the ideal location for this display, but if there is a table for desserts, it could form the focal point there. Make sure there is plenty of space around the arrangement for guests to help themselves to food without knocking against it. Make sure, too, that there is plenty of fresh fruit on offer on conventional serving dishes, so no-one is tempted to pick from the display and spoil the effect.

Looking after the display

This is a short-term arrangement, because cut fruit resting against saturated florist's foam soon rots in a warm room. Equally, the ethylene gas that is given off by fruit shortens the life of flowers such as gypsophila and freesia. After all the guests have gone, or the next morning, carefully take apart the display. Wash all the whole fruit thoroughly, as harmful sap from the spurge may have got to it, and use to make a fruit salad. Discard all the cut sections of fruit.

Transfer the long-stemmed pieris and euphorbia to a tall vase. Carefully slice a round section from the base of the florist's foam to make an instant 'posy pad', and insert the short-stemmed flowers for an attractive and long-lasting reminder of the occasion.

CLEVER PARTY FLOWERS

For a children's party this pretty floral display is completed with bright and cheerful crayons. Perfect for youngsters, the arrangement is also easy to adapt for a more formal setting.

hildren, as much as adults, deserve attractive flower arrangements to mark the high spots in their lives – and birthday parties surely rank among the highest! Bright colours are always popular with children, and the anemones featured in this display provide a blaze of primary colours.

Set aside at least half an hour out of the time you've allowed for general preparations to tackle the flower arrangement. Once it's finished, keep it in a cool but draught-free spot until just before the party starts. That way, you'll get maximum 'life' and pleasure from the cut flowers.

A word of warning! Young children's enthusiasm can quickly overwhelm their 'party manners'. When the time comes for each guest to choose a coloured pencil prize, try to have them do it one at a time. You might even be able to make a game of it – putting numbered cards randomly under each place setting, for example, and having the children choose in numerical order, or conducting a simple quiz, with the winner choosing a prize. Hold the base of the display while prizes are being selected, or

stick it to a convenient spot on a low table with some blue tacky clay.

Choosing the flowers

Although there are traditional birthday flowers for each month – roses for June, carnations for January, and so on – this is too sophisticated an idea for most children, who simply want something bright and colourful to look at. If the birthday girl or boy has a favourite colour, however, you may want to base your display around that alone.

Some of the flowers used in this display are sold all year round; others, such as anemones, are seasonal, but can be easily replaced with equally beautiful seasonal flowers (suggestions are given below). All are relatively inexpensive and popular, and are widely available from florists, flower stalls and some high-street chain stores.

The florist's anemones (*Anemone coronaria* hybrids), often called 'de Caen' or 'St Bridget' anemones, provide the bright focal colour in this display. Sold from autumn through to spring, they are especially popular after Christmas. The goblet-shaped, black-centred flowers come in both single and

double forms, and in mixed shades of purple, blue, red, pink and white – as well as in single-colour bunches. Here, a bunch of mixed colours and a bunch of deep violet-blue anemones are used – about 25 stems in all – with the violet-blue providing the main colour theme. Or, you could use two mixed bunches, two single-colour bunches – an all-white display would be particularly effective – or two single, but different-coloured bunches – say, one white and one blue.

If you do choose mixed colours, check that the mix is an attractive and balanced one – single blooms of a different colour can stand out like a sore thumb, and be difficult to incorporate into the chosen colour scheme.

When you get the anemones home, condition them by re-cutting the stems, dipping the ends in boiling water for a few seconds, then following with a long, cool drink of water, ideally overnight, before arranging them.

If you can't get anemones, china asters, with their round, flat flowers in shades of pink, rose, white, mauve and blue, would be good substitutes, as would godetia, or satin flower, in its range of pinks and reds.

Sweet scented flowers

Freesias are included for their sweet scent as much as for their colour. Fortunately, they are available all year round, in a range of pretty mixed colours – whites, yellows, oranges, pinks, mauves, blue-violets and reds – or in single colours.

When choosing freesias, look for bunches with the lowest bud on each flower spike open or about to open. In cold winter weather, this is especially important, as buds that are too tightly closed when you buy them may fail to open altogether. Lily of the valley, though more expensive, have an equally beautiful, lingering fragrance, and delicate charm. You could use them instead, perhaps combined with open 'Sweetheart' roses as the main flower. Or try the delicate pink flower spikes of *Schizostylis coccinea*, or Kaffir lily – scentless, but long lasting.

Sprigs of gypsophila and spray carnations complete the floral palette. The spray carnations are creamy white, rimmed with red, to contrast with the

Making a two-tiered party display

1 *25 anemones*
2 *bunch of freesias*
3 *small bunch of carnations*
4 *a few sprigs of gypsophila*
5 *2 stems asparagus fern*
6 *a few trails of ivy*
7 *a few sprigs of golden yew*
8 *large block of florist's foam*
9 *florist's adhesive clay*
10 *prong*
11 *2 cup-shaped pedestal glasses*
12 *coloured pencils*
13 *floristry scissors*
14 *knife*

1 Use the prepared containers. Cut 10 leaves, each with a short piece of stem attached, from the main trails of ivy. (Larger, thicker, mature leaves will last longer than the young, thin ones at the tip of the stem.) Insert the ivy leaves, evenly spaced apart, but overlapping, into the sides of the lower foam blocks, to form a horizontal 'collar', overhanging the rim.

2 Break off the leaf-like fronds from two stems of asparagus fern. Insert about half of them, again evenly spaced apart, into the sides of the foam block, just above the ivy-leaf 'collar'. Visually, this helps to lighten the solid, heavy appearance of the ivy leaves. Using the remaining asparagus fern, make another horizontal 'collar' around the edge of the upper container.

3 Insert a small anemone with a 10cm (4in) long stem in the centre of the upper tier, to set the height. Shorten the remaining anemone stems to 5-7.5cm (2-3in). Use small anemones in the upper tier and larger ones in the bottom tier. Insert a ring of large anemones above the ivy, then work upwards, turning the display as you proceed, to build a dome.

4 Cut the golden yew into sprigs roughly 7.5cm (3in) long. Remove the lower needles from each sprig, and begin filling in the spaces between the anemones, to conceal the foam block. Prepare about 15 carnation flowers and buds with 7.5cm (3in) stems. Insert them randomly with smaller flowers in the top tier and larger ones below.

5 Cut the freesia stems to a similar length, leaving some a little shorter, others a little longer, for variety. Use them to add lighter areas of colour between the intense reds, purples and blues of the anemones. The yellow freesias stand out especially, so keep them well apart. Add bunched sprigs of gypsophila here and there, as needed.

6 When you are satisfied with the all-over density of the display, insert the coloured pencils, angled upwards towards the top, and out and downwards towards the bottom. (Don't leave gaps specially for the pencils, as they're easy to insert between the stems.) A dozen pencils are used here, but you may use more or less, depending on the number of guests.

more solid-coloured flowers, but white, pink, or scarlet spray carnations would be equally effective. (Remember, when you shorten the stems, to cut between the nodes.) Gypsophila, the most popular 'filler' of all, is at its best in the pure white form, as used here. Choose sprigs with about two-thirds of the flowers open.

Variegated ivy and golden yew (*Taxus baccata* 'Aurea') are used to off-set the warm floral colours. The yew is definitely a garden plant rather than a commercial one, but sprigs of cypress, though darker, could be used instead.

You can order variegated ivy from your florist, but will probably have to buy a bunch much larger than you need for this display. Plant some of the extra stems in the garden, in a patio tub or even in an indoor pot. If fresh, they should root, and from the following year onwards, you'll have your own private supply. Don't just bury the cut end, though; cover the entire length of the stem with 1.5cm (1/2in) of soil with the leaves above ground and keep well-watered in dry weather.

Asparagus fern (*Asparagus plumosus*) completes the trio of suitable foliage.

This is a florist's standby – you should be able to buy it by the stem. In an emergency, you could nip off a few fronds of Boston fern or the popular house plant fern, *Asparagus sprengeri*, if you have one to hand. You may need to shorten the fronds of Boston fern a little, before using them.

Choosing the container
In this display, the container is made up of large and medium-sized dessert or coupe pedestal glasses, one inside the other, and they are all but hidden by the flowers and foliage. Using a stemmed container is very effective, as it lifts the display off the table surface, allow-ing some material to trail and arch gracefully, and prevents the arrange-ment from looking heavy or dumpy.

Fixing up the two-tiered container couldn't be easier (see the 'How-to' box). But you could, instead, use a two-tiered cake stand with moistened florist's foam block impaled on florist's prongs, round the central stem. Two-tiered or even three-tiered Victorian stands for fruit, cakes or flower arrangements could also be used, but these antiques are few and far between, and are usually too ornate for this particular display and occasion.

Alternative prizes
Brightly-coloured pencils, toning in with the flowers, are featured here, but there are all sorts of alternative prizes you might like to try. Cellophane-wrapped barley sugar sticks, or, at Christmas-time, old fashioned red and white striped candy canes, would be ideal. Instead of inserting them directly into the florist's foam, wrap medium-gauge stub wire around them and insert

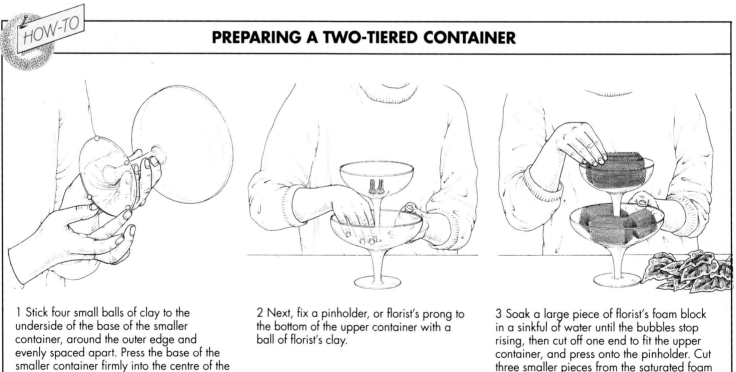

HOW-TO
PREPARING A TWO-TIERED CONTAINER

1 Stick four small balls of clay to the underside of the base of the smaller container, around the outer edge and evenly spaced apart. Press the base of the smaller container firmly into the centre of the larger container, until it feels secure.

2 Next, fix a pinholder, or florist's prong to the bottom of the upper container with a ball of florist's clay.

3 Soak a large piece of florist's foam block in a sinkful of water until the bubbles stop rising, then cut off one end to fit the upper container, and press onto the pinholder. Cut three smaller pieces from the saturated foam block, and wedge them firmly into the bottom container, around the stem of the upper container – you shouldn't need any pinholders, provided the foam blocks are well and truly snug.

the end of the wire into the foam. Lollipops can be inserted directly into the florist's foam block, but do this at the last minute, so the cardboard stick ends don't get soggy.

For very young children choose decorative pencils topped with heads of favourite cartoon or television characters. Older children are fascinated by curled transparent plastic drinking straws – these add just the right hint of 'trendiness' that an adolescent longs for. For an adult cocktail party, attractive or jokey swizzle sticks would be ideal. And for the centrepiece of an Oriental dinner party, chopsticks are the perfect finishing touch.

Choosing a location

This flower arrangement is a genuinely moveable feast. It's first job is to grace the birthday party dining or buffet table table, as shown, but it's far too attractive to dismantle once the party is over. Being an 'all-round' display, it is ideal for a coffee table or bedside table; the birthday boy or girl may want it in his or her room afterwards, as a reminder of their 'big' day.

As with any fresh flower display, it will last longer if you keep it away from heat, draughts, and direct sunlight. Because freesias and gypsophila are particularly vulnerable to ethylene gas damage, keep the display away from any bowls of ripe fruit and vegetables.

Looking after your display

After the young guests have gone, you might want to adjust the flowers to close any gaps caused by the removal of pencils or the actions of young hands generally.

Anemones are heavy drinkers, so keep the florist's foam block well saturated, adding more water daily. Anemones also have a habit of turning towards the light – charming in theory, but awkward in an all-round display, such as this one. If the light source comes from one direction – say, a nearby window – give the arrangement roughly a quarter-turn every day, to keep the flower stems relatively straight.

The asparagus fern will quickly drop its needles in a dry atmosphere, so an occasional spray-mist will keep it intact for two weeks or more. If you've used Boston fern or *Asparagus sprengeri*, the

same applies. Cut ivy will also last longer in a humid environment than in a dry one. You can also increase the humidity locally by standing the display in a shallow dish of water. (If you don't like the way this looks, even placing the display in a dish of water overnight helps extend its life.)

Anemones can be relied on to last at least four days, longer if well cared for. (Shortening their stems also helps prolong their life.) For freesias, a week is usually their outer limit. Longest lasting of all are the spray carnations, up to three weeks in cool conditions. Gypsophila, of course, dries as it ages,

ABOVE When the birthday party's over, and the prizes are removed, the display takes on a new lease of life. Here, it is used as the sophisticated focal point in a modern living room, but it would be equally attractive in a less formal scheme, or as a pretty, scented feature on a bedside table.

so you need never throw it away. Once the shorter-lived flowers die, re-use carnations and gypsophila with any remaining foliage to make a tiny posy, perhaps in a wine glass or an egg cup.

SPOTLIGHT

OUTDOOR PARTY TABLE ARRANGEMENTS

Flower arrangements, indoors or out, should always match the mood of the occasion, whether it is an informal barbecue or a wedding reception. The more casual the party, the more unconstrained the flower arrangements can be. The opposite is also true – if you're going to town on an outdoor wedding reception, the flowers should rise to the occasion – loop evergreen swags around the table cloth or twine them around the pillars or posts of the marquee.

If you have a colourful patch of garden, such as a border with a tall, bright strip of foxgloves, lupins or hollyhocks, place the table or a drinks trolley against it, so that the flowers form a natural background. If this isn't possible, stand some large potted plants on a raised surface behind. Brightly coloured geraniums are particularly effective displayed in this fashion.

If you have to arrange flowers at short notice, make the most of whatever plant materials you have growing plentifully in the garden. Cut an armful of gypsophila, golden rod, ornamental grasses, ferns, cow parsley, hogweed, beech leaves or privet. Strip off any leaves that come below the water level and place the stems in a large jug, a deep cylindrical vase, an enamel bucket, or a large casserole dish.

Complement this leafy framework with a few bright flowers, such as poppies, lush stems of pink and white mallow or larkspur, and position the display prominently at waist height so that it can be seen by all your guests who will probably be standing or walking round for much of the time.

Whatever impression you create with background flowers, a colourful display on the buffet table is all important. Display a jug of bright-blue cornflowers colour matched to a gingham tablecloth or napkins, a bunch of sweet peas or a pot of tumbling wild roses and golden tansy. Once thought out these displays take only moments to arrange but create striking effects.

LEFT A party in the garden is all the more enjoyable for a table that's decorated attractively. The hanging swag is made of smilax and yellow and white daisy chrysanthemums to match the jug of carnations and lilies.

BELOW For an informal but attractive table arrangement for a meal in the garden, display white single roses and heads of aromatic and golden tansy in a blue and white swirly patterned vase.

PARTY
EXTRAVAGANZA

This huge, rustic basket, brimming with colourful, fresh flowers and foliage is ideal for a special spring dinner party or celebration that demands a show. If you prefer, you can easily use a smaller basket and create a cheaper version based on the same flowers and colour scheme.

Spring is an especially good time to make this kind of brimming display as there is a fine range of flowers available. The sheer quantity of flowers in this arrangement make it an expensive project, so make it for a special occasion such as a wedding anniversary, special birthday or christening.

Creating an all-round display

The display is an all-round massed design with no focal point, front or back, although if you're displaying it against a wall you could concentrate the flowers towards the front. The arrangement is built up with flowers and foliage springing from a central source and arching gracefully up and out in all directions. The simple design can be scaled up or down, depending on the size of your container and amount of flowers and foliage available.

Choosing the flowers

The colour scheme of the arrangement includes yellows, pinks, oranges, reds and white. Most of the flowers used are available in plain white, so for a cool, sophisticated look you could limit the colours to white and green. A pink and white scheme is suitable for a baby girl's christening. For a boy, you'd probably have to have a blue, lavender and white scheme, since the range of blue fresh flowers is limited.

Arum lilies, also called calla lilies or zantedeschias, are the most exotic and expensive flowers used in this display. The impressive size and bold outline of their flower spathe make arum lilies excellent for large-scale displays, especially those meant to be seen from a distance, such as church flowers. Arum lilies are sold by the stem and will almost certainly have to be ordered in advance. Most commercially-grown arum lilies are white, but yellow, orange, pink and green-flowered varieties are also available. Buy arum lilies when the spathes are fully open and evenly

Creating a lavish party display

WHAT TO DO
WHAT YOU NEED

1 1 large branch of Laurustinus
2 7 bunches of freesias
3 15 – 20 stems of triangular-leaved eucalyptus
4 9 lilies
5 22 parrot tulips
6 1 bunch of bear grass
7 12 arum lilies
8 3 bunches of anemones
9 9 stems of forsythia
10 10-12 stems of narrow-leaved eucalyptus
11 large basket, 60cm x 30cm (2ft x 1ft)
12 1m (3ft) of chicken wire
13 2 large blocks of florist's foam
14 1 plastic bin liner
15 scissors

1 Line the basket and secure the foam and chicken wire (see 'How-to' box). Place small groups of narrow-leaved eucalyptus in the centre of the basket as though growing from a central point and longer stems trailing over the basket rim. Position stems of laurustinus along the basket edge and throughout the display. Introduce triangular-leaved eucalyptus below the handle and over the basket rim.

2 Trim the white section from the bottom of the bear grass. Group into clusters of about eight stems for impact and intersperse them throughout the eucalyptus foliage to give a wispy look. As before, position the shorter stems in the middle of the display and the longer stems to the sides. Their arching shape will accentuate the domed display. Spray the foliage with a fine mist of water to keep it fresh.

3 Cut 5cm (2in) from stems of the parrot tulips and remove their foliage. Work outwards from the centre of the display and place the tulips throughout the arrangement. Allow the tulips to follow their natural line. Use those with slightly longer stems in the centre and those with shorter stems towards the front edge of the display. Make sure you achieve an even colour balance throughout the basket.

4 Introduce nine orange lily stems. Remove the bottom 12cm (5in) from the stems and place them evenly throughout the display. Angle the stems as you work to follow the domed shape of the basket. Using large blooms is more economical. Spray the flowers with a fine mist of water to keep them fresh. Check the display from every angle to ensure that you have not neglected any areas.

5 Trim the anemones, but leave them as long as possible. Place as single stems throughout the display, allowing them to stand slightly higher than the other flowers so that their small flowerheads are visible. Add the freesias as a light touch. Make sure that their thin stems enter the foam. If you are making a design which is front-facing, concentrate the freesias in the front of the basket.

6 Add the arum lilies to pick out the colour of the orange lilies. Their stems will naturally follow the line of the display. Place them throughout or at the front of the arrangement. Cut side shoots from a branch of forsythia and add these to give line and definition to the mass of flowers. Stand the forsythia slightly above the other flowers. Check that the flowers are evenly distributed throughout.

opaque; brown or transparent edges indicate that a flower is past its best. Anthuriums, or painters' palettes, have a similar shape and exotic appeal, but are also expensive. Paeonies are completely different in shape, but are equally large, and would make the same impact, at less cost.

Adding scent to the display

Large, creamy-white 'Fantasy' freesias provide scent as well as soft colour in the arrangement. You also could use mixed-colour freesias, although in this colour scheme the purple blooms might clash. If you place your order in advance, you can get bunches of single-colour freesias in white, yellow, pink, crimson or lavender. Buy them when the lowest florets are open and the others are just showing colour. Small, creamy-white, multi-flowered narcissi could be substituted; they are less expensive, but shorter lived.

Florists' 'de Caen' anemones repeat the white theme; their dark centres add depth to the display, and their ruffles of foliage under the flowerheads provide a lacy touch. Anemones also come in scarlet, lavender, violet and pink, and in mixed and single-colour bunches. Buy anemones when their petals have started to open, but before they are fully flat. Turk's-cap ranunculus come in a similar range of colours, plus yellow.

From the garden, white daisies could be used, or early, single, white roses.

Orange lilies are illustrated, but lilies also are available in white, pink, yellow and crimson. Buy lilies which have one flower open per stem, and the other buds showing colour. On a tight budget, omit the arum lilies and use extra lilies, day lilies or alstroemeria as an alternative.

Parrot tulips, with their large size, fringed petals and stripes and splashes of colour, look more extravagant than ordinary florists' tulips, and they are usually more expensive. As a more economical alternative, use ordinary tulips. To make them look more special, ease their petals open and backwards, which makes them look eye-catching. If you have garden tulips in flower, these will look equally effective.

Adding linear contrast

Upright branches of forsythia add line definition and contrast in form as well as a spring-like touch to the display. Buy or cut forsythia branches in tight bud. Use branches of mock orange (*Philadelphus*) as an alternative or arching branches of deutzia or broom, for a more rounded effect.

Bear grass, laurustinus, or *Viburnum tinus*, and two types of eucalyptus foliage are used. The bear grass and eucalyptus have a natural grace and

provide a dense, arching background of greenery for the flowers. From the garden, *Iris sibirica*, waterside rushes, or day lily foliage can be used instead. Senecio 'Sunshine', with its rounded, grey leaves, can replace the eucalyptus, although it is more upright than arching.

Laurustinus is used as filler material. Alternatively, use small branches of Portuguese laurel (*Prunus lusitanica*).

Choosing the container

A large, woven-wicker, rustic basket is used, 60cm (2ft) across. Although not waterproof, it is easily converted with a plastic bin liner, a trick that works with most other porous containers (see 'How-to' box). Initially, the handle helps establish the middle of the display, but eventually it is almost obscured by the flowers and greenery, and so it is just as good to use a handle-less basket. You can use a large soup tureen instead, or a serving bowl. The lower part of the container is visible, so make sure its colours and any patterns on it complement the flowers and the intended final location.

With these flowers and foliage you can scale the container down to 20cm (8in) across, and still get much the same effect. To achieve an even smaller display, substitute smaller flowers for the arum lilies and tulips.

Choosing the setting

Before you embark on this project, make sure you have space for it. You need three times the length of the basket to allow room for the flowers and foliage to spread out and to leave space around them. A low coffee table, entrance hall table or uncluttered sideboard position is ideal, but if the display has to share a table with food or drink, try to leave a substantial gap between these and the flowers so that the display can be seen.

Caring for your flowers

To obtain the maximum life from your fresh materials make sure they have been well conditioned before arranging. Leave a slight gap at the back of the display, towards the basket rim so that once the arrangement is in position you can top up the florist's foam easily with water. Spray the materials regularly to keep them looking their best.

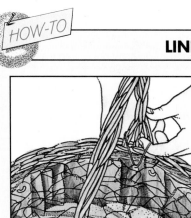

HOW-TO

LINING A BASKET

1 Line the inside of the basket with half a plastic bin liner. Secure the plastic to the basket with pieces of wire bent into a hair pin shape. At regular intervals, push each wire from the outside through the basket weave and the plastic lining and twist the ends together inside the basket.
2 Place two large, rectangular blocks of soaked florist's foam into the basket to cover the basket base completely. The foam is held in position by its own weight so prongs are not required.
3 Fold 1m (3 ft) of chicken wire into a cylindrical shape to fill the mouth of the basket and place in position. Secure it to the basket handle with stub wire, as before.
4 Pull up the top of the chicken wire to form a dome and set the shape of the display. Open out the holes in the chicken wire so that you can insert the flowers and foliage more easily.

SPOTLIGHT

FIREPLACE DECORATIONS

At Christmas time the fireplace is rightly the focal point of a room. After all, this is Father Christmas's doorway to your home, and as such has a very special place in the family's affections. Make sure the hearth and its surround live up to traditional expectations by giving it a high priority decoration scheme.

Swags and ribbons of evergreens, cones, baubles or false fruits looped over the fireplace surround – though not in reach of stray sparks – are a decorative way to frame this important architectural feature. All you need is a length of strong rope or thick string, a roll of fine wire, and a handful of ingredients! Dried flowers, artificial berries, loops of tinsel, ribbon bows, they can all enhance a 'trail of leaves'.

If your fireplace has a mirror above it, the kind that is known as an overmantel, work that into your scheme of things, too, with a slender version of the fireplace decoration outlining its frame.

Some fireplaces just weren't built for loops and drapes – there may not be space to spare above the aperture. Such features look especially attractive with a simple hanging decoration on each side, a ribbon of evergreens, a posy of dried flowers on a pretend wood carving made up of cones, nuts and seedheads wired to a base. The plaited frame used for garlic strings makes a perfect base for this type of hanging.

The wall area above a fireplace is too precious to ignore. Make it the focus of attention by adorning it with a hanging wreath of Christmas tree trimmings, other evergreens and dried flowers, or a glittering version composed of tinsel and baubles. Make a Christmas card collage on a piece of softboard outlined with sprigs of holly, or string a spare set of fairy lights in loops and fix small baubles along the wire to maximise the effect.

If you don't have a fireplace, you may be able to treat another architectural feature – an alcove, arch or even a doorway – in a similar way.

ABOVE Just because a fireplace is not in use, there's no need to leave it out in the cold! These bright and cheerful swags make sure that it retains its rightful place as the focal point of the room. Cones, silk leaves and brilliant red fruit look-alikes are tied to scarlet ribbons to make an original and festive design.

ABOVE If the shape of your tree leaves something to be desired, cut off the offending branches, and use the 'off-cuts' to make a cheery wall decoration.

HOLIDAY PARTIES

Christmas wouldn't be Christmas without a big dinner or a party. It's a time for being specially creative with your flower arrangements. Here are some ideas to get your guests into a party mood.

ecorating your home for a Christmas dinner? Inviting a few friends and neighbours to drop in for a festive drink and a chat? Organising a formal party down to the last careful detail? Giving a boisterous party for young children or a get-together for older ones? Whatever your plans for the holiday season, it is fun to dress up your home in its party best.

Space is usually a commodity that comes under enormous pressure throughout the holiday period. We all know that feeling of despair when, having issued invitations for a party, we are convinced that there just isn't going to be enough room to shoe-horn everybody through the front door and certainly nowhere to put anything down.

So, for most of us, the smartest ideas for party-time decorations are those which take the space factor into account.

The Christmas dinner table

For most families, Christmas dinner is the meal of the year. With such a high profile, the table setting deserves to be planned with as much attention to detail as is given to the meal itself.

To make sure that the dinner table not only looks as pretty as you can make it,

but that it will actually 'work', stage a dress rehearsal. Set out the plates and side plates, the carving dish and vegetable dishes, the sauce boats and butter dishes, the wine glasses and bottles or carafes, and then take stock.

First, make sure there is enough room for your guests to sit comfortably. Then look at the table setting. If the arrangement itself looks too cramped for comfort, consider carving and serving from a sideboard or a table brought in for the occasion.

Assess how much space there is for table flower decorations, and then decide how to make the most eye-catching use of it. Perhaps there is space in the centre of the table for a hoop of evergreens and candles or a bowl of nuts decorated with trails of holly and ivy.

There may be limited space, but enough for one, two or three slender candlesticks. In this case, turn them to decorative advantage, and trim the candlesticks with greenery or dried or fresh flowers. Remember that tall designs – candles and flowers arranged in a dish secured to the top of a long candlestick or tall vase, or a dried flower tree in a small container – save precious table space because you can push plates and dishes beneath them.

A long thin 'ribbon' of greenery, small cones and baubles with or without candles, in the centre of a narrow table can be particularly effective as well as practical. Cut thin strips of foam and put them in the longest, narrowest containers you can find, such as corn-on-the-cob dishes or wooden date boxes lined with foil (to save moisture seeping on to the table's surface).

More space-saving still, are trails of ivy and long sprigs of holly – the more the merrier – along the centre of the table or wherever there is a tiny space. Add a few baubles – the hanging loops will prevent them from rolling off – or cut-out gold or silver paper stars for a dash of glitter.

Decorative place settings

As an alternative, or a pretty addition, consider taking the decorative action to each place setting – certainly a more personal touch than any central design. A tiny posy of holly, mistletoe and a mini-bauble tied with ribbons and standing in a narrow glass or an egg cup (a pretty 'take home' present) or a tussie mussie – a lovely old-fashioned word for nosegay – of a few leaves and flowers surrounded by a paper doily: these designs leave the centre of the table completely clear for your dishes.

If there is really no space on the table at all, the food itself may be the only place left for a deft touch of floral art. Stand the vegetable dishes on plates and edge them with rings of holly or tinsel:

LEFT A triangle of red spray carnations, roses and hawthorn berries, white spray chrysanthemums and chincherinchi, is high on impact but economical with table space. The crystal candlestick is fitted with a 'candle cup' holder and foam. A simple glass candlestick has a cascade of hawthorn berries and a single flower. The stems are pushed in a cube of foam wrapped in foil and taped to the candle base. The brass 'bedroom candlestick' holds sprays of holly and a few berry-red flowers.

turn out the pudding on to a large plate or a pedestal cake stand, and surround it by a circle of holly with brandy.

Present small ramekin-desserts such as chocolate mousse or blancmange on plates lined with leaves or ringed with dried flowers and, for good measure, decorate the top of the dish with a single flower and leaf.

If you hand round after-dinner coffee and mints on a tray, add a very small floral decoration, just a couple of blooms such as freesias in a small glass, or a trail of leaves around one edge of the tray.

Buffet parties
Many of the same considerations of space apply to a table set for a buffet party – and many of the decorative solutions can be applied too. A tall, central flower arrangement that can be easily seen from the other side of the room is an additional come-hither to the buffet table and will remain as a decoration when the meal has finished.

Be sure to use a sturdy and steady container for even in the politest of circles, people reaching across a table can spell disaster to any container that is delicate and vulnerable. If you are in any doubt, secure the base of the container by pressing a few dabs of blue tacky clay and then pressing them firmly to the table surface.

Keep lit candles and any candle arrangements well away from the edge of a table, or any position where guests will have to reach over them.

Putting elaborate flower decorations on food isn't a particularly good idea at a help-yourself buffet. The dishes can soon look bedraggled and a spray of yellow statice floating in a sea of blackcurrant mousse can be slightly off-putting! It is best to confine the floral garnishes to the

LEFT These shelves, bedecked with trails and sprays of ivy and baubles, makes an ideal 'away-from-it-all' serving table. The white pottery jar holds a selection of evergreens including cypress, ivy and holly, a bunch of golden lilies and a few stems of fake blackberries.

table-top. A few dried flowerheads scattered on the cloth look remarkably pretty – and help to hide the inevitable crumbs and spills.

Children's parties

Bright, colourful placements cut from shiny paper or, more practically, from plastic can set a theme for the event, and quick-to-make paper flowers are more in tune with the children's ideas, and certainly less vulnerable, than 'real' flower arrangements. So that everyone – parents, young hosts and hostesses and guests alike – can have a carefree time, remove and put away anything, including special flower arrangements, that might come to grief once the excitement of the moment becomes infectious.

Fresh or dried flowers?

With so many occasions to plan for in such a short space of time, dried flower arrangments have the built-in advantage that they can be made-up and ready and waiting for any occasion. Choose colours that harmonise with your room, or neutral shades that blend with more than one of your furnishing schemes, and a dried flower arrangement can be a portable feast for the eyes, moved from dining room to hall to living room as the occasion demands.

Pretty-up existing dried flower arrangements by adding a few special blooms – a trio of dried peonies, perhaps, in a pink and blue design, or splash of white flowers to one that looks a little too subtle. Give a design a party face by tying a ribbon around the container and finishing it with a flourish, or tie several bows and fix them to the rim of the container. The basket of gypsophila

(below) with its white and gold ribbon trim, shows how effective this can be.

For some people there will never be anything to replace the beauty – and at this time of year luxury – of fresh flowers for the party season. Sometimes the most expensive buys – lilies and gerberas for example – can prove to be the most economical in both cash and time-saving terms. If properly acclimatised to your house for the long holiday period, and given a good long drink in tepid water, both species should last for the twelve days of Christmas and beyond.

Evergreens last even longer. A good tip is to make a lovely full arrangement of foliage, then add the flowers. When these fade, the foliage can be left in place

ABOVE Dried flowers have a great deal going for them throughout the party season. You can arrange the grasses, larkspur, seedheads and everlastings some time in advance and be confident that the flowers won't wilt.

and new flowers added.

Bring pot plants into the decorative act and you combine the best of both worlds, long-lasting properties and fresh blooms. Make a pot-et-feuilles design (an adaptation of pot-et-fleur, using foliage rather than fresh cut flowers) by 'burying' a pot of poinsettia, cyclamen or begonia among evergreens and it will become the star of the occasion.

Making elbow room

With a party looming and the pressure on space rising, think thin as far as decorations are concerned. If there really isn't room for a Christmas tree, even a table-top one, cut your design according to your cubic capacity. Hang a large tree branch flat against a wall and adorn it with baubles and bows, or go fully one-dimensional and cut out a huge paper tree to hang, with suitable paper decorations, on a wall, door or window.

LEFT As crisp and evocative as a flurry of snowflakes, a basket of dried gypsophila makes an unusual and highly seasonal decoration for a buffet table. Choose a deep, wide-necked container – a brown earthenware casserole dish would be an attractive alternative – and cut the stems in graduating lengths so that those in the front trail over the rim.

This handsome, front-facing display combines the delicacy of lilies, the elegance of tall candles and the cheerfulness of gold-tinted larch branches, pine cones and holly sprigs. The striking combination of pure white, rich red and a whole spectrum of pinks is an exciting variation on the more traditional Christmas colour scheme of red and white. It would make an ideal centrepiece for a buffet table, or an eyecatching focal point on an entrance hall table.

A CHRISTMAS WINNER

For a Christmas buffet table, hall table or sideboard, here is the perfect, front-facing display. The conifer sprays and holly give it that special festive touch.

ntertaining is as much a part of Christmas as buying presents, and when you've worked hard sorting out menus and preparing party dishes, what better way to enhance the spirit of the occasion than with flowers? This formal arrangement on a glass cake-stand couldn't be more perfect, with its elegant lines and generous proportions it has just the right 'Christmassy' feel. Though the display looks expensive (and it would be if you bought it), relatively few flowers are used, so it's surprisingly economical to make yourself.

All the flowers used in this display are available during the Christmas season, and if bought fresh and properly conditioned, should remain attractive for at least a week. When they start to fade, carefully remove them and replace them with fresh flowers, so you get twice as much pleasure for your efforts.

Choosing the flowers
Pink lilies provide the focal point for this composition, but you could use creamy white or pure white ones, instead. And although they are fairly expensive, only three stems are needed. Choose stems with a mixture of open flowers and buds, but make sure that the buds are showing a little colour.

Alstroemeria, or Peruvian lily, is available all year round – in spite of its deceptively summery appearance! Again, pink is used here, but alstroemeria also comes in yellow, purple, scarlet and creamy white tones, often attractively streaked, splashed or striped with second colours. Alstroemeria is often sold by the stem, so you can choose, if you prefer, flowers in colours that best fit in with your decor. As before, go for a mixture of buds and open flowers.

Choosing sedums
It is unlikely that you will find sedums growing in the garden at this time of year, but your florist should be able to order them if given plenty of advance warning. There are many colourful rockery sedums, but larger herbaceous perennial types, such as those used here, are especially valuable in arrangements. The tightly-packed, flat flowerheads start as green buds (charming with summer roses), then open into starry pink flowers, ideal with autumnal asters; and finally mature to rich pink or red – perfect for winter displays.

Sedum flower stems often take root in water, so check the stems when taking the display apart and plant (in the garden) any that have rooted. Sedums are happy in sun or light shade, and any well-drained soil. Grow them either in containers or the open ground.

Even the tiniest corner flowerstalls stock a good selection of carnations, and at Christmas time, red carnations are everywhere. Graceful spray carnations are used here as they are more suited to this kind of display than the larger, single-flower varieties. And though their bright red emphasises the Christmas theme, pink, pale yellow or white carnations would be just as effective. (If you choose another colour than red, change the candle colour accordingly.) Spray carnations are sold in bunches,

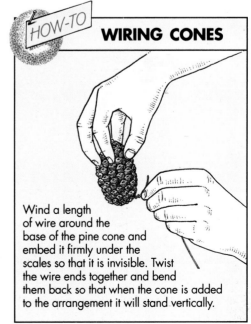

HOW-TO WIRING CONES

Wind a length of wire around the base of the pine cone and embed it firmly under the scales so that it is invisible. Twist the wire ends together and bend them back so that when the cone is added to the arrangement it will stand vertically.

rather than singly, but the extra sprays are sure to come in handy over the Christmas period. Always cut carnation stems between the swollen joints, or nodes, otherwise, they won't absorb water properly.

Chincherinchees are imported from South Africa, especially at Christmas time, and last for weeks in water. It is said that their unusual name comes from the sound the wind makes as it blows through their stems. Choose bunches where the lowest flowers are open, and a third of the rest are showing colour.

Spraying cones and foliage

The wired-up pine cones and lichen-covered larch branches in the display are sprayed gold with florist's spray paint designed specifically for dried and artificial flowers. It gives cones and branches a subtle, three-dimensional gleam, rather than an over-all, flat-looking coating. You can buy branches ready-sprayed, but it is more economical to spray them yourself.

Two types of foliage are needed for this arrangement. As well as fir pine, you could use sprigs of dwarf conifers or conifer hedging such as Leyland cypress or *macrocarpa* – or any other foliage that you like the look of. Matching candles and ribbons, and artificial holly sprigs complete the picture. If real holly is available, so much the better, but if spraying fake holly gold, as here, remember to take off the plastic berries beforehand, and allow plenty of time for the paint to dry.

DISPLAY CARE

• The unopened lily and alstroemeria buds should open after a few days. At this stage, remove or 'dead head' any faded, older flowerheads to give the young blooms more space. It is also important to do this because the dying blooms give off a gas which is harmful to the development of nearby flower buds, and can even prevent them from opening properly.

• The foliage of lily and alstroemeria turns yellow long before the flowers fade. To keep your display looking its best, inspect it regularly and carefully snip off any yellowing leaves. If you use cut-flower food in liquid form only add a drop; too much makes the leaves turn yellow.

WHAT TO DO
WHAT YOU NEED

Formal festive display

1 *3 dusty pink lilies*	**11** *glass cake stand*
2 *5 alstroemeria*	**12** *florist's foam block*
3 *10 chincherinchee stems*	**13** *stub wires*
4 *3 sedum stems*	**14** *red ribbon*
5 *3 red carnations sprays*	**15** *florist's gold spray*
6 *dried larch stem with cones*	**16** *prong*
7 *2 holly sprigs*	**17** *florist's adhesive tape*
8 *3-4 fir pine sprays*	**18** *wire cutters*
9 *3-4 sprays of conifer foliage*	**19** *4 thin red candles*
10 *5-6 cones*	**20** *florist's adhesive clay*

1 Soak the foam block then, using a prong and florist's adhesive clay, fix it to the cake stand. Shape the block into two roughly horizontal 'steps', cutting a corner out of the upper 'step'. Cut medium-strength stub wire into 12 pieces, each 7.5cm (3in) long. Tape three wires to the base of each candle, to form prongs. Firmly insert two candles on each level, in staggered rows.

2 Spray the pine cone, larch branches and holly gold (optional). When dry, break the larch into 15-30cm (6-12in) lengths. Starting on your left-hand side, insert a long piece, slightly angled downwards, into the lower-level foam. Repeat on your right-hand side, but angle it slightly upwards. Place a third, steeply-angled branch at the rear, on the right.

3 Divide the fir foliage into 7.5-15cm (3-6in) lengths, and the conifer foliage into 10-20cm (4-8in) lengths. Insert the fir sprigs horizontally into the front and sides of the block, and angled upwards in the back. Insert the floppier, darker conifer foliage underneath the fir. Concentrate the large conifer sprigs on your left-hand side, to create a waterfall of greenery.

4 Remove the lily stamens and shorten the stems to 15cm (6in) lengths. Insert a stem facing front, between the candles, to build up the centre and set the height of the display. Shorten and insert the other stems clustered amongst the candles, placing one stem at the back. Divide the sedum heads into clusters. Insert one tight mass in front, one diagonally at the back.

5 Cut the chincherinchee stems to 5-20cm (2-8in) lengths. Inserting the longest stem first, create a tight cluster on your left-hand side, carrying through the diagonal line of the larch. Cut the alstroemeria stems to 7.5-15cm (3-6in) lengths. Insert them downwards, on the rear opposite side, to balance the chincherinchees.

6 Shorten the carnation stems to 6-17cm (2-7in) lengths. Insert them in the centre front of the display. Run a staggered row of wired cones (see How-to), alternating small and large, along the front, between the carnations and alstroemeria. Make four bows with the red ribbon, and insert them near the candle bases. Insert the holly off centre, one in front and one at the back.

Garland GREETINGS

What better welcome is there than a Christmas wreath or garland – and one that you create yourself is extra special. Here's a traditional wreath to make, with simple instructions, lots of variations and unusual display ideas.

hristmas wreaths and garlands are on sale from the end of November onwards but it is just as easy to make your own. It's also cheaper – for the cost of a plain ready-made wreath, you can buy what you need to make your own, including the festive decorations such as the brightly coloured wooden cherries and holly berries used here. And, if you have plenty of evergreens in your garden, you could even make one or two extra wreaths as presents for your friends.

Choosing the material

Foliage is the mainstay of most Christmas wreaths and garlands and there is a long tradition of using holly, ivy and conifers at Christmas-time. Of the broad-leaved evergreens, plain-leaved ivy and variegated holly are best. There are dozens of

LEFT A gloriously traditional Christmas wreath made of holly, ivy and conifer foliage, displayed on an antique wooden chair. Dark green leaves on their own can be rather sombre but here, blue cedar, variegated holly, ribbons and artificial fruit provide festive flair.

variegated hollies, with silver or gold splashes, stripes or edges, any of which are fine. Or you might choose variegated ivy – again, there are dozens available – partnered with plain-leaved holly. Keep away from too many different variegations, though, or you'll end up with a confused effect. If you can't get variegated ivy or holly, variegated elaeagnus would be a good substitute.

Cupressus, or true cypress, and its close relatives, chamaecyparis, or false cypress, and Leyland's cypress also make good foliage, and branches of these quick-growing screen and hedging plants are often included by florists in mixed bunches so they're fairly easy to buy. Blue cedar also features in this wreath, but is less common in the shops. Fortunately, florists are now starting to stock more unusual conifer foliage, and you could use blue spruce instead.

Whatever foliage you choose, it helps to lay it all out in separate piles in front of you when you work. Buy generous sized bunches – you can always use what's left in other floral displays, and it's better than running out halfway through. However, if you're using holly from your garden, remember that it is quite slow growing, so don't go overboard. You can always nip outside for a few extra sprigs.

Holly berries are a traditional Christmas decoration, but birds tend to strip holly berries long before December 25th. You can pick some berried sprigs in advance and keep them fresh in a polythene bag in a cool place. If the berries start to shrivel, spray them lightly.

Adding festive ingredients.

Once you have formed the basis of your wreath you can let your imagination and creativity run wild when deciding on additional materials to make it both sumptuous and eye-catching for Christmas. Use traditional red and gold coloured ingredients; red and gold ribbons to make large bows, and short candles for a table-top arrangement, or tall

WIRING CANDLES

Table top garlands make wonderfully festive dining table centrepieces. Add short red candles to provide bright highlights to a predominantly green base. Cut a piece of thick stub wire, approximately 15-20cm (6-8in) long, in half. Insert the two pieces, spaced evenly apart, into the base of the candle. Don't insert them too near the rim, or the wax may chip off.

173

ones for a sideboard, to add light and lustre to your design. Wire nuts and cones and spray them gold and silver, or sprinkle them with a covering of glitter so that they shimmer in the candlelight, or simply varnish them if they are to be mixed with brightly-coloured flowers.

Kitchen wreath materials

Spices and herbs are ideal ingredients for a more unusual, sweet-smelling Christmas wreath to hang on your kitchen door or at your window. They are an attractive natural way to display nutmeg, cinnamon sticks, lemon sticks, and star anise. Choose complementary herbs so that the wreath fills the kitchen with a delicious aroma. Don't include anything too overpowering that will cancel out the more subtle smells of other herbs. If you look after the wreath carefully and do not use too many of its ingredients in your cooking, your wreath should last well into the new year. Our kitchen arrangement is built upon an ivy base but as an alternative you could use laurel leaves. Long spikes of rosemary also look lovely in winter arrangements and would mix well with holly and ivy featured here. Lastly, the seedheads of fennel, caraway and dill could also have an aromatic part to play in long-lasting Christmas wreaths.

Choosing the frame

There are many types of frame for Christmas wreaths and garlands but we have used the simplest here – copper wire formed into a rough circle. Don't worry about a perfect shape – once you get a thick cover of foliage over the wire, any unevenness is less obvious, and the slight variation on a perfect circle gives it character. If you're really keen on a perfect circle, you could use a wire-frame lampshade base instead.

RIGHT This elegant wreath is made of long stems of ivy, arranged in a circle and secured with stub wire. It is important to use woody stems, thick enough to hold their shape, but flexible enough to bend. Golden bows, top and bottom, add glitter.

RIGHT This variegated and plain leaved holly wreath is made as shown in the 'step-by-steps', but using only two types of foliage. With its bright red ribbons, it would be as decorative in a living room, dining room or hallway as on a front door. If hung in a warm room, spray it lightly from time to time.

LEFT This aromatic nut and herb kitchen wreath is pretty all year round. Straw moulded into a sausage shape, bound with natural string and tied together at the ends, forms the circular base. Ivy leaves, clusters of whole nutmegs, cinnamon sticks, wheat and lemon grass are glued on, then golden bows added to finish.

You can buy plastic-backed foam rings, in a range of diameters and in oval or round shapes: our dining table wreath is built on a foam ring. A more traditional foundation is wire-mesh netting formed into a circular tube and stuffed with moss. Unfortunately, moss tends to stain white paint or wallpaper so is often unsuitable for indoors. For a rustic, informal dried wreath, teased-out straw (available from pet shops) can be bound into a long sausage shape with natural twine, then tied together at the ends to form a circular base.

Displaying your wreath

The front door is the traditional location for Christmas wreaths but they look equally as nice on internal doors. Wreaths made with dried flowers or herbs must be kept under cover, as rain or even a damp atmosphere will ruin them. Indoors, you can hang a wreath over a mantelpiece mirror, from a picture hook on a wall, or on an ornate and decorative piece of furniture.

LEFT A flat wreath makes a perfect dining-table display. Here, a plastic, pre-formed ring is covered with fresh moss, then studded with ribbons, pine cones and candles. Real and fake holly, complete with berries, ivy, fake silver leaves and red-dyed dried moss, add tone and texture. Dried artichokes and a lotus seed pod form unusual focal points.

WHAT TO DO
WHAT YOU NEED

Traditional Christmas wreath

FOLLOW OUR STEPS TO CREATE THIS CHRISTMAS WREATH AND ADD A FESTIVE TOUCH TO YOUR FRONT DOOR. EASY TO MAKE, ITS PROFESSIONAL LOOK AND WELCOMING APPEARANCE WILL DELIGHT YOUR VISITORS.

1 *variegated holly*
2 *blue cedar*
3 *ivy*
4 *cupressus*
5 *fake holly berries*

6 *large and small cones*
7 *wooden cherries*
8 *copper wire*
9 *scissors*
10 *green twine*

11 *red ribbon*
12 *transparent glue*
Optional
13 *plate moss*

HOW-TO

HANGING YOUR CHRISTMAS WREATH

To make a hook for your Christmas wreath, cover a piece of stub wire in green gutta-percha tape.

1 Twist a circle in the middle of the wire and push ends into the back of the wreath at the top.

2 Pull the wire ends back under the wreath, then push each end into each side of the wreath to secure.

3 The loop should be fixed in the middle of the wreath on the top back, with the ends neatly tucked in.

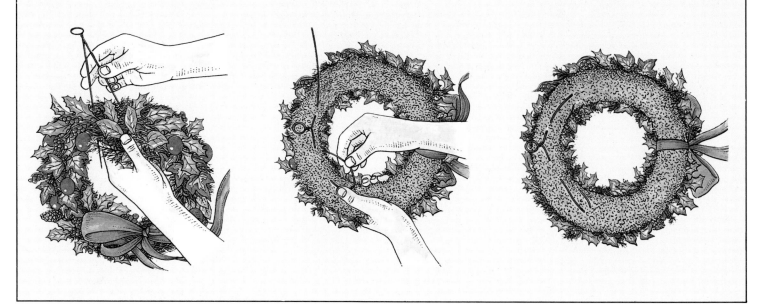

1 Bend copper wire (length depends on how big you want your wreath to be) into a circle, then firmly bind with uncut green twine. Take five or six sprays of foliage from the cupressus and strip some of the lower fronds to leave bare stems. Bunch two or three stems together, then hold them against the bound wire, and start binding onto the wire with the twine still attached to the reel.

2 Using the same uncut twine, keep binding overlapping bunches of foliage and moss, if used, to the frame. Select three or four long-stalked ivy leaves, then add them, as a tight group, wrapping the twine round the stalks five or six times. Break off small lengths of blue cedar, strip the lower stems, then bind a small bunch overlapping the ivy. Keep following the curve of the ring as you work.

3 Divide the holly into small sprigs, then secure a bunch of five or six sprigs to the wire ring, in the same way. Use small bunches of holly to give a more interesting shape. You should now be roughly half-way round the ring, but if not, don't worry – you simply repeat the ingredients in the same order, and carry on adding more material until the entire ring is completely covered with overlapping foliage.

4 Once the ring is completely covered, cut and knot the twine. Inspect the wreath from all sides and trim off any stray pieces that don't follow the general line and 'flow'. Don't tidy up too much though or the wreath will look artificial and the final effect spoilt. If there are bare patches, you can usually gently manipulate the foliage to cover them, or at least make them smaller.

5 To add colour, glue on the red-painted wooden cherries in clusters or pairs, using quick-drying transparent glue. Fake holly berries do not always look authentic but real berries tend to shrivel after a couple of weeks. Glue on fake berry clusters instead of, or as well as, real berries evenly spaced apart. Glue pine, fir or larch cones onto the cedar branches.

6 Hold the wreath up or prop it on the mantelpiece, so that you can decide which way up it looks best. Then, when you have decided where the top of the wreath is, glue on a large bow, both for decoration and to disguise the hook. Glue another ribbon, with long trailing ends, onto the bottom, and glue small bows all around the greenery for added Christmas sparkle.

ALL THAT GLITTERS

If you want to cheer up your home for the New Year, make a display that dazzles using shiny containers and bright flowers.

All that glitters may not be gold, but in the short, dark days of winter any additional shine or sparkle, glint or glitter you can add to your home will bring a welcome glow.

Gather together a group of shiny containers and ornaments; arrange them on a surface you can almost 'see your face in'; invest in a handful of dried or long-lasting fresh flowers for an arrangement with a difference and you can create an eye-catching still-life.

Shiny surfaces

This is not the time for best linen table-cloths. Concentrate attention instead on a highly-polished wooden surface, whether an occasional table, a sideboard, a glass shelf or coffee table.

Look out for bargain lengths of shiny-coated plasticised cotton, the up-dated version of the old-fashioned oilcloth, which is sold to match conventional cotton furnishing fabrics in a wide range of modern and classic patterns.

Give new, if temporary, prominence to a brass or copper tray or large plate or improvise by using sheets of gold, silver or brightly-coloured foil paper.

Sparkling containers

Once you have decided on the base for your attention-grabbing display, look around your home for imaginative containers with a high gloss factor. If you happen to have a glass vase, particularly one of the pearlised type, or an old lustre jug or teapot, that's fine. If not, use a shiny stainless steel pan or an enamel saucepan from the kitchen.

If utensils are at a premium at this busy time of year, create your own glittering containers. Cover a washed and dried food can or coffee jar with strips of sequin press-outs, or with smooth or crumpled kitchen foil – a completely smooth surface has a higher glint count, but it's harder to achieve a perfect finish. Another possibility is to paint throwaway food containers with clear glue and sprinkle with glitter.

Dress up your chosen container with shiny extras. A double bow of parcel ribbon tied around the neck of a vase and finished off with long, curling, trailing ends; a string of golden or silvery decoration beads wound round a cylindrical container; a few sequined flowers or shiny beads struck at random over a simple glass jar all add some jazz.

Glossy flowers and foliage

Seek out the shiniest specimens among everlasting and dried flowers, preserved and evergreen foliage, and fresh flowers. Each category has some which have a higher gloss factor than others; these are the ones you want.

Everlasting flowers, which dry naturally on the plant or hung up in a warm, airy room, have more built-in sparkle than other dried flowers. Pick of the bunch must be strawflowers, which grow in many lovely colours, and rhodanthe (also known as helipterum) which grow in shiny sugar-almond pink and snowy white. Both of these are pretty daisy-shaped species and blend well with other dried materials.

When it comes to seedheads there is no contest. Honesty, those translucent, silvery-papery 'moon petals', stand out a mile. Stems and clippings of honesty are excellent mixers and provide pretty highlights in arrangements of both dried and fresh flowers. And a casual bunch of honesty (once you have rubbed off the drab beige outer covers of the seed carriers) will brighten a dark corner almost as a cluster of candles.

Evergreen leaves and most foliage preserved in glycerine is good for shine. Ivy, magnolia, laurel, elaeagnus, pittosporum, camellia, pyracanthus and many other evergreens will fit perfectly into your design, as will preserved beech, oak, maple and many other types.

BELOW Look in your kitchen for any shiny utensils. A stainless steel saucepan cooks up a high-rise dome of yellow strawflowers, blue dried love-in-a mist and pale green frondy, fluffy lepidium. The stems are held in crumpled wire mesh netting placed in the neck of the container. A strip of insulating tape stuck below the rim protects the pan from scratching.

LEFT A single stem of Singapore orchid provides six blooms and two buds; two sprays of pink and yellow spotted alstroemeria, and three two-tone carnations provide contrastingly round shapes that give the design weight and depth. It adds up to a glossy arrangement that should last for weeks.

It is well worth giving any slightly weary-looking foliage a bit of 'spit and polish'. Dust large leaves with pot plant leaf-shine wipes. Alternatively, use a soft dry cloth. Then for extra gloss, polish the leaves with a cloth sprinkled with a couple of drops of salad oil. It makes all the difference. One word of warning though; leaves treated with this special dressing do tend to attract and hold the dust, so it is not suitable for a dusty environment. Fortunately, some of the shiniest fresh flowers also have the longest vase life. Lilies of all kinds, including alstroemeria, orchids and, as the season merges into spring, tulips, all have glossy wax-like petals which act like reflectors to every shaft of sunlight or lamplight. It is not necessary to buy a lot of these – if you plan your arrangement carefully a few stems will go a long way.

Not quite natural
You don't have to rely on nature – a can or two of spray paint and a few brushfuls of clear varnish can turn a collection of lack-lustre seedheads, twigs and foliage into a dazzlingly different display. Spray love-in-a-mist seedheads silver, stately poppy 'urns' bright, blushing red and tough little windfall apples golden.

Find some teasels and spray them very lightly with silver paint so they have a frosted appearance. Spray spare apples and pears and a few oranges with a touch or two of red paint. Leave to dry, then touch up with silver, gold or bronze. Bunches of plastic grapes also take well to this treatment, and add an interesting change of size and shape to a decorative bowl of sprayed fruits.

Polished wood
With woody-looking subjects such as cones, nuts and seedheads, all you need is a coat of varnish. Choose a clear, colourless type – you can buy it in bottles, tins or spray cans – and apply a thin, even coat to your chosen materials. Cones look like intricate and highly polished wood carvings; walnuts, chestnuts and hazelnuts glisten like tiny baubles, and stems or sideshoots of seedheads – hollyhock or delphinium, for example – sparkle as never before. Do keep treated fruit out of children's reach, as it is poisonous to eat.

Keeping up a pretence

Artificial flowers, whether they are made of a glazed silky material or shiny-bright plastic, are highly suitable for this sort of scheme. Realistic-looking silk flowers, many of them indistinguishable from real-life blooms, are not. Go for the mass-produced and frankly fanciful flowers: if their colouring is a bit over the top spray them with paint of a more suitable colour.

QUICK TIP SPRAYING FRUIT

To make the job of paint spraying fruit and seedheads easier, follow these simple steps for a cleaner finish.
• If you are going to spray paint, remember to use the aerosol in a well-ventilated room.
• Pierce the fruits with wooden skewers or cocktail sticks, and secure them in a firm base such a metal pinholder or even a large potato.
• Stand the base on newspaper to prevent paint spray from falling on the floor or furniture – or put it into a cardboard box turned on one side and spray it there.
• Spray the paint as you turn the base in an even, all-round motion.
• Leave the fruits to dry thoroughly overnight before arranging them.

ABOVE From the metallic thread in the tablecloth to the sugar frosting of the grapes, this is a group that is designed to dazzle. Pale and deep pink everlasting strawflowers are mingled with not-so-shiny dried peonies and rose-buds in a fluted glass vase. Sprays of honesty and pink ribbon bows held on twists of wire provide sparkling highlights. A single white rose in a pearlised glass vase adds a fresh touch.

ABOVE LEFT Nestling in coils of glossy ivy leaves, apples and pears, cones and tiny teasels show themselves in a new light. Spray the fruits with one gloss paint – we chose red – and then overspray with a metallic one for an interesting finish.

LEFT Maximum impact of these fresh and dried plant materials arranged in a red enamel teapot is achieved by standing the design on a sheet of metallic foil. Even without this, the group has sparkle and style. Three fresh scarlet gerberas and a couple of stems of rosehips are contrasted with silver and red-sprayed Chinese lanterns and teasel, honesty, and stems of fake blackberries.

There are endless possibilities for your false flower arrangements on a fan theme: a clutch of tall, slender wine bottles each holding a white plastic arum lily; an old shopping basket painted with varnish or sprayed silver and gold to take a handful of scarlet plastic poinsettias; a discarded teapot spilling over with a synthetic trailing plant and a few false flowers.

Accessories after the fact

Now you have chosen the three main ingredients – the surface, the container and the flowers – increase the effect with a few accessories.

Baubles and tinsels are obvious and cheerful candidates. Parcel ribbons, especially ones with a metallic thread, snaking in and out of the items in the group visually link the components and add extra colour. For the finishing touch, a dish of the brightest, brashest boiled sweets or chocolate in gold-foil wrappings make stunning accessories.

HEARTS AND FLOWERS

What could be more romantic on Valentine's Day than dinner for two by candlelight? Here's an elegant fresh-flower display that will help to set the mood for that special evening.

n occasion like Valentine's Day gives you the perfect opportunity to treat yourself, and a loved one, to an intimate dinner for two. This lovely fresh flower arrangement will get the evening off to the best possible start, and it's a thoughtful way of showing off the flowers given to you for Valentine's Day.

It's an unusual, two-tiered display, with a central vertical feature of long-stemmed red roses, and a low 'all-round' base of foliage, tulips and gypsophila. The design effectively combines two approaches; the lower section is constructed according to traditional guidelines while the starkly upright roses add a distinctly modern touch.

Choosing the flowers

Long-stemmed red roses form the upper focal point. Although in many displays you can get by with less expensive, short-stemmed, sweetheart-type roses,

here, stem-length is important, and are worth paying a little extra for. Red roses are the perfect colour for Valentine's Day, but you could use deep or pale-pink, apricot, peach or creamy white roses instead. Yellow roses have a coolness of colour which is not really in keeping with the spirit of the occasion, though they might be just right for another evening.

If possible, buy the roses in fairly tight bud the day before you need them. Condition the roses as soon as you get them home. Cut a tiny bit off the stems, to prevent air locks from forming, then put them in a bucket or tall container of water in a cool place overnight. Conditioning is doubly important for this display, as the stems and flowers have to stand upright, and if not full of water, they will quickly droop.

Beautiful blooms

Pale-pink tulips are the main flowers in the 'lower' display. Because it can sometimes be difficult to find tulips in the shops that are anything more than buds showing colour, look around a few days before the big day, and buy tulip buds if necessary, in advance, so they'll be fully coloured when you need them. Keep them somewhere light and warmish, but not hot as they will dry out.

You could use deep-pink tulips instead, or the beautiful pink parrot tulips, if you can get them, tinged with green and red. Matching the reds of roses and tulips is tricky, and if one is

LEFT This elegant and unusual two-tiered display makes a memorable and romantic dining table centrepiece for a Valentine's Day dinner for two. Long-stemmed roses, tulips, gypsophila, ferns and euphorbia foliage are combined to create a delicate, feminine-looking arrangement, perfect for the occasion.

Creating a Valentine's Day display of romantic red roses and tulips

1 *12 red roses*
2 *6-8 euphorbia stems*
3 *10-12 tulips*
4 *bunch of dyed pink gypsophila*
5 *20-30 fern fronds*
6 *block of florists foam*
7 *floristry knife*
8 *low china container*

1 Soak a foam block until bubbles stop rising, then cut it to snuggly fit the container standing about 3cm (1½ in) above the rim. Cut off the tips of the stem ends of 20-30 fern fronds, then remove the lower frondlets, for ease of insertion. Push the stalks into the sides of the foam block, angling the fronds downwards. Overlap the fronds, and insert them to form a bushy collar around the foam.

2 Shorten the rose stems to 30-45cm (12- 18in), cutting the stems at an angle. Remove the thorns and leaves from the lower half, then insert the stems as deeply as you can into the foam block. Place the tallest stems in the centre, the shorter ones clustered around them. Insert the roses close together, to form a tight mass, but splay them out slightly. Trim any leaves that are damaged.

3 Cut off the leafy tops from 6-8 euphorbia stems, which should be 5-10cm (2-4in) long. Euphorbia bleeds milky latex when cut, so cut each stem and immerse it in boiling water for a few seconds, or insert it at once into the foam, to block the flow. Insert the euphorbia tight against the foam block, to make a dense, frilly covering of foliage from the fern collar to the base of the rose stems.

4 Cut the stems of 10-12 tulips back to 7.5cm (3in), reserving the tulip foliage for use later. Carefully insert the tulip stems, here and there, in between the euphorbia foliage. The tulip stems should be hidden by the foliage, and the flowerheads should stand a just a little above the surrounding leaves. Check that the tulips are evenly distributed and angled outwards.

5 Cut small sprigs of gypsophila, about 7.5cm (3in) long, making sure the stalks are stiff enough to insert. Bunch several sprigs in your hand, then insert the bunches among the tulips and euphorbia. Place the gypsophila horizontally around the sides of the block, gradually angling the bunches upwards towards the top. Check the display from every viewpoint, and fill any gaps.

6 Break off the reserved headless tulip stalks so that just the curly leaves remain (see 'How-to' box). Insert the leaves as close as you can at the base of the bare rose stems, carefully entwining some of the tulip leaves around the stems. The leaves act as 'transitional' material, filling the space between the roses and the mass of gypsophila, ferns, euphorbia and tulips.

slightly more orange than the other, the effect can be unpleasant. You could, however, reverse the display colours, and use pink long-stemmed roses along with red tulips.

Because the appearance of tulip and rose foliage is so important in this design, check that the leaves are in perfect condition before buying. Avoid any that are limp, torn, brown or shrivelled round the edges. Long-stemmed roses are usually sold by the stem, so you can easily inspect the leaves. Bunches of tulips in tight transparent wrappers may prove a bit more difficult to examine, but a helpful florist will probably check them for you.

Dyed pink gypsophila is used in its usual 'filler' role. Though your florist is more likely to stock this speciality around Valentine's Day than at any other time of year, you might still need to order it in advance. At a pinch, white gypsophila could also be used, in its large or small-flowered varieties. Dyed gypsophila is more expensive than white, but you can dry it when you take apart the arrangement, once the other fresh flowers have faded. You can also do the same with any roses that wilt while still in bud – just cut off the wet ends of the stems, and hang the roses upside down in a warm, dry and airy spot. If the roses have opened and faded, they will be unsuitable for drying and should be discarded.

Choosing the foliage
Leatherleaf fern and euphorbia foliage supplement the rose and tulip leaves. Leatherleaf fern, *Dryopteris erythrosora*, has shiny, stiff, dark-green fronds. The fronds are tougher than many other, more delicate ferns (hence its common name), but it still needs frequent misting to retain its freshness. It's also a good idea to totally submerge the ferns in water for several hours, or overnight, before use. Buy a large bunch of 20-30 fronds, and keep them cool and damp until you're ready to begin your display.

Ferns and foliage
Leatherleaf fern is imported, but you could substitute the native male fern, *Dryopteris filix-mas*, to which the leatherleaf fern is related; or the evergreen hard fern, *Blechnum spicant*, which also has tough, leathery fronds, and tolerates dry air.

The euphorbia, *E. marginata*, has white flowers, but they are so tiny that they make no impact. Its green and white variegated foliage and leaf-like bracts, however, are strikingly fresh-looking, and especially attractive used all together, as here. It's a hardy annual garden plant, known as 'snow on the mountain'. Its flowers appear in late summer, so at this time of year, you'll have to buy imported stems from florist shops.

Choosing the container
As the sides of of the container will be visible below the display, it is important to use an attractive one. A low, round, straight-sided china dish is used, about 20cm (8in) across. Our featured container is white, but it could be pink or red, though matching it to the red of fresh flowers can be difficult!

The container should be deep enough to keep the foam block in position.

Alternatively, you could use a shallow wicker basket sprayed white (use car enamel aerosols available from car accessory shops). Remember to allow time for the paint to dry, and line the basket with polythene or kitchen plastic wrap before use.

Choosing the setting
A dining-room table is the obvious spot for this display, and if you have a pink tablecloth and napkins, this is the time to bring them out. If your tablecloth is white, you could buy inexpensive pink or red paper napkins, to reinforce the colour scheme and mood. Though tall flower arrangements on dining room tables are not usually recommended, this one is narrow enough to look round, rather than having to look over.

If you have young children you might want to move the display to a safer spot on a sideboard in the dining room, or corner table in the living room, when Valentine's Day is over. Two pairs of hands are better than one for this task, to prevent the roses from toppling over.

Flower language
Flowers have always had a language of their own, and over the centuries different meanings have been attributed to them.

The flowers featured in this arrangement were not only chosen for their decorative qualities but also for their particular romantic message. The message of love and affection has always been expressed through gifts of red roses, and tulips also carry the same meaning. What better way of creating a romantic atmosphere than with a quiet dinner for two and beautiful flowers!

REMOVING TULIP STEMS FROM LEAVES

You can often make good use of cut-off tulip leaves, either with their own flowers or in another display. When you cut the flowers short, as here, stumpy stems remain attached to the pairs of leaves. Don't use scissors to cut away the rest of the stems: they won't reach deep enough, and you'll be left with a shorter, but just as unattractive stump. Instead, bend back the leaves as far as they will go, then cleanly break off the stem with your fingers, and you're left with a neat edge.

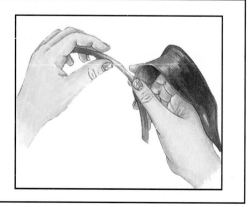

Easter Parade

Take Easter as your inspiration and decorate your home with festive spring flowers. With a little imagination, you can create delightful novelty displays.

raditional colour and festive accessories give the lead to Easter flower arrangements that are both seasonal and fun. Whether you take time over decorating individual eggs for use in a display, or simply place a variety of budding branches in a vase and watch them slowly open out, Easter should be a celebration of spring flowers within the home.

Easter hues

The easiest way of adding an Easter touch to your floral displays is to opt for a traditional colour scheme. The Easter colours are purple, blue, yellow and white and these are also the shades of some of the prettiest bulb, hothouse and wild flowers available at this time of year, so if you want to use the traditional colour theme, there is plenty of material to choose from.

Purple is the colour associated with Lent, the period immediately before Easter. The altar drapes and vestments worn in Church are purple until Easter Sunday, when they are replaced by gold or yellow and white. Purple orchis is sometimes known as 'Gethsemane' because its spotted leaves were said to be stained with Christ's blood. Seasonal purple-coloured flowers include violets, anemones, freesias, hyacinths, irises, lilac, wallflowers and crocuses.

Yellow for spring

In addition to its religious connotations, yellow is the predominant colour of spring flowers and is represented by showy blooms such as tulips, lilies, irises, daffodils and narcissi, but don't overlook branches of forsythia and mimosa, spray carnations, chrysanthemums, alstroemeria and primroses.

Blue also has religious significance as it is the colour associated with the Virgin Mary and in legend the pretty blue speedwell grew on the side of the road to Calvary. Use anemones, freesias, hyacinths, grape hyacinths, irises, lilac and crocuses in your arrangements for their delightful shades of blue.

Pure white and cream flowers have an ethereal quality and a special serenity when used on their own, and, of course, are perfect mixers in a varied arrangement. The list of white or cream flowers is broadly similar to that for yellow with the addition of some fruit or ornamental blossoms and snowdrops, glorious white and cream anemones, lilies of the valley and roses.

Festive eggs

Eggs and their shells are the perfect accessory for an Easter arrangement as eggs have a traditional association with this holiday. One of the most charming ways to use empty egg shells is to turn them into a tiny vase for a nosegay of delicate flowers.

Break each egg close to the top, as you would a boiled egg, and neaten the edges to give a smooth look. Wash the egg shells thoroughly and check that the eggs are watertight and have not been accidently cracked. Fill the shells about half full with water and stand them in egg cups or napkin rings brimming with a collection of primroses,

LEFT The criss-crossing gypsophila stems hold the daffodils and freesias in place to create an elegant floral display which is perfect for a festive Easter table setting.

RIGHT A slightly-tapered purple pottery vase is the perfect container for a floral celebration in traditional Easter hues. The purple of the vase is repeated in the hyacinths.

snowdrops, primulas or violets.

Whole egg shells can be decorated to make a festive accompaniment for an Easter flower arrangement, and a unique, colourful design can be achieved easily using cans of spray paint and small tins of matt or gloss paint. Uncooked eggs can be used, although don't attempt to eat them afterwards, but it is safer to hard-boil or blow the eggs first.

Blowing eggs

This involves emptying their shells of the white and the yolk. Use a sharp, fine-pointed needle to pierce a hole in each end, at the top and bottom of the shell. Hold each egg over a bowl and blow through one hole. The egg will emerge through the hole at the opposite end, and can be used for cooking.

Hold the blown egg shells under the tap and run hot water through them until it runs clear. Shake the shells to remove any water left inside. They are now ready for decorating.

In order to prepare the egg for painting, wash the shell thoroughly to make sure there is no grease on the surface, then rinse and dry it well. Place it on a flat surface covered with newspaper and apply a coat of paint. Leave this to dry, then spatter-spray it with short bursts from an aerosol paint can or use a small brush.

DECORATING BLOWN EGGS

In order to be painted or sprayed, blown eggs need to be raised so that you have access to the whole egg. Cut a potato in half and place it on a flat surface covered with newspaper. Push a medium-gauge wire through the hole in one end of the egg and make a small kink in the wire on which the egg can sit. Insert the free end of the wire into the potato base.

To paint hard-boiled eggs, work on one end at a time. Stand the half-painted egg in a cardboard egg carton. Leave it to dry, then turn upside down and paint the other end. Return the eggs to the carton and leave until dry.

tree of TREATS

*Everyone loves Christmas trees, but here's
something new to try. Branch out with
a cheerful Easter tree, 'growing' from a
base of fresh spring flowers and sparkling
with foil-covered treats and
festive decorations.*

ive your children or grand-children a special Easter
this year, with this unusual
Easter tree. It's easy and
inexpensive to make, and
large enough to create an impact in any
room. By omitting the fluffy toys, you
can give the tree more sophisticated
overtones, perhaps for an Easter dinner
party.

Most of the ingredients used give
double value for money: the flower pot
container can go in the garden after-wards, the sweet decorations can be
eaten, and the Easter trinkets put away
for use next year.

Choosing the flowers

Traditional Easter colours, yellow and
white are used here, but you could use
pastel colours, in a monochromatic or
multi-coloured room scheme.

You will need a bunch of large yel-low daffodils. Our featured blooms have
orange-tinged trumpets, but yellow,
yellow and white, creamy-white trum-pets or the scented, small-flowered
'Paperwhite' or 'Soleil d'Or' could be
used. Buy a bunch with leaves as well as
flowers, to re-create the look of a
clump of daffodils growing in the wild.

Fully-open blooms are pictured to
show the finished effect, but for the
best value buy daffodils in green bud or
with the barest touch of colour show-ing. The small-flowered narcissus
should be just starting to open. When
you get the flowers home, snip off the
lower, white stems to the required dis-play length and soak them separately
from other flowers. This is because
daffodil stems exude a slimy sap that can
block the stems of other flowers, not
allowing them to take in water, which
shortens their lives.

Use a bunch of white tulips or bright
yellow ones, especially if you're using
white daffodils. Instead of ordinary, sin-gle tulips, you could buy the more
expensive double-flowered blooms,

**RIGHT Celebrate Easter in
style, with this unusual
Easter tree. Made of
hazel branches adorned
with gifts and inserted
into a foam-filled flower
pot, the tree has its own
sunny garden of tulips,
mimosa, daffodils and
shasta daises, nestling in
a bed of bun moss.**

such as the yellow 'Monte Carlo'. Buy tulips closed, but with the buds showing colour. Again, condition them in a tall container with water halfway up their stems, ideally overnight.

Selecting mimosa

Buy mimosa, the most expensive ingredient, with about half the buds open. Re-cut the stems and give them a long drink of water. A budget alternative is forsythia, from the florist or the garden. Combine it with ferns or other dark-green, delicate foliage. For a pink and white display, mix white daffodils and pink tulips with sprigs of pink chaenomeles, or japonica, instead of the yellow mimosa branches.

Shasta daises from a florist add to the informal touch. Choose fully-open flowers with hard centres; fluffy centres indicate an over-mature flower. Leopard's bane, or doronicum, a bright-yellow daily, should be out in the garden in late spring; these last well as cut flowers, and could be used instead.

As a variation, you could fill the flower pot with potting mixture and, instead of using cut flowers, plant polyanthus, pansies or hyacinths. Hide any potting mixture with moss and insert the 'tree' in the centre.

Choosing the tree and moss

Hazel, with its elegant branches and delicate catkins, makes an ideal choice. The catkins will continue to grow, even when the branches are cut. A few green leaves may appear, as the warm conditions in your home force the branches into new spring growth.

Alternatives include alder, beech, birch or even lilac. Oak branches would give the effect of a stubby tree, like a miniature oak, while Peking, or contorted, willow has a sophisticated, oriental-style appeal.

For a more unconventional tree, use branches of the unusual-looking *Salix sachalinensis* 'Sekka'. This has distinctive paddle-shaped stems. It is not available from florists, so grow your own in the garden or buy dried branches from dried-flower stockists.

Try to choose attractively forked branches as straight ones provide no hooks for the decorations, and they would simply slide to the base. Avoid conifer branches, as they have

Preparing your festive Easter tree

1 *1 hazel branch with catkins*	**7** *assorted hanging sweets and novelties*
2 *8 yellow and orange daffodils*	**8** *floristry scissors*
3 *5 white tulips*	**9** *block of wet florist's foam*
4 *1 large bunch of mimosa*	**10** *15cm (6in) stub wires*
5 *10 white shasta daisies*	**11** *terracotta pot*
6 *1 large clump of bun moss*	**12** *polythene film*

1 Prepare your terracotta pot as shown in the 'How-to' box, taking care when securing the moss to leave enough space to insert the assorted flowers. Place the hazel branch with catkins into the centre of the pot and push it firmly into the block of moss-covered florist's foam. The branch should stand around 75cm (30in) high and have plenty of forked twigs on which to hang the festive decorations.

2 Begin adding the spring flowers to the arrangement. Insert the ready-cut daffodils of various lengths. Make sure that the stems are not too long, otherwise you won't be able to view the decorations on the branches. Arrange the daffodils in the foam as they would grow naturally, clustered vertically around the base of the branch. Tie a few loose leaves together with wire and push them into the foam.

3 Trim the tulips to different lengths and remove most of the leaves. For a neatly-finished edge, cut firmly around the base of the leaf with a sharp knife and snap off the foliage. Wrap some of the leaves around your finger to make them curl and push them in between the daffodil stems. Arrange the tulip blooms and the remaining leaves evenly around the outside of the display.

4 Cut most of the leaves off one large stem of mimosa and snip off the sideshoots so you have a cluster of smaller sprigs. Mimosa provides good value in this display as one stem will yield many smaller pieces. Insert both flowers and foliage around the rim of the pot, making a collar for the arrangement. Place a few stems upright and angle others outward so they drape naturally over the edge.

5 Trim the lower leaves off the shasta daisies and scatter them in a circle throughout the other flowers. Remember to keep the other stems fairly short so the lower twigs of the hazel branch are still visible. You could arrange the flowers at the base into a tighter cluster, but spring flowers are more suited to a looser arrangement. You could use primulas from the garden instead of shasta daisies.

6 Finally, hang the Easter novelties from the hazel branch. Place the lighter chocolate coins and miniature baskets on the higher and more flimsy branches. Then hang the heavier novelties – the foil-covered eggs, marzipan fruit and chocolate animals – onto the larger, stronger branches. Arrange the fluffy chicks among the flowers to complete your Easter woodland display.

Christmas overtones, even in spring. Conceal the top of the foam block with bun moss, and continue the wild garden theme. You can order bun moss from your florist. Fresh sphagnum moss or dried reindeer moss can be used instead and are also available in bags from florist shops or garden centres.

Choosing a container

An ordinary, terracotta flower pot, 15cm (6in) across, is used here. Inexpensive and heavy enough to balance the top-heavy weight of the tree, a flower pot adds to the informal, garden appearance. For a more sophisticated look, spray a flower pot, with one or more colours, to tone in with the yellow and white theme, or the colour scheme of the room. Alternatively, you could use a glazed ceramic storage jar or simple vase, in a suitable colour, or a cylindrical glass storage jar or bowl lined with moss, to conceal the foam block.

Plastic flower pots aren't really suitable, as they are lightweight and liable to topple over. When you put a lot of effort into a display, you should to show it off to its best advantage; you wouldn't cook a beautiful meal and serve it on plastic or paper plates.

Choosing decorations

Here, foil-covered chocolate coins and eggs, unwrapped chocolates, marzipan

---

MARZIPAN FRUIT

Marzipan fruit is expensive to buy but easy to make and can be tinted with food dye to the desired colour. Handle marzipan lightly at room temperature, as it gets oily if over-worked. Form grape-sized pieces into fruit shapes such as apples and pears. Stick in cloves as stalks and paint detail on the fruit with a fine brush and diluted food colouring. Roll the fruit in caster sugar for a crystalline surface. With a large needle, pierce a hole through the top, a quarter of the way down. Place in a dry, cool, airy spot for one or two days to harden. Hang from gold thread.

---

fruit and tiny wicker baskets are hung from the branches.

You could fix foil-covered sweets or tiny, fluffy, chicks to the branches – they often have flexible wire feet which can be bent into any shape. Or buy narrow ribbon, in white, pale and deep yellow, and tie little bows on the branches. If you intend to eat the unwrapped marzipan and chocolates, don't hang them too far in advance, otherwise they may get dry and dusty.

Choosing a setting

The Easter tree, like a Christmas tree, should be given pride of place, with plenty of space around it to allow

---

people to walk by without damaging it. If it is safe from young children and pets, you could use it as a floor-level display, otherwise place it on a low table or chair. If you place it next to a window, passers-by can also enjoy its festive appearance, and sunlight filtering through the bare branches will create attractive shadow patterns.

Place the tree in a cool position as mimosa doesn't like heat. Mimosa is also vulnerable to ethylene gas, so keep it well away from fruit, vegetables and wilted flowers.

Looking after the display

If children want to remove the trinkets and sweets, a bit of gentle guidance will keep them from knocking the display over in their enthusiasm.

Even after the decorations are removed, the tree on its flowery knoll remains an attractive display of colour.

Remember to top up the water, and mist-spray the moss regularly, to keep it fresh and green. Daffodils are short-lived; once the flowers turn papery, carefully remove them and replace with fresh buds. Gather any mimosa flowers that fall from the branches, and discard or save them for potpourri. When you dismantle the display, save the hazel branches to support sweet peas or herbaceous perennials, such as delphiniums, in the summer garden.

HOW-TO

PREPARING THE TERRACOTTA POT

1 Line a clean pot with polythene or a plastic bag to prevent water from leaking out of the porous terracotta. Fit in the trimmed and soaked florist's foam. Ensure that none of the foam shows over the pot edge.

2 Trim the edges of the plastic back to the level of the pot rim. Add a little more water into the pot to ensure the foam is wet enough.

3 Cover the top of the foam with small clumps of bun moss to create a natural woodland effect. Fix in position with hairpin-shaped stub wires. Leave gaps to insert the flower stems.

SPOTLIGHT

EASTER TABLES

Make sure your table is prepared for the Easter holiday by planning one or two unusual flower arrangements.

If possible, compose a couple of designs which are completely different in appearance; one a casual grouping of bright and cheerful spring flowers to reflect the festive atmosphere at Easter, and another more elegant arrangement to signify the serious religious aspect of the celebrations and to serve for an evening dinner party.

Flowers for the breakfast table should not look contrived, so a jug of spring blooms carefully chosen to complement one key colour in the room is really all that is needed. If you want something slightly more adventurous, try a mixed nosegay put together in the hand and just placed in water.

In order to make the nosegay, you will need a deep, wide-necked container such as a jug or storage jar. Choose a combination of irises, tulips, daffodils, anemones, hyacinths, broom or periwinkles for your Easter nosegay and ensure that the stems are of varying lengths. Start using tall buds and flowers for the centre. Hold them in one hand and place slightly shorter stems around them. Continue in this fashion until you have included the shortest stems. Once you have achieved a pleasing look, place in water, with the lowest bloom just resting on the rim of the container.

Select your most stylish container for the formal Easter arrangement. If you think it will help you, sketch the shape and direction of the flowers that will complement it best. A basket with a low handle will look attractive with flowers in a graceful curve, and a shallow bowl lends itself to flowers arranged in a gentle mound.

Foam-filled rings are available from florist shops and can be transformed into a dried or fresh-flower hoop for the table centre, with smaller versions at each place setting. For an Easter display with religious overtones, create a dramatic ring with twigs to represent the crown of thorns.

LEFT Blue, purple and yellow flowers are traditional for Easter. Here they are arranged in pale brown pots which look like loaves. Pottery dishes or jars would give the same effect.

BELOW A graceful swan and cygnet vase is treated as a seasonal substitute for a basket – with the joined beaks taking the place of a handle. The pink broom links the red and white of the tulips and narcissi.

WONDERFUL WEDDINGS

*Make the walk up the aisle especially
magical with this cascading display
of pink and white flowers to
decorate the pew ends.*

ling bouquet, and creates a waterfall ffect of flowers and foliage. Because ou don't want the flowers or branches ɔ catch on the bride's dress or be damged by guests, keep the display fairly ɔmpact, no more than 25cm (10in) deep. his is especially important in the case ᵢ a narrow aisle.

esign considerations

any churches have pews made of natu-lly dark or dark-stained wood, and ɔst churches are dimly lit. In this set-ɩg, white or pale-pastel flowers show ɔ best, especially from a distance, and course they should carry through the ʋridal colour theme. Avoid deep-blue or

bea
The
wec
rail,
dov
entr
e rou
part
can
wan
and
    U   iie iiuiiic, aiiy
floral display in a church has to be sub-stantial to be seen. If you are working on a limited budget, use branches, foliage or flowers from your garden or a friend's garden to keep your florist's bill to a minimum.

Even if you're working to a budget and have to buy all the flowers and foliage from a florist, you can still put on a good show. Under these circum-stances it's better to do fewer pew-end displays and make them really generous than to do a number of sparse ones. You could decorate just the pair of pew ends closest to the altar; or in a large church, every second or third pair; the front, middle and back pairs or the front two or three pairs.

The featured pew-end arrangement is teardrop-shaped, like an informal wed-

violet flowers when decorating the church, even if they form part of the bridesmaids' or flower girls' bouquets. Deep blues and violets, and dark reds for that matter, are visually recessive, and tend to look gloomy. They don't photograph well either, which is an important consideration.

Most churches have neutral colour schemes, whether dark wood, stone or rendered and painted walls, so the choice of floral colour scheme depends on personal taste and the colour scheme of the bridal party.

For church flowers, and wedding flowers generally, use a high propor-tion of open blooms. Wedding displays

---

HOW-TO

WIRING A RIBBON BOW

Cut the ribbon to a length of 60cm (24in). Holding one end firmly in one hand and leaving a small tail, loop the ribbon into a figure of eight. The size of the loop determines the size of the finished bow. Hold the central point firmly. Make a second figure of eight on top of the first. Continue building up the layers of ribbon loops. Bind a stub wire around the central point to secure the bow. Twist the wire together to form a stem for insertion into the display. Leave the ribbon tails long and trailing or cut short, as required.

have a different time scale from ordinary flower arrangements in the home, which are meant to last as long as possible, and are often made up entirely of flowers still in bud. Wedding flowers on the other hand are expected to look beautiful for that day, and that day alone. After the ceremony, some people like to leave the flowers in the church for others to enjoy, or contribute them to a local hospital or old people's home. This is still possible but the arrangements will not last for as long as usual.

Planning in advance

As soon as the date is set, try to meet with the verger or whoever is in charge of organising church flowers. You can take measurements and sort out the best time to deliver and arrange the flowers, find out what vases are available, where the water tap is, and so on. Look at the pew ends carefully, since they vary in their design. Some have horizontal indentations through which securing ribbons can be slotted; with others, the display is hooked over the top.

Always discuss your wedding-flower needs with your florist as soon as the date is set. He or she will be able to tell you what will be available at that time of year, and what the cost is likely to be. They can also arrange to order your flowers early to avoid any last-minute disappointment.

It is usual to make up and position the church flowers the day before the wedding, so they are still fresh on the day, and you have time to enjoy yourself without feeling pressurised. If you are doing all the flowers yourself, try to enlist the help of a friend or two, hopefully with some experience in flower arranging. If you are doing the flowers at home, make sure you have adequate transport to get them to the church on time and in good condition. It is easy to underestimate the amount of space you will need to pack all the arrangements safely into the back of the car. It might be worth hiring or borrowing a small van just for the day.

Choosing the pew-end flowers

You may want to use the same type of flowers for pew ends that you use for the bridal bouquet, perhaps without the more expensive lily of the valley and orchids that are usually included.

Making a fresh-flower pew end

1 *18-20 stems of pink roses*	**7** *5-6 cyclamen leaves*
2 *2-3 stems of gypsophila*	**8** *3 trailing stems of variegated ivy*
3 *10 stems of cherry blossom*	**9** *foam base for pew ends*
4 *2-3 stems of pink broom*	**10** *fine stub wires*
5 *16-18 stems of spray chrysanthemums*	**11** *scissors*
6 *6-8 stems of laurustinus*	**12** *white ribbon*

1 Soak the foam ball base. Place upright on the working surface. Insert three pieces of ivy at least 46cm (18in) long into the base of the foam ball so that they trail downwards. Make a wired bow from the white ribbon (see 'Quick tip') and insert it in the middle of the ivy. Wire five or six cyclamen leaves and make a ring of leaves around the foam ball.

2 Cut off the lower flowers from the cherry blossom stems. Leave two stems long and cut the remaining stems in half. Make a slit in the base of all the woody stems to increase water uptake from the foam. Insert the short sprigs into the top of the of foam ball in a spiky fan shape. Place the two long cherry blossom stems at the bottom of the ball, following the line of the trailing ivy.

3 Cut several pink broom stems off their main stem to the same length as the ivy. Insert them in the base of the foam so that they spray in a cascading waterfall effect, fanning out slightly from the downward line of the ivy and cherry blossom stems. Be careful when inserting woody stems into foam, especially into a small foam ball. If the stems are pushed in too far, the foam will break up.

4 Cut eight or ten open rose stems approximately 20cm (8in) long. Make a fan shape radiating downwards and outwards from the base of the foam ball. Cut the remaining roses shorter at slightly varying heights and insert in the foam to form a rounded, dome shape, covering most of the foam. Place the most open roses in the centre of the display, facing outwards to form the focal point.

5 Cut the spray chrysanthemum stems to the same length as the roses, leaving an upper floret of four or five flowers. Remove most of the leaves from each stem. Intersperse the chrysanthemum florets between the low-lying roses. The open faces of the chrysanthemums make them good 'filler' flowers and the white groupings make an interesting contrast with the pink roses.

6 Cut off little sprigs of laurustinus and intersperse randomly throughout the design, covering any visible foam. Finish off with the gypsophila. This is best inserted last throughout the display as its delicate flowers fill out the arrangement, giving it a light, natural look. As an important finishing touch, insert a second wired ribbon bow into the foam at the top of the arrangement.

The main pew-end arrangement shown is made up of a combination of branches from flowering shrubs and herbaceous perennials: cherry blossom, pink broom, single-flowered chrysanthemums, pink roses and gypsophila. The woody branches give length and elegance to the display, while the roses and perennial flowers add colour, mass and delicate detail.

Woody stems

Forced cherry blossom comes in pink and white-flowered varieties, and in single and double forms. Normally, for home display you buy the stems in tight bud, but for wedding work buy them at a later stage of development. Remember, too, that churches are usually cooler than normal room temperature, and the buds need warmth to open.

For a yellow colour scheme, you could use forsythia branches instead. Branches of white, pink, orange, apricot or scarlet flowering quince, or chaenomeles, could be substituted; and branches of white *Philadelphus*, or mock orange, would provide a suitably romantic fragrance, traditionally associated with late spring and early summer weddings.

Broom has charming flowers, but they are small and unevenly distributed. The leafless stems contribute as much, if not more, to floral displays; their graceful, cascading curves add elegance and a sense of movement. There are broom varieties with white, creamy-yellow, deep-yellow and red flowers, as well as the pink-flowered variety shown. It's a popular and easy-going garden shrub, thriving in well-drained soil and full sun. When you get the broom home, re-cut the stems, dip them in boiling water for a few minutes, then follow with a long drink. Broom flowers are short lived and, again, it's important to get the timing right so that they look their best on the day.

Floral choices

Spray chrysanthemums are available all year round, in white, as shown, and many different pastel colours. Single-flowered chrysanthemums always look charming, unpretentious and 'fresh from the garden'; their strong stems make them easy to insert in florist's foam, and stay where put. For a modern, sophisticated-looking display, use white spider chrysanthemums instead; for a formal, imposing display, use semi-double or double spray chrysanthemums. You could also use shasta daisies from the garden, or in late summer and autumn, masses of Michaelmas daisies.

Pink, short-stemmed, hybrid tea roses provide the main colour; pale-yellow, apricot, creamy-white or white roses could be used instead. On a budget, substitute spray carnations in a similar colour range, with the added bonus of fat, unopened buds as fillers. As with cherry blossom, buy roses for wedding work at a more mature stage than you would normally.

Filling out the display

Gypsophila – white, dainty, long-lasting and available all year round – probably appears at more weddings than any other flower. Luckily, it's less expensive in spring than in winter, but you may find that sea lavender is cheaper still. Pale-pink, dyed gypsophila is an alternative, but you'll probably have to order it well in advance. Be careful that the pink of the gypsophila doesn't clash with the pink of the roses; try to see a sample of both flowers together before placing your order.

Pew-end floral displays need foliage to add bulk, grace and contrasting

---

HOW-TO — MAKING AN INFORMAL PEW-END DISPLAY

If your florist cannot supply a specially-made floral foam pew-end base, it is still possible to create attractive pew-end displays. An elongated, front-facing hand-tied bunch is easy to make and very informal in style which would suit a country church wedding. To prevent wilting, position the flowers on the morning of the ceremony rather than the day before.

1 Working with your chosen flowers and foliage, lay the longest, trailing stems, such as bloom or blossom, flat on your working surface.

2 Build up the other flowers and foliage in groups placed in graduating layers, so that they don't obscure one another. Position the flowers for maximum contrast of colour and

texture. Make a focal point of the most open flowers in the centre of the arrangement.

3 Gather the stems together, snip them off to even lengths to make a neat finish, and tie securely with a piece of twine. Cover the twine with a ribbon bow and a long length of ribbon with which to attach the display to the pew end.

colour and form to the flowers. Here, ivy, laurustinus and cyclamen leaves are used, but almost any attractive leaves will do, provided they can stay fresh-looking for a day or so. Large-leaved, white-variegated ivy is shown, but you could use all-green, or yellow-variegated ivy instead; or any of the smaller-leaved varieties. The ivy, like the broom, adds sweeping, linear grace, and a feeling of informality. Evergreen clematis, such as *C. armandii*, or the small, pointed evergreen leaves of Chinese jasmine, *Trachelospermum jas-minoides*, could be substituted. Asparagus fern is another option, but its delicacy is less effective in church-flower work than bold, large ivy leaves, and you need an enormous amount to make an impression.

Cyclamen leaves are an unusual addition, and repeat the green and white theme of the ivy. You can use hardy, garden cyclamen leaves, or those from a cyclamen pot plant. If you take just a few leaves from a healthy plant, it

doesn't matter, but if you strip a plant completely, it is liable to die. Though they lack the pretty marbled colouring, camellia leaves could be used instead.

Laurustinus, or *Viburnum tinus*, is an old-fashioned, hardy evergreen shrub, its clusters of pink-tinged, white flowers attractively set off by its dark-green leaves. Here, sprigs help build up a central focal point; evergreen Mexican orange leaves *Choisya ternata* could be used instead.

Alternative foundations

Florists sell specially-made, half-globe, florist's foam pew-end bases, complete with a clip, as shown. These come in just one size, but by varying the length of the flower and foliage stems, you can create smaller or larger displays in a range of silhouettes, using the same-sized base. If you can't get pew-end bases, florist's foam blocks with plastic backing and pierced handles for hanging are available in a range of sizes.

You can also create lovely, informal

ABOVE This ribbon-tied bunch of broom, solidaster, freesias, gypsophila and matricaria is the simplest of all possible pew-end displays. Upside-down bunches have no florist's foam to keep them fresh, so choose long-lasting material and condition it well before positioning the display.

pew-end displays without any founda-tions. Build up an elongated, front-facing, hand-tied bunch, (see 'How-to' box for details). Incorporate plenty of trailing material, and layer the flowers so they don't obscure one another. Cut the stems evenly, then tie securely with a ribbon, making a pretty bow. White ribbon is the best choice to stand out against a dark wooden pew, but you could also use pastel-coloured ribbon to match the arrangement. Tie the flowers to the pew end with more ribbon, and fix another ribbon bow to the back of the pew to finish off.

TO TOP IT ALL

Cutting the cake is the high point of every wedding reception, so add to the moment with a cake that is beautifully decorated with fragrant flowers.

 here is a growing trend at many weddings to carry through the fresh flower theme from the bridal party and church decorations to the cake itself, dispensing with more traditional decorations, such as a miniature bride and groom, wedding bells, silver horse shoes or sugar-paste flowers. Fresh flowers add to the sense of occasion and photograph well, which is important for wedding pictures.

The featured decoration is a two-tier floral display, repeating the tiers of the cake. The lower tier of the decoration is a flat, round circle of flowers, resting on the top of the cake. On the smaller, upper tier, an elegant floral spray is supported by a slender wire foundation. (For details on how to make your own wire foundation see the 'How-to' box.)

Choosing the flowers

When selecting your wedding-cake flowers, repeat the combination of flowers used for the bridal bouquet and

LEFT Roses, chrysanthemums, lilies, ixias, tracheliums and ivy leaves and berries form a two-tier decoration, echoing the tiered elegance of the cake.

reception hall decorations. Traditional flowers for a wedding cake decoration include lilies of the valley, orange blossom, gypsophila, miniature gladioli, heathers, gardenias, camellias, stephanotis, rose-buds, spray roses, spray carnations and spray orchids.

Most wedding cakes are white, but if pink or peach-tinted icing is used, pick up the tint in some or all of the flowers. However, do not leave anything to chance. Discuss the cake decoration with your florist so that your chosen flowers can be ordered well in advance.

In the featured display, peach-pink lilies are the most eye-catching flower. White or cream lilies, such as *Lilium longiflorum*, or white iris could be substituted. Large white orchids also would look stunning.

Pure pastels

The featured pale-peach, single spray chrysanthemums add a delicate hint of colour to the display. Alternatively, you could substitute single florist's chrysanthemums, shasta daisies, field daisies or marguerites from the garden. White trachelium, or throatwort, adds

dense mass but white or pastel-coloured carnations, white achillea, pale-pink bouvardia or pale-pink sedum from the garden all make suitable alternatives.

White spray roses are featured here, but pink, salmon pink, cream, peach or pale-yellow spray roses; single miniature roses; or florets of alstroemeria in similar pastel colours could be substituted.

Ixia, or African corn lily, gives this arrangement linear elegance. For a similar effect, use chincherinchees, miniature gladioli, freesias or sprigs of white broom or heather. For an unusual touch, use the pink-purple hanging blooms of the wand flower (*Dierama pulcherrimum*).

Choosing the foliage and berries

Variegated ivy leaves are wired and overlapped to form a flat, circular base. Your florist should be able to get hold of variegated ivy, but plain ivy, or small Portugal laurel or elaeagnus leaves could be used instead. For a lovely fragrance, choose scented geranium leaves or, for an unusual marbled effect, cyclamen leaves.

Ivy berries (artificial pearls, wired into bunches, similar to berries, could be substituted) and plain-green ivy leaves provide dark contrast for the paler flowers together with florist's galax leaves. Galax has rounded,

---

HOW-TO

MAKING THE WIRE BASE

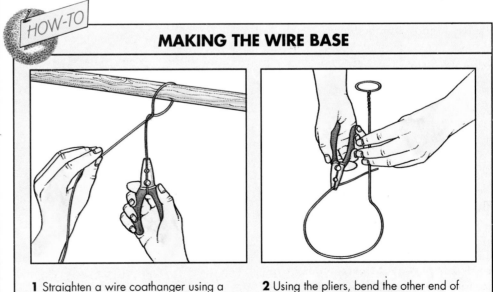

1 Straighten a wire coathanger using a pair of pliers. Make the small circular top tier by wrapping one end of the wire around a pole. Twist the ends together, bend the wire round at a 90° angle to the circle; straighten out to 25cm (10in).

2 Using the pliers, bend the other end of the wire into a circle 15cm (6in) in diameter to fit neatly on the top tier of the cake. Cut off any excess wire. Cover a surface with newspaper and spray the whole base with white paint.

evergreen leaves, suitable for cutting, and bears tiny white flowers in summer. Artificial berries and stamens are available from craft shops. Spray them white for inclusion in the decoration.

Decorating the cake table

If you have time to decorate the table holding the cake, use the same flowers as in the cake decoration and make up two or three small posies. Attach them to the table at even intervals, gathering up the tablecloth to give a ruched effect. Alternatively, place a garland of matching flowers round the edge of the table or a smaller garland round the base of the cake.

Keeping the flowers fresh

There is no foundation of florist's foam in the floral cake decoration; the flowers are glued in place so have no water source. Make up the decoration as close as possible to the time of the wedding. If you have to assemble it the night before, cover the display with a piece of damp tissue paper and store in a cool place. Spray-mist it regularly with water, but not once it's on the cake as the droplets of water will stain the smooth surface of the royal icing.

Easy alternatives

If you are concerned that you won't have enough time to make up a wedding cake decoration on the actual day, you can buy slender silver bud vases specially for wedding-cake flowers. A small posy display arranged in a bud vase will last much longer than those in the featured decoration, so it can be made up a day or so in advance. If you're having the cake made professionally, ask the baker or caterer about hiring a bud vase. Otherwise, fill a small tumbler, stemmed wine glass or white china egg cup with saturated florist's foam, then build up an informal, all-round posy of flowers and foliage.

Ribbon and foliage cascades

Create a backdrop of trailing sprigs of ivy, asparagus fern or periwinkle and narrow, 6mm (¼in) satin ribbon, in white or pastel colours, as streamers cascading down the sides of the vase. Complete the display with a simple bunch of white freesias and cow parsley or a few romantic white roses.

WHAT TO DO
WHAT YOU NEED

Decorating the cake with flowers

1 *28 variegated ivy leaves*	**7** *3 stems of white trachelium*
2 *small bunch of garden ivy with berries*	**8** *wire base*
3 *2 stems of white spray roses*	**9** *scissors*
4 *2 stems of peach spray chrysanthemums*	**10** *green reel wire*
5 *3 stems of white ixia*	**11** *clear-based glue*
6 *3 peach lilies*	**12** *gutta-percha tape*

1 Wire 24 ivy leaves with fine reel wire. Cut the wired stems to a length of 1.5cm (1/2in) and cover with gutta-percha tape. Glue underneath 12 larger leaves and stick them onto the bottom wire ring, with stems pointing inwards. Overlap each leaf as you go. Make an inner ring of 12 smaller ivy leaves facing in the opposite direction. This forms a base on which to secure other flowers. Leave to dry.

2 Pull apart two stems of white trachelium and wire them into about 12 small florets. Cover the wire with gutta-percha tape and cut each stem short. Place a little glue on each of the larger ivy leaves and stick one trachelium floret firmly on the top of each leaf, the stems pointing inwards. This will form a tightly packed ring in which you can insert more open flowerheads.

3 Wire together five small bunches of ivy berries, together with two or three ivy leaves, binding the stems together with tape. Make a smaller inner ring of ivy berries inside the circle of trachelium florets, with stems facing inwards. Cut the heads from eight peach daisy chrysanthemums, leaving a short length of stem. Apply a little glue to each stem length and place amongst the ivy berries.

4 Cut seven stems of white spray roses, just beneath the flowerhead. Apply a little glue to each short length of stem. Dot the roses amongst the trachelium, berries and chrysanthemums with the flowerheads pointing upwards. Cut the stems of two peach lilies just underneath the flowerhead. Apply a blob of glue to each short stem and stick them on either side of the upright wire.

5 Strip the leaves from two or three stems of ixia and wire them together. Tape over the exposed wire with gutta-percha tape. Wire the ixia bunch securely onto the top tier of the frame with fine reel wire so that the bunch leans in the same direction as the two lilies on the layer below. Stick two trachelium florets and a single daisy chrysanthemum at the base of the ixia stems.

6 Glue a bunch of ivy berries to the top of a variegated ivy leaf and stick beside the trachelium on the top tier. Cut a single lily flowerhead and stick it down beside the trachelium. Glue two or three more ivy leaves and use them to cover the mechanics and strengthen the flower base. Finish by sticking a bunch of ivy berries alongside. Spray the leaves and berries with house plant leaf shine if desired.

INDEX

Page numbers in *italic* refer to the
illustrations

ACKNOWLEDGEMENTS

Caroline Arber 131, 133(BL). Steve Bicknell (Octopus Picture Library) 2-3, 8-9, 98-99. Anthony Blake Photo Library 167(TR). Camera Press 21(BR), 87(TR), 101, 129, 135(BR), 158(BR). Tommy Chandler 104, 106-107. Chris Crofton 172, 174-177. David Garcia 62(C), 63-65, 108, 110(R), 111, 152, 154-155, 157, 196, 197, 201. Will Giles (Artwork) 105, 150. Nelson Hargreaves 11(TL), 14-16, 32-33, 54, 56-57, 71-73, 84-86, 92, 103(TC), 126-128, 130, 132-135, 142-145, 158(T), 163(B), 164, 166, 167(BL), 178, 179, 180-181, 187-189, 195. Jon Harris (Octopus Picture Library) 13. Marilyn Leader (Artwork) 38, 46, 58, 62, 66, 112. Roy McMahon 25, 34-37, 38(L), 39-41, 42(L), 43-49, 50(L), 51-53, 58(L), 59-61, 88-91, 112(L), 113-119. Mondadori Press 83, 87(BR). J. Pickering (Artwork) 23, 27, 50(BR), 82, 124-125, 137, 186, 194. Sandra Pond (Artwork) 20, 30, 42, 110, 112(BR), 156, 162, 169, 176, 200, 203. Annick Regnault 30, 32, 100, 102. Malcolm Robertson (Octopus Picture Library) 6-7. M. Smallcombe 17-19, 22, 24, 26, 28-29, 66-69, 79-81, 95-97, 120, 122-123, 125(T), 136, 138-140, 168, 170-171, 183-185, 190, 192-193, 198-199, 202, 204-205. J. Suett 159-161. Syndication International 10, 12, 163(T). Rosemary Weller 146-149, 151. Elizabeth Whiting Associates 11(BL), 21(TC), 103(B). Shona Wood 74-77.